ART HISTORY AND APPRECI

Henry J Sharpe

ART HISTORY
and appreciation

Gill and Macmillan

Published in Ireland by
Gill and Macmillan Ltd
Goldenbridge
Dublin 8
with associated companies throughout the world
© Henry Sharpe, 1976
© Diagrams and maps, Gill and Macmillan Ltd, 1976
7171 0789 2
Print origination in Ireland by
Richview Press Ltd, Dublin

Front Cover:
'Lant' by Victor Vasarely,
reproduced by kind permission of the artist

Back Cover:
'Notre-Dame de la Belle Verrière'
(detail) from
Chartres Cathedral (Photographie Giraudon)

Acknowledgments

In addition to those credited in the text, the publishers wish to thank the following for their
assistance in finding illustrations: Rod Tuach, David Hendricks, Anne-Marie Ehrlich and Peter
Larrigan. The publishers have made every effort to locate copyright holders in each instance.
They will be glad to make the necessary arrangements at the first opportunity with copyright
holders traced after publication.

Photocopying
prohibited
by law

For Anne

Contents

General Introduction

Art is a complex matter and may be viewed from a number of vantage points. Sometimes its function is purely decorative, sometimes religious or magical, sometimes political. Always art is a mirror of the society which produced it.

Part I is set out with this idea very much in mind. Rather than seeking to produce a text which would amount to a series of lists of artists' names, dates, works of art, etc. (and some potted art histories do just this) I have attempted to show what it is that makes each period distinctive and therefore why art took a particular form at a particular time.

The text should be seen as an introduction to a given period or topic, which hopefully will lead the student, with the art-teacher's guidance, to further research. At the end of each section a list of books will be found. These should be fairly easily obtainable, many from public libraries. Charts setting out the names of important artists, works of art etc. are also provided. Maps are included in Parts I and III.

Some practical exercises will also be found at the end of each chapter. These relate directly to the ideas already encountered in the text. Although optional, such exercises, if carried out in the art class, should help to reinforce and add interest to ideas which otherwise might remain too theoretical.

The Middle Ages

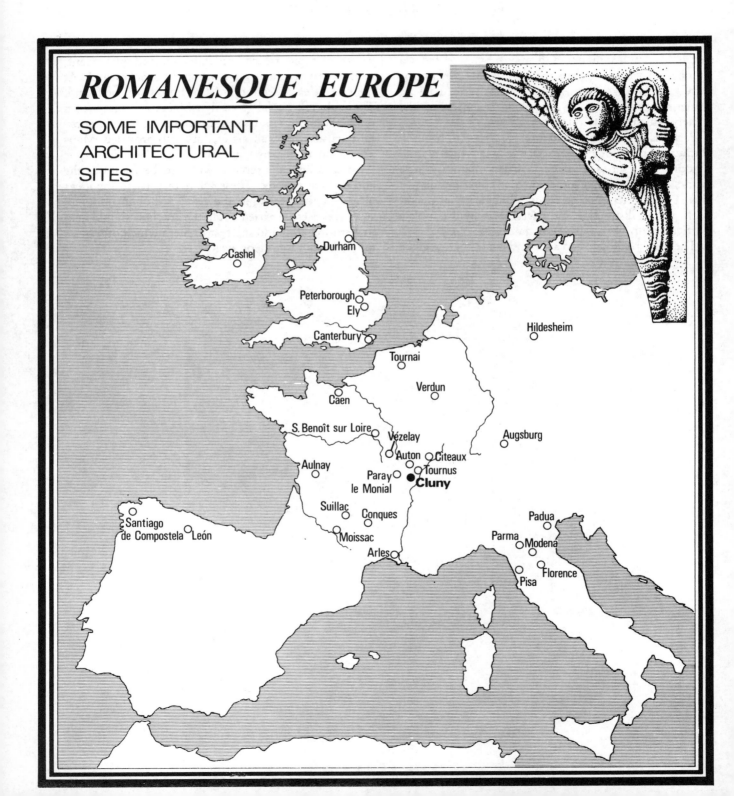

ROMANESQUE EUROPE

SOME IMPORTANT ARCHITECTURAL SITES

Cashel
Durham
Peterborough
Ely
Canterbury
Tournai
Verdun
Hildesheim
Caen
S. Benoît sur Loire
Vézelay
Augsburg
Auton
Cîteaux
Aulnay
Tournus
Paray le Monial
Cluny
Suillac
Conques
Padua
Santiago de Compostela
León
Moissac
Parma
Modena
Arles
Florence
Pisa

Romanesque

Look at the illustration on this page. Perhaps it is a rather macabre note with which to begin but nevertheless it is certainly a dramatic one.

A naked man hangs by his neck from a curiously fragile-looking tree. His mouth is wide open in a scream of pain or terror; two winged monsters or demons squat at his feet tugging viciously on the rope which throttles him. The carving represents Judas Iscariot, the betrayer of Christ, who hanged himself in a fit of remorse. It hardly impresses us as a work of sophistication or representational accuracy. The carver of the piece seems to have taken an almost child-like delight in the sheer gruesomeness of his subject. His knowledge of human anatomy was rudimentary and his trees are merely decorative symbols. Yet the carving has some powerful quality which is not easy to define. Certain aspects of it may be child-like but it is certainly not childish.

The Death of Judas is a product of an age very much simpler than our own. We have grown used to endless complexity, to hidden meanings (even in the simplest things), to the polish and ultra-sophistication of a highly mechanised society. The eleventh and twelfth centuries, the period we are about to discuss, were not at all like that. Life had a roughness and a rawness which we are unlikely to experience, and art assumed a simplicity and a directness which we can only envy.

Now look at the photograph once more. A gruesome subject is presented in a gruesome manner, without any whitewash. A 'bad man' has received his just deserts and the artist does not suppress his satisfaction.

The artist in question was called Gislebertus and the carving, along with many more from his hand, is to be found in Autun Cathedral in France. Gislebertus lived during a period when architecture almost totally dominated the other visual arts. The pages that follow will therefore be largely concerned with the development of buildings.

Historical Background—The Eleventh Century

The eleventh century was a period of painful and perhaps miraculous recovery for Western European civilisation. The glories of the Roman Empire had long since been submerged beneath centuries of barbarism and fragmentation; only vague memories of past greatness and a variety of crumbling monuments remained. And to those regions where civilisation had retained a tenuous foothold came the Vikings from the cold lands of the north, at first in the role of pirates on the make, but later as fully fledged invaders who wanted good land for themselves. In Ireland their desires were thwarted by the efforts of King Brian Boru, but elsewhere, particularly in France, fortune seemed to favour them. It is one of the ironies of history that the

The Death of Judas *by* Gislebertus. *Autun Cathedral. First half of the twelfth century. (Giraudon)*

Viking territory in France, the Dukedom of Normandy, should rapidly have become a primary force in the rebuilding of a stable Europe. The Normans had a curious respect for law coupled with the energy and will to extend their influence. By the end of the century the Kingdom of England had been added to the Norman sphere of influence, as had the Kingdom of Sicily, a small and relatively unimportant country in itself, but nevertheless of considerable importance to the advancement of Western European civilisation. Sicily opened a gateway to those well-established cultures of the East, the Eastern Empire with its centre at Byzantium, and the great Islamic Empire.

Yet the greatest single power in Western Europe was the Christian Church. The abbots and bishops of the Church were men of considerable power and often great wealth, comparable indeed in their social stature to the great feudal lords of the time. It was the Church, in the person of Pope John XII, which declared the German Otto I Holy Roman Emperor, thus making possible at least in theory, the unification of a vast area of central Europe and northern Italy. And it was the Church which spearheaded the great revival of interest in building. The monk Raoul Glaber, writing in 1048 tells us, 'In the years that followed the year 1000 we witnessed the rebuilding of churches all over the Universe, but especially in Italy and Gaul. Even if there was no need for it, each Christian community resolved to build sanctuaries more sumptuous than those of its neighbours, as if the world, anxious to cast away its rags, wished to dress in a beautiful white robe of churches.'

Glaber notes the year 1000 as marking the beginning of the revival, and perhaps it is worth mentioning here that this particular date possessed a significance above and beyond that of being a nice rounded figure. For it had been a widely held belief throughout Christendom that Christ would return to earth in the year 1000 thus heralding the Day of Judgment. But the last trumpet was not sounded and folk heaved a collective sigh of relief and returned, perhaps with renewed vigour, to the task of living.

The Rise of the Churches

The first buildings to emerge were not particularly impressive, in terms of size, workmanship or design. Indeed much of the new construction work simply entailed the restoration of older existing buildings. The reason for this is simple: men skilled in building techniques, master masons, were very scarce in Western Europe. Only in Lombardy, northern Italy, could a pool of such craftsmen be found.

In Lombardy some vestiges of Roman building tradition had remained alive although much had been lost. Not surprisingly therefore, we hear of Lombard masons making frequent trips abroad to supervise the work of local builders. The style of architecture which emerged during the eleventh century, founded as it was on old Roman structural principles, we refer to as 'Romanesque'. Strictly the term should apply to any architecture based upon Roman precedents built during the period stretching from the fifth to the twelfth centuries. It was only during the eleventh and twelfth centuries, however, that Romanesque architecture became a truly living form, fully capable of creative development.

The Basilica Form

The churches were constructed along the lines of the old Roman basilicas, long rectangular buildings with central nave and side aisles, originally designed to serve as meeting places or closed markets. To this basic

Romanesque church at Germigny-les-Prés. Begun early ninth century. View from the east. (Bulloz)

rectangular form a transverse nave or 'transept' was added, so that the building would form a cross in plan. The altar was placed at the junction of nave and transept and beyond the altar itself lay a semi-circular or polygonal recess called the 'apse'.

1. The Romanesque Basilica

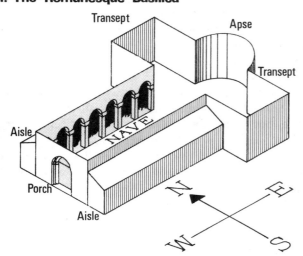

Interior view of the church of St Philibert, Tournus. (Giraudon)

Church at Paray-le-Monial, about 1100. View from the west. (Giraudon)

As the eleventh century progressed many refinements were added to this extremely simple form. Churches sprouted great towers and clusters of semi-circular chapels. Naves were widened and made higher, and an extended east end or 'choir' was developed for the sole use of the clergy. Above all, the art of sculpture, and to a lesser extent painting, began to appear on walls and capitals.

The Problem of Vaulting

No true equivalent of the modern architect—the man who plans a building on paper in detail and who then hands over the plans to a builder—existed during the period we are discussing. Instead there were the 'master masons' already referred to. These men probably did a certain amount of planning on paper but their chief function was to strike out the plan accurately on the ground. They had to supervise the construction of adequate foundations, direct the building of the walls, ensuring that certain simple proportions governing the height etc. were adhered to. They had to direct the work of carving and painting, and, perhaps most difficult of all, overcome the many engineering difficulties of spanning the space between walls with ceiling and roof.

In early churches the wide span across the nave was covered entirely with timber. Forests were very extensive during the eleventh century and it was possible to obtain quantities of timber beams up to twenty metres or so in length. It was a comparatively simple matter to

Church at Paray-le-Monial. View from the east. (Bulloz)

place and secure a series of such beams at regular intervals above the space to be spanned. The resultant downward thrust was a simple vertical one and even poorly constructed walls could take the strain. Timber presented a considerable fire hazard, however, and largely on account of this it was found necessary to replace it with stone. Thus were incurred some very difficult structural problems.

A system borrowed from the Romans called 'barrel vaulting' had been employed very successfully for small spans. Barrel vaults, as the diagram shows, were half-cylindrical in form and were built up of wedge-shaped stones called 'voussoirs'. Cutting the voussoirs

2. Barrel Vault

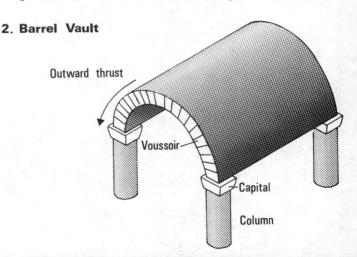

Outward thrust

Voussoir

Capital

Column

3. Groin Vault

Formed by the intersection of two barrel vaults

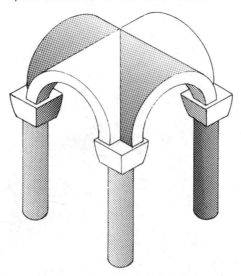

accurately was only one of the problems. A problem of much greater magnitude was the nature of the thrust exerted by the barrel vault shape—it tended to push the walls outwards—and stone is a heavy material in any case. The most obvious answer to this problem, albeit the crudest, was to build walls so thick that the extra weight of stone ceilings and the angle of thrust were adequately compensated for. Thus walls of two to three metres in thickness resulted, pierced by very narrow windows. Windows of any great size would of

course weaken the structure unduly. These massive walls had a core of rubble and were faced with cut stone or 'ashlar'. The builders themselves worked from scaffolding made entirely of wood instead of the steel pipes used today. Wooden poles were lashed together, and platforms of woven willow twigs provided flat horizontal surfaces where the men could stand to work. All stones, timber beams and mortar had, of course, to be lifted painfully by man power usually augmented by crude pulleys. When the wall had been built to a sufficient height it was then necessary to prepare the 'centring'. This was a wooden mould upon which the vault was constructed. Centring was difficult and time-consuming to make, and was usually constructed in such a way that it could be removed from under completed sections of vaulting and moved on to the next to be built.

The Importance of the Crusades

As the eleventh century advanced, competence in dealing with these purely technological problems improved, leading inevitably to an increasing diversity and degree of imaginative design. This advance on all fronts accelerated rapidly with the dawning of the twelfth century. It is hardly a coincidence that at this very time the western world was re-establishing contact (albeit of a largely belligerent nature) with the civilisations of the Middle East.

The Crusaders who travelled the long and dangerous road to the Holy Land to do battle with the Infidel (and, by the way, to aid their Christian—though heretical—half-brothers in Byzantium) brought back to Western Europe vivid memories of a civilisation vastly more sophisticated and luxurious than their own. They were not slow to borrow from their enemy. Many of the secrets of Muslim building technology and design were imported into Europe. Drawings of Muslim architecture were painstakingly made and superior building machinery was eagerly copied. Occasionally actual builders were captured and pressed into service.

Architecture, indeed, was by no means the only aspect of western culture which benefited from the Crusades. The Muslim civilisation possessed a superior knowledge of mathematics, medicine, philosophy, astronomy and chemistry. Important writings from Ancient Greece, which the west had largely lost track of, had been carefully preserved by the Muslims. The works of Aristotle and Euclid were foremost among those restored to the west. And perhaps the germs of those curious medieval virtues, chivalry and courtly love, were likewise imported from the East at this time and added to the melting pot.

Barrel vault and columns in the church of St-Benoît-sur-Loire. (Bulloz)

A glance at the map will give you some idea of how widespread was the upsurge of Romanesque building. A number of styles emerged and we shall now examine two of the most distinctive.

The Norman Builders

The great energy and strength of purpose which characterised the Normans found concrete expression in their buildings. Look at the photographs on this page, particularly the view of Durham Cathedral. How weighty and majestic those great square towers look, looming over the trees and river like some massive natural outcrop of rock. But there is surely an element of menace here also, a show of overwhelming strength by a conqueror to a conquered people.

The last quarter of the eleventh century saw a very extensive campaign of building throughout much of England by the new Norman overlords. The building of castles was deemed necessary as the surest means of entrenching the new landlords in their estates. Existing Saxon churches tended to be built on too modest a scale for Norman taste. So energies were directed to the task of cutting and hauling timber and stone on a scale unknown in England since the time of the Romans. Building materials were hauled in great wagons at a painfully slow pace along almost non-existent roads or, where possible, carried by sea or river. Some building stone was actually imported from France. When we consider that almost all the builders were Saxons, men quite unused to large-scale working, directed by Norman masons who were themselves rather vague about many of the basic structural problems, we begin to glimpse something of the sheer determination behind such a campaign of building. Not surprisingly mishaps did occur and a number of the great Norman towers collapsed under their own weight.

Anglo-Norman cathedral at Durham. (Camera Press)

Norman church of St Etienne, Caen. Begun towards the end of the eleventh century; towers completed early in the thirteenth century. (Bulloz)

Anglo-Norman castle, Harlech. (Camera Press)

Anglo-Norman doorway, St Michael's, Tudenham, Suffolk. (Camera Press)

Interior of Peterborough Cathedral showing the painted wooden roof, still the largest Norman decoration of its kind to be found in Europe. (National Monuments Record)

Norman buildings were massive but there was an austere, almost puritanical, quality about them. Sculptural decoration was often purely geometrical. The rounded arches of doorways and windows were carved with rows of zigzag 'teeth' and even the shafts of the massive columns became criss-crossed with chevron and diamond patterns. Figurative sculpture did of course exist, but remained relatively unimportant.

The interior walls of Norman churches were plastered and painted, often with geometric patterns, but occasionally with figures of saints. Prevailing colours tended to be cream and light red. Wooden ceilings were also decorated in a rigid geometrical manner. The great painted ceiling of Peterborough Cathedral remains the largest Norman decoration of its kind in existence.

The art of making pictures from pieces of coloured glass—the stained-glass window—was in its infancy. Great difficulty was experienced in making large pieces of glass; the glass itself was thick and unwieldly and colours were very limited in range. Stained-glass windows were therefore a luxury and reserved only for the most important churches.

The problem of decorating the great bare expanses of wall in both castles and churches was probably best solved by the use of fabric hangings. Most of these wall hangings, tapestries and embroideries, have long since crumbled to dust, victims of dampness and moth, but one superb example does remain. This is the 'Telle du Conquest d'Angleterre', better known to the English

speaking world as the 'Bayeux Tapestry' (although it is, in fact, an embroidery).

This embroidery, which measures some seventy metres in length by about half a metre deep, is stitched in coloured wool and relates the history of the conquest of England by William, Duke of Normandy, in 1066. Bishop Odo of Bayeux (the Conqueror's half-brother), may have ordered the hanging for his cathedral, where it was traditionally hung up on St John's day. Although we are not certain who the creator of the Bayeux Tapestry was, the credit is usually given to the Conqueror's wife, Queen Mathilde.

A small section of the Bayeux Tapestry.

Cluny—the Flowering of the Romanesque Style

The greatest single Romanesque church, at least in terms of size and grandeur, was the abbey church built at Cluny in the Rhône valley during the last decades of the eleventh century and the opening decades of the twelfth. The building was over one hundred and twenty-five metres in length and the nave vaulting rose to the then remarkable height of twenty-seven metres. The floors were said to have been decorated with vast mosaic designs; many stone carvings adorned the capitals and a magnificent relief carving, reaching to fifteen metres in height, imposed itself above the main entrance. Sadly, we can now only speculate about this for it was demolished in 1811.

Splendid as the church at Cluny was, its chief claim to fame lies in the fact that it was the central church of the most powerful monastic order of the Middle Ages, a period when such orders wielded very real power, both spiritual and temporal. The Clunaic order held sway over some two thousand satellite churches in France, Spain and Italy. Among other things it catered for the medieval passion for pilgrimages—journeys made, often with great difficulty, by the faithful rich and poor to the shrines of a variety of saints. Travellers to the holy places of Jerusalem were helped on their way by the hostels along the route provided by the order, as were those to the greatest pilgrimage centre of all, Santiago de Compostela in Spain.

But from our point of view the most important aspect of the Clunaic order was its role as patron of the arts, for it helped to foster the rise of a sculptural movement which would compare well, in terms of sheer exuberance and invention, with anything in European history. Capitals no longer merely transfer stress from arch to column; under the chisels of the late Romanesque carvers they burst into life. And what life—figures from the most primitive depths of the subconscious, concocted of fish, fowl, vegetable, animal and human parts, writhe and twist like voodoo dancers. That such delightful monsters should virtually rub shoulders with figures of Christ, his saints and angels, was more novel still.

The Abbey church at Cluny, seen from the east. (from a nineteenth-century print)

Capital sculpture from the church of St Madeleine, Vézelay. These figures holding bellows are symbolic representations of the winds. (Bulloz)

Capital sculpture from the church of St Madeleine, Vézelay, early twelfth century. The carving depicts Samson strangling a lion. (Bulloz)

Tympanum carving from the church of St Pierre, Moissac: **Christ Enthroned between Two Angels, the symbols of the Evangelists and the twenty-four Elders.** *Early twelfth century. (Giraudon)*

The large semi-circular area between lintel and arch above the main doorways—the 'tympanum'—frequently gave the sculptors the opportunity to display their skills fully. Often great figures of Christ in the fullness of his majesty and surrounded by a panoply of evangelists, prophets, saints and angels, gaze down upon the faithful as they enter their church to worship. Such sculptures may have been painted in bright primary colours. To the minds of ordinary medieval folk, far less sophisticated than ourselves and, unlike us, virtually starved of images, they must have seemed impressive indeed. To so many of us, products of an age of mass media bombardment that we are, they may simply remain dusty curios from the distant past.

Contemporary medieval opinion was not, however, unanimous in its approval of these Clunaic sculptural efflorescences. St Bernard of Clairvaux expressed his opinion of them thus: 'Why place these ridiculous monsters, those beautiful horrors and horrible beauties, under the eyes of monks who should read and meditate? What is the use of these unclean monkeys, these ferocious lions and monstrous centaurs? Here you see a quadruped with a serpent's tail, there a fish with a goat's head. Will it be more profitable to study these marbles than to read the sacred books, to pass days in successive contemplation of these sculptures instead of meditating the law of the Lord?'

Medieval men were not obsessed, as we in the twentieth century are, with the 'authentically signed work of art'. Painters and sculptors were simply tradesmen paid to do a job of work, like blacksmiths, bakers or carpenters. Many artists did sign their work however, but mainly for their own personal satisfaction and often in very unobtrusive places. The Master of Autun, Gislebertus, whose work we have already briefly discussed, was a notable exception, for beneath the feet of the Christ from the tympanum of Autun Cathedral's west façade may clearly be read the words: 'Gislebertus Hoc Fecit.' We know very little about Gislebertus apart from the fact that he worked in Autun during the early years of the twelfth century and seems to have accomplished all the carving in the Cathedral by himself. He was a great individualist certainly and it has seriously been suggested that the prominent positioning of his signature may have been at the behest of the clergy, so impressed were they by his work.

The Weighing of Souls *by* Gislebertus. *Autun Cathedral. Early twelfth century. (Bulloz)*

Gislebertus and his contemporaries, who were working during the early decades of the twelfth century, up to about 1140, helped to bring the Romanesque style to its fullest flowering. Yet as they worked a new style had already emerged in the Ile-de-France, a style so revolutionary and so explosively vital that it was soon to supplant the Romanesque in almost every part of Europe.

This was the Gothic style.

A. *The nave of Salisbury Cathedral, mid thirteenth century. (Camera Press)*

B. *West façade of Cologne Cathedral. Begun in 1248 and not completed until the nineteenth century. (Bundesbildstelle Bonn)*

C. *Part of Rheims Cathedral showing the flying buttresses. Begun 1211. (Camera Press)*

The Gothic Revolution

Study the three photographs reproduced on this page. Compare them with views of buildings in the first part of this chapter. Would you agree that there are certain distinct differences between the two styles—between the Romanesque and the Gothic?

There is a full rounded quality about Romanesque buildings—a product not merely of the quirks of fashion but more the result of methods and materials used in their construction.

The Gothic buildings, on the other hand, seem to be all ribs and points and to lack the heavy Romanesque feeling.

Look at the nave in photo A.

The surging vertical thrust of all those lines is overwhelming—reminiscent of a pathway through a forest of very tall and slender trees whose branches meet far overhead.

The façade shown in photo B conveys that same vertical thrust and distinctly linear quality. And all the arches are pointed!

The view in photo C is more distinctive still. Here is a phenomenon quite unlike anything we have met so far, a building which seems to be sprouting shoots like certain plants—or are they crutches?

How these new Gothic forms evolved from the Romanesque, how they flourished and finally went to seed and withered we shall now attempt to discover.

More about vaults

The Norman architects of Durham cathedral first hit upon the happy idea of using stone ribs to lend stability to their vaulted ceilings. Whether they borrowed the idea from the East or not is a matter for speculation. The fact remains that in Western Europe it was the builders of Durham, during the first few years of the twelfth century, who discovered that if they reinforced the groins of their vaults with narrow, independent arches or ribs they could fill in the areas between such ribs with much lighter stones than were usually necessary.

The pointed arch was also introduced into a number of Romanesque buildings, notably Autun, during the first few decades of the twelfth century. Presumably a further import from the East, its introduction led to greater flexibility of design in that pointed arches of differing spans may attain the same height, unlike the semi-circular shape.

Only when architects began to add up the implications of various isolated steps like these was a true leap forward in design made possible. And the principle of design which did finally emerge was beautifully simple. It consisted of the discovery that if ribs can both strengthen and lighten a vault they can also carry most of the stresses to the ground, and thick heavy walls could therefore be dispensed with. The 'flying buttresses' (see photo C) were a further, and later, refinement of this principle. They were really external ribs whose function was to carry the thrust from the roof—and Gothic roofs became much higher than Romanesque—over the tops of side aisles and down sturdy pillars into the ground.

With a system of ribs and flying buttresses to carry most of the weight, the walls of churches were pierced increasingly by even larger windows and the interior gloom of Romanesque buildings gave way to interior radiance.

Where Romanesque building was often a triumph of the will, a dogged desire to build on a grand scale despite faulty technique, Gothic building was a triumph of the understanding. Techniques for cutting stone with great accuracy, improved tools and lifting machinery combined with a much wider understanding of geometry and of natural forces, led to a form of building which could best be described as organic. As a tree grows it overcomes the forces of gravity by thrust and counter-thrust. It becomes the inevitable expression of the forces which shaped it and the forces which were overcome in the course of its growing. Virtually the same could be said for Gothic buildings.

Perhaps it should be pointed out at this stage that 'Gothic' architecture and art have nothing to do with the 'Goths'. The word was coined by later men of the Renaissance period who felt that the products of ages

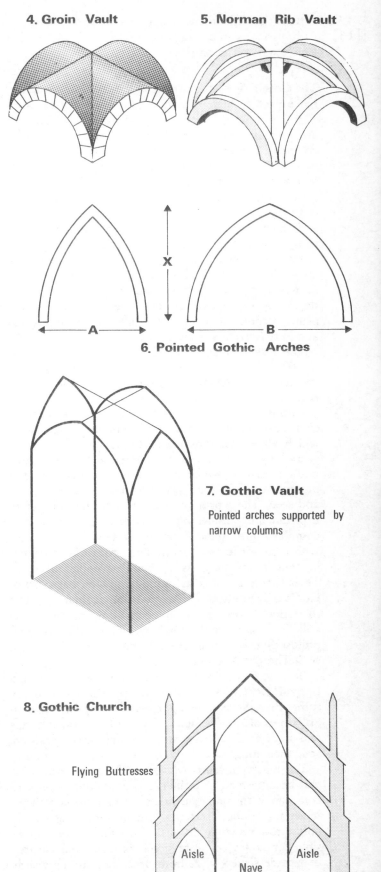

4. Groin Vault

5. Norman Rib Vault

6. Pointed Gothic Arches

7. Gothic Vault

Pointed arches supported by narrow columns

8. Gothic Church

Flying Buttresses

Aisle

Aisle

Nave

[14] earlier than their own were barbaric or 'Gothic'. Although we can certainly no longer agree with such a view the name has stuck.

The Gothic Age—the twelfth and thirteenth centuries

No aspect of human culture functions in a vacuum. This is a point we shall continually return to. That an art form so logical, so filled with energy and the confidence to grow and change should emerge in the mid 1100s is a powerful indication of a real step forward for western man. So we should not be surprised to learn that the age which saw the development of the Gothic style also witnessed the growth of towns and cities, with all that implies in terms of trade, prosperity and learning. Scholarship, once the stock-in-trade of monks, was rapidly moving to the new universities—to Paris, Oxford and Cambridge. In such centres, but particularly in Paris, the works of Aristotle, newly translated and available to western Europeans in complete form for the first time since classical antiquity, were eagerly studied.

The task of reconciling the teachings of the great pre-Christian philosophers to orthodox Christianity was left to the acute and powerful mind of St Thomas Aquinas.

During the twelfth and thirteenth centuries medieval civilisation achieved that enviable plateau of certainty which all civilisations aspire to. For a time at least everything in the universe appeared to have its place; nothing existed which could not be explained. The presence of God, the Great Architect, was clearly felt and seen. The works of man existed only in order to explicate and parallel the perfect harmony of God. The complex harmonies of the great Gothic cathedrals, with their intricate structure and profusion of images in stone, paint and glass, were understood in this light. Their function was to echo the far greater harmony of God's universe and perhaps to bring ordinary mortals that much closer to an understanding of the divine will. Something similar might be said for the crowning philosophical work of the era, the Summa Theologica of St Thomas Aquinas.

Because God was perfect harmony the world which he had created might also be approached with joy rather than the fear and apprehension of previous ages. St Francis of Assisi taught the love of all created things and made an art form of his own life; the troubadours sang their songs of courtly love and knightly honour.

The master masons who built the great cathedrals had become men of influence, wealth and culture. In common with many other trades they formed themselves into guilds, fraternal organisations not wholly unlike today's trade unions. The guilds were responsible for codes of professional practice and ensured that trade secrets were both protected and efficiently

Thirteenth-century masons at work, from a French manuscript, about 1240. Notice in particular the machinery used for hoisting the blocks of stone. The man on the ladder is carrying mortar on his back. (Pierpont Morgan Library)

passed on to the rising generation. Master masons frequently spent periods abroad following their trade, and sometimes they borrowed ideas from each other.

The position of sculptors, painters and other artists —craftsmen in enamel, glass and metal—remained comparatively lowly.

The Gothic Buildings

Gothic building first made its appearance soon after 1125 in the Ile-de-France, the Domaine Royale of the Capetian kings. We do not know the name of the designer of the Abbey church of St Denis, usually designated the first true Gothic building, but we do know a good deal about the Abbot Suger whose enthusiasm and sheer imagination lay behind the building's conception. Suger was a man of many parts, a prominent politician (he was chief minister to Louis VII), a collector of *objets d'art* and precious materials, and a poet. He took a direct personal interest in the work of architects, sculptors, painters and other craftsmen whose skills he had commissioned. He was not above personally conducting his workmen into the forest to ensure that the timber they felled for one of his projects was to his satisfaction.

The new style of building first flourished in the Ile-de-France but its spread was rapid. Long before the end of the twelfth century it had reached England, while during the thirteenth and fourteenth centuries it took root in countries throughout Europe. The style was received with least enthusiasm by the Italians whose development was taking a rather different course to that of the rest of Europe. We shall return to that particular theme at the end of this chapter.

In very simple terms the Gothic style passed through three major periods:

(a) A period of experiment; roughly the period from the building of the Abbey church of St Denis to the opening decades of the thirteenth century.

(b) The great Classic period which spans the entire thirteenth century.

(c) The Flamboyant period which extends into the sixteenth century.

These three photographs give some indication of how Gothic buildings developed over several hundred years. In each case the view shown is of the west façade.

Compare them for yourself.

The cathedrals which were built during the second half of the twelfth century still had a Romanesque 'feel' about them. Look at the photo of Laon cathedral. Would you agree that the building has a ponderous, weighty quality? Those two great towers are impressive; the craftsmanship, for instance, is obviously very competent indeed. But how massive they appear. There is little of that sense of uplift—the sense of reaching towards heaven—which Gothic buildings sought so consistently. Even the arches shown in this view are hardly pointed at all in the Gothic manner and are far more reminiscent of the Romanesque style.

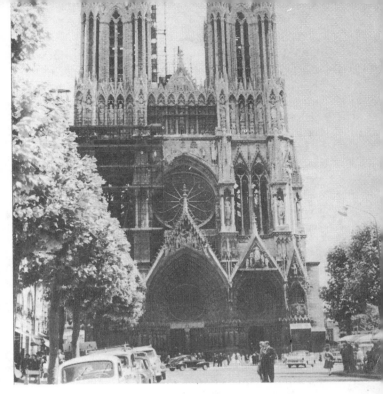

West façade of Rheims Cathedral, late thirteenth century. (Camera Press)

West façade of Rouen Cathedral, early sixteenth century. (Mansell)

The west façade of Laon Cathedral, about 1170. (from a nineteenth-century print, Giraudon)

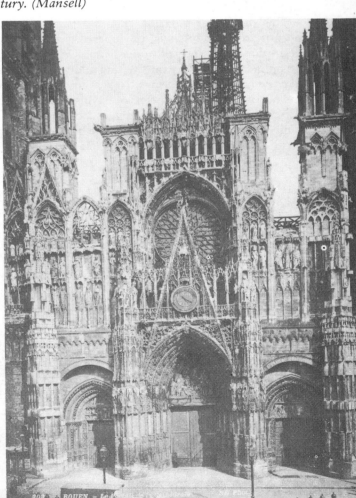

Now look at the photo of Rheims cathedral, which was built almost a century later. Rheims is a product of the 'classic' century of Gothic building, a period of poise and perfect confidence. All of the ponderousness of Laon has been left behind; here the overwhelming feeling is one of soaring verticality.

Look at the photo of Rheims once more and try to note all the various elements which add up to this vertical feeling.

The term 'Radiating' or 'Rayonnant' is often given to Gothic buildings from the latter half of the thirteenth century, the period when Rheims was built. This name is derived from the radiating stone tracery of the circular 'Rose' windows which were such an important feature of the style.

The final phase of the Gothic style has been called 'Flamboyant'. What does that term suggest to you? Something lively with perhaps a touch of showmanship thrown in for good measure? Look at the photo which shows the west façade of Rouen cathedral. This façade really is a great work of virtuosity—or showmanship if you like—it seems hardly credible that all of that fine lacy detail is actually cut from stone. We are left with the impression that the masons who carved this façade found no difficulty whatsoever in shaping the stone exactly as they pleased. We have come a very long way from Romanesque building and indeed from early Gothic buildings like Laon.

This display of amazing skill is typical of Flamboyant architecture, as is the apparently irrepressible desire for detail and still more detail. Windows took on an increasingly 'organic' feeling and begun to look like the habitat of luxurious tropical ferns. Some give the overwhelming impression of having been attacked by some particularly virulent fungus. Several architects built open-work spires where a stone creeper seems to grow on a pyramid of stone-work poles.

The rose window in the west façade of Amiens Cathedral. (Camera Press)

Not unexpectedly, inside the buildings themselves the ribs and columns also ran the risk of metamorphosing into gigantic ferns. This is particularly true of that English specialty the fan vault, one of the last creations of the Gothic style before the fire of invention finally died.

We have seen that Gothic building passed through three distinct phases. All artistic movements seem to develop in a similar fashion. The first phase—usually referred to as 'Archaic'—when a new idea is struggling to assert itself, often produces work which appears clumsy and which probably retains strong traces of whatever idea it is attempting to supplant. This is true of a building like Laon cathedral which has a certain clumsiness about it and which retains strong Romanesque elements.

The second, or 'High' phase emerges when an idea is fully established; the artist knows what he is doing and proceeds with complete confidence. This is true of Rayonnant Gothic building.

The High period of confidence eventually gives way to one of flagging inspiration usually coupled with technical virtuosity. The artist has arrived at a stage of such mastery that materials seem to bend to his every whim, but unfortunately his appetite has grown jaded, he loses himself in even greater excesses of decorative detail and pure showmanship. This last phase, when an art idea 'goes to seed' is usually referred to as 'Mannerist', and is of course exemplified by Flamboyant Gothic.

The Bishop's Eye *rose window in the southern end of the transept, Lincoln Cathedral, about 1330. (Camera Press)*

Fan vaulting in the King's College Chapel, Cambridge, about 1508. This highly decorative form of vaulting was an English speciality. (Camera Press)

The Development of Sculpture

Romanesque building produced its own sculptural offshoot and so too did Gothic. Gothic sculpture, like Gothic architecture, was a vastly more supple form than its Romanesque predecessor, having much greater potential for development.

These curiously elongated, still figures were carved approximately fifteen years after Gislebertus had completed his work at Autun. What can we say about them?

Certainly the artist who carved them was no dramatist like Gislebertus; there is no attempt here to capture our attention with dramatic gestures, intriguing subject matter or violent facial expression. The figures from the west façade of Chartres are tall and still like so many candles. The only movement is extremely subtle—the delicate linear rhythm of drapery, the simple hand gestures, the curling of hair—and the facial expressions are just as subtle: these faces give very little away. At best there is the hint of a smile and no more. The figures carved by Gislebertus fairly shout their message to us; the figures from Chartres require a great deal more effort from us. It is we who must approach them in a spirit of contemplation.

There are several other very marked areas of contrast between the two. The distortion of natural proportions so noticeable in the Chartres figures is a

device in the service of architectural harmony rather than dramatic expression. Then there is that curious hint of the Ancient Greek civilisation; the suggestion of tall reeded Greek columns, and indeed of certain Greek sculptures, which is such a far cry from the barbaric earthiness of so much Romanesque carving. Whether they were consciously modelled on Greek sculpture, as Kenneth Clarke suggests, is not of the greatest importance. What is far more important is the desire for far greater emotional subtlety which they exemplify.

Some of the carved figures from the central porch in the west façade of Chartres Cathedral about 1150. (Bulloz)

[18] Before a century had elapsed figures like these were beginning to appear in Gothic cathedrals. The confidence which western man felt in his world during the thirteenth century meant that artists could once again look directly to nature for their inspiration without fear or revulsion. Capitals broke into leaf and even sprouted branches. The everyday toil of man was recorded with great candour and freshness of vision. Above all, human expression and gesture was studied with penetration and thoroughness.

Carved figures of a later period from the north façade of Chartres. From the left: Simeon, John the Baptist, *and* St Peter. *(Bulloz)*

Foliage capital from Rheims Cathedral, thirteenth century. (Giraudon)

One of the Labour of the Months *carvings from Amiens Cathedral, thirteenth century. (Giraudon)*

Klaus Sluter

By the closing decades of the fourteenth century the art of sculpture had won its freedom from the maternal ties of architecture. This was most dramatically evident in the work of the great Dutch sculptor, Klaus Sluter, who did his most important work in Burgundy. Sluter's massive figures refuse to cling to walls or obediently stand in allotted niches; they demand the right to dominate the space around them. They are often swathed in great folds of drapery which both articulate them and create dramatic rifts of shadow. Add to this Sluter's mastery of facial expression—his Daniel from the Well of Moses is a superb example—and it is not surprising to learn that his influence rapidly spread throughout Southern France, Germany, Spain and Portugal.

Uta *from Naumburg Cathedral about 1260. (Mansell)*

French ivory Virgin, fourteenth century. (Louvre/ Giraudon)

Part of the Well of Moses *by* Klaus Sluter *(active about 1380–1406, in which year he died). This carving, in the Chartreuse of Champmol, was made during the period 1397–1405. (Bulloz)*

GOTHIC EUROPE
SOME IMPORTANT ARCHITECTURAL SITES

independent art form did not begin to develop seriously until the second half of the fourteenth century (again, Italy is an exception). Before considering this development we must first examine briefly an extremely important branch of the 'art of colour' which emerged tentatively during the late Romanesque period and rose to prominence during the Gothic. This was the art of stained glass.

Interior of the Sainte Chapelle, Paris, 1243–48. (Bulloz)

Stained-glass windows are essentially pictures constructed of pieces of coloured glass (not stained!) held together by a lattice work of lead strips. Details such as drapery, human features, foliage etc. may be painted, and then fired, onto the surface of the glass pieces. What makes the stained-glass window so different from any other form of painting is not so much the manner of its construction as the quality of light and colour which emanates from it. Colours, set as they are in lines of deepest black, become jewel-like and almost hallucinatory. Even the simplest images, composed of such colours, would have taken on an almost magical quality to the folk of the thirteenth century.

The Development of Painting

The painter of the twelfth and thirteenth centuries was almost indistinguishable from any other tradesman in terms of wealth, status and the type of work which was most likely to occupy him. He might decorate the accoutrements of war: saddles, shields, helmets and banners. He might design tapestries, paint the walls of churches and palaces or illustrate books. Painting as an

Illustrations from La Somme le Roy *about 1290 by Master Honore, the most distinguished manuscript illuminator in Paris during the late thirteenth century. The figures shown here represent* Humility *(standing on a unicorn),* Pride *(having a fall),* The Repentant Sinner *and* Hypocrisy. *(British Museum)*

This special quality of light and colour, of course, is almost wholly lost in reproduction (but see the back cover), particularly in black and white. There is also the matter of scale; many thirteenth-century windows were very large indeed and highly complex in terms of subject matter. A single window might be composed of dozens of small panels, each telling its own story.

As the Gothic style of architecture developed, so the walls of the churches were steadily reduced to a skeleton of stone ribs. Thus the stained-glass windows were given space to grow. Some Gothic churches became, in effect, vast green-houses, as the photograph of the Sainte-Chapelle in Paris, shows.

passion while the young king, although sumptuously dressed, kneels with an air of great humility and dedication. Richard's long delicate fingers and soft, almost girlish face suggest great piety and aesthetic refinement but not quite the regal authority we might expect from the monarch of a powerful land.

The intriguing quality of its subject matter aside, the painting has much more to recommend it. The surface has been worked with great delicacy, from the finely detailed textures of the drapery, hair and facial features to the tooled gold work of the background. The gentle curves which flow from figure to figure are likewise handled with considerable finesse and light-

This photograph shows a beautiful example of the kind of painting which emerged during the second half of the fourteenth century, the Wilton Diptych. A diptych is a painting made on two separate panels which are hinged together in the centre. This one is both a religious painting and a royal portrait. The right-hand panel shows the Madonna and Child surrounded by attendant angels, and the left panel shows the kneeling figure of the English King, Richard II who is being presented to the Virgin by three patron saints. The painting may strike us on several levels simultaneously—the great calm suggested by the entire composition and the wonderful richness and delicacy of the surface. The Madonna seems to be all gentleness and com-

The Wilton Diptych, *about 1396. (National Gallery, London)*

ness of touch. Does all of this suggest a civilisation of almost utopian perfection where piety, gentleness and affluence reign supreme? Is it a surprise to note that England was embroiled in her Hundred Years War with France when the Wilton Diptych was painted, that heresy and rebellion were rife in the land and that Richard himself was brutally murdered in the Tower of London while still in his early thirties?

In fact the Wilton Diptych was painted during a period when not only England, but Western Europe generally, was undergoing a period of severe hardship and self-doubt. The Black Death, an extremely virulent form of bubonic plague, ravaged the continent between the years 1347 and 1350; the young and the fit were often most vulnerable and estimates indicate that up to a quarter of Europe's population perished. A catastrophe on such a scale must have done much to undermine the confidence which had brought into being the cathedrals of the Rayonnant period and the philosophy of Thomas Aquinas. Even the Universal Church did not emerge from the crisis unscathed; the Great Schism, when rival Popes vied with each other for the affections of the faithful, undermined the fabric of the Church during some four decades at the close of the fourteenth century and the beginning of the fifteenth.

What is of considerable interest from our point of view is the fact that the Wilton Diptych was by no means unique. Between the years 1375 and 1425 a large number of pictures, very similar in style to the Wilton Diptych, appeared in many Western European countries. These pictures, whether they were miniatures or murals, stained glass or tapestries, religious or profane, all bear a strong stylistic resemblance to one another. Human figures, animals, trees, rocks, buildings etc. are all treated with a light delicate touch which emphasises rich texture and fluid curves. This style of painting has been called 'International Gothic'.

Now look at this picture: a winter scene—some

peasants warm themselves before a fire, a farm-yard behind its neat woven fence where crows peck in the snow and sheep huddle together for warmth in the fold, and that peaceful little village with its snow-capped roofs far in the distance.

What has this painting, a book illustration depicting the month of February, got in common with the Wilton Diptych? (They are both regarded as examples of the International Gothic style). There are certainly some similarities; the reverence for detail and texture is common to both as are the sense of pattern and the feeling of utopian calm. There the similarities appear to end. The subject matter in the second picture is obviously drawn lovingly from life and instead of a flat decorative background we are given a very commendable rendition of three-dimensional space. The book from which this picture was taken, the 'Très Riches Heures' of the Duke of Berry was a sort of pictorial almanac prepared for the Duke by Pol de Limbourg and his brothers Hermaun and Hennequin. The book is full of wonderfully observed detail. The Duke sits down to dinner surrounded by his courtiers, servants and animals, while his chamberlain bids a suitor to approach the great man. The Duke's beautiful castle acts as back-drop both to springtime sowing and to lords and ladies in all their finery enjoying a summer canter.

With artists of the calibre of the Limbourg brothers painting was beginning to assert its independence, as sculpture had done. Soon the 'art of colour' would be free of books and walls; the era of the easel picture was just around the corner.

Page from Les Très Riches Heures du Duc De Berry *by the Limbourg brothers. Early fifteenth century. (Giraudon/Musee Chantilly)*

The Development of Art in Italy
The triumphant Gothic style made relatively few inroads onto the Italian peninsula, an area of small independent states, each evolving its own form of government and its own local culture. The greatness of her classical past seemed to linger in the Italian soul. (We have already discussed the revival of Roman building skills by the masons of Lombardy.) Elements of Roman law found their way into the political structures of various Italian states—consuls appeared in Pisa towards the end of the eleventh century—and a number of attempts were made to recapture something of the weighty grandeur of Roman monumental sculpture as early as the beginning of the twelfth century.

[23]

Carving by Benedetto Antelami from Parma Cathedral, second half of the twelfth century. (Mansell)

The Pisan Sculptors

The thirteenth century, which saw the rise of many of the finest Gothic buildings in northern Europe also witnessed the rise of what might be called the 'Italian artistic personality'. This was probably most powerfully exemplified by the work of a group of sculptors based in the Tuscan city of Pisa during the second half of that century. The founder of the Pisan school, Nicola (called 'Pisano'), came from southern Italy. His first authenticated work was completed in 1260. This was the great marble pulpit in the baptistry of Pisa cathedral. The pulpit, a hexagonal structure supported on seven pillars (one in the centre) looks Gothic enough in its entirety. However when we look more closely, at one of the five relief panels on the side for instance, a very different impression is gained.

This photograph shows the panel representing the Nativity. The first thing you may notice is how heavy the various figures appear; there is very little of that light, springy feeling which we associate with French Gothic sculpture from the same period. Look at the drapery, how it hangs in heavy folds about the figures and helps to anchor them to the ground. Notice the faces, particularly that of the Madonna. Her face is very definitely that of a rather solemn Roman matron with its very straight nose, full cupid's bow mouth, firm jaw and severe hair style. There is no doubt that Nicola Pisano had paid very careful attention to work which had survived from the great Roman past and was very capable of applying the lessons he had learned to his own work. He was very much more than an antiquarian however, as further examination of his work soon demonstrates. Nicola's greatness lies in the use to which he put his various borrowings from the past. Although it is true that a number of his individual figures have a rather stiff, antique, flavour—he was, after all, attempting the very difficult task of reviving a long dead artistic language—many of his compositions are vividly dramatic and genuinely moving. His pulpit in Siena cathedral, for instance, features a very impressive Crucifixion. The figure of the dying Christ is quite alien to the classical world. His face is a curiously subtle blend of pain and sorrow while the grief and

Carving of The Nativity *by* Nicola Pisano *(born about 1220, died about 1284) from the pulpit in the baptistry, Pisa. (Mansell)*

bewilderment shown by the group of disciples who gather beneath the cross are admirably portrayed. One might also cite the 'Massacre of the Innocents' from the same pulpit as a further demonstration of Nicola's dramatic ability and skill in conveying human emotion through gesture and facial expression.

The later artists of the Renaissance regarded Nicola Pisano as one of the foremost of those medieval artists who had 'rescued' Italian art from the influence of Byzantium—('the rude manner of the Greeks', as the Florentine Giorgio Vasari put it, writing in the sixteenth century). They saw in his work the beginning of their own path to 'true art'. The men of the Renaissance had mixed feelings, however, where the work of Nicola's son Giovanni was concerned. Giovanni Pisano was at least as great an artist as his father. Even Vasari admitted that 'although Nicola had passed away, Giovanni remained . . . the heir to his virtues as well as to his abilities.' Giovanni's work suffered by comparison with that of his father, at least in Renaissance eyes, simply because the younger sculptor attempted to blend the dynamic, fluid quality of French Gothic sculpture with the dramatic forcefulness he had learned from Nicola.

If you compare the version of the Nativity by Giovanni with that of his father you may perceive the difference of approach in the work of the two sculptors. Giovanni's version, less weighty and full of sinuous movement, will probably appeal far more to the twentieth-century eye. Judge for yourself. In any case we should not be over influenced by what can only be regarded as a Renaissance prejudice against the Gothic style (which was referred to as 'Tadesco' in Italy).

At least a century was to elapse before the classical style, pioneered by Nicola Pisano, was to make further dramatic headway in Italy. During that period sculpture, painting and architecture in Italy were strongly tinged by Gothic influence. There is one very important exception to this: curiously not another sculptor but a painter, the Florentine Giotto.

Madonna and Child with Angels by Cimabue (born about 1240, died about 1302). (Louvre/Giraudon)

Carving of The Nativity by Giovanni Pisano (born about 1245—died about 1320) from the pulpit in Pisa Cathedral. This pulpit bears a lengthy inscription, part of which reads: 'He (Giovanni) would not know how to curve ugly or base things even if he wished to do so!' (Mansell)

Deposition *by* Giotto *(born about 1266, died about 1337). Fresco in the Arena Chapel, Padua, 1305—9. (Mansell)*

Giotto (c. 1266–1337)

We have only to compare this work by the painter Cimabue with that of Nicola or Giovanni to appreciate how great a gulf existed between the arts of painting and sculpture during the latter half of the thirteenth century. This is not at all to denigrate Cimabue, but when we compare him with the Pisans his work seems both excessively flat and rather coldly remote. It is curious therefore that the classical concept should be carried on by a painter, and a pupil of Cimabue's at that! This painter was Giotto, one of the greatest innovators in the entire history of European art. In adopting the visual language of the sculptors—by lending his figures volume and weight and by attempting to imbue them with the full spectrum of human emotions—Giotto virtually had to re-invent the art of painting single-handed.

To his contemporaries, Giotto's paintings were miracles of naturalism, a fact which may seem hard to credit in the twentieth century. Again we should remember that our concept of what constitutes a naturalistic image must differ very greatly from that of a citizen of the thirteenth or fourteenth century. We live in a society which is inundated with photographic images and in any case we have several centuries of naturalistic paintings and sculpture to look back upon. We cannot see Giotto's paintings as his contemporaries did; we must make a much greater effort than they in our approach to them. The photograph shows one of the panels which Giotto painted on the walls of the Arena chapel in Padua (the chapel is so called because it was built in the centre of an old Roman arena).

To step into the Arena chapel is a remarkable experience, for the walls seem covered by what looks like a gigantic comic strip. In a sense they are! Giotto's sequence of paintings, made during the years 1305–9, which are set out on the walls exactly as they would be on the pages of a comic book, tell one long story. They relate how the Virgin Mary was conceived by her parents, Joachim and Anna, and later how Joseph was chosen to marry the Virgin. Then we are in more familiar territory with the retelling in visual form of the life of Christ.

Our picture shows the dead Christ with the mourning figures of his mother and his disciples. Their grief is echoed by the group of angels who hover overhead. The subject, of course, is a very familiar one. Let us examine how Giotto has tackled it.

In a painting like the Wilton Diptych each figure is treated as a flat, decorative symbol—a structure of flowing rhythmic lines and texture. This is obviously not the case with Giotto's painting; look at the two figures sitting with their backs turned to us. They are certainly not decorative. Giotto has painted them like great bulky sacks of potatoes with extremely simple outlines for maximum clarity. Light and shade, and drapery folds, are employed almost exclusively to emphasise the bulk and sheer weight of the figures. The use of foreshortening further emphasises the three-dimensional quality of certain of the figures. The figure standing in the centre of the composition stretches his right arm backwards into space in a gesture of grief. Some of the angels in the top half of the picture plunge head first towards us.

The landscape, what there is of it, must seem particularly unimpressive to most twentieth-century eyes. It is important to note here that, although Giotto went to some pains to convince his public of the 'reality' (i.e. the solid existence) of everything he painted, he was hardly at all concerned with mere 'illusionism'. He put in just enough landscape to act as a solid stage for his figures, in this case consisting of a solid-looking slab of rock and a single, leafless tree. And the landscape is painted to look every bit as solid, and therefore 'real', as the figures.

The creation of solid, weighty figures and landscapes was only one side of Giotto's talents. Like the great Pisan sculptors he was also a master of the dramatic presentation. If we take the trouble to study Giotto, his talents as a superb stage manager become increasingly apparent and his various shortcomings —the lumpiness of many of his figures, the facial expressions which do not always quite work, the over sparse landscapes etc.—seem almost trivial. We no longer have to remind ourselves that, after all, he was virtually the first painter to attempt these things. His version of the 'Betrayal of Judas', also from the Arena chapel, is probably one of the finest renditions of that subject from any period. The same might be said of his 'Massacre of the Innocents'.

Most of Giotto's paintings have survived the ravages of time as have many of the legends and anecdotes concerning his life. There is almost a touch of Hollywood about the story which relates how the master painter Cimabue, while walking through the fields one day, discovered an ugly little peasant boy making a drawing of one of the sheep he was tending, on a flat piece of rock with a sharp stone. Cimabue invited the boy to join him as an apprentice and, in true Hollywood fashion, the boy grew to outshine his master. In 1334 he was honoured by the city of Florence by being made City Architect (no position of 'City Painter' existed at the time, a further indication of the lowly status of the painter during most of the medieval period).

Giotto never seems to have lost touch with his humble origins; his earthy sense of humour and his endearing ugliness seem almost to have gained him as much fame as his painting. He mixed with the greatest in the land with the greatest of ease. The poet Dante, whose portrait he painted, was a close friend. When Pope Boniface VIII sent a messenger to his studio requesting a sample of his work Giotto drew a perfect circle in red paint on a piece of paper and handed it to the startled messenger. Vasari tells us that on receiving this drawing, 'the Pope instantly perceived that Giotto surpassed all other painters of his time'.

And the great artists of the High Renaissance several centuries later shared the Pope's opinion. Michelangelo was sufficiently impressed by Giotto's figures to copy some of them. And Michelangelo's friend and contemporary Giorgio Vasari could write 'Giotto alone, in a rude and inept age, when all good methods in art had long been lost, dead and buried in the ruins of war, set art upon the path that may be called the true one'.

However much we may disagree with Vasari's contempt for the fourteenth century, the fact remains that Giotto did set art upon the path which led to what we call 'The Renaissance'.

Practical Exercises

The study of medieval art suggests a number of ideas which might find practical application:

1 Stained glass

The flat, brilliant colours, heavy black lead-lines and highly stylised drawing found in medieval glass might be interpreted in several ways:

(a) As large wax crayon drawings on white paper. Linseed oil brushed onto the back of the paper when the crayon work is complete tends to make the work more translucent and suitable for display, taped to a large window.

(b) In cardboard and coloured tissue paper (or cellophane). The lead-lines are painted onto the cardboard in black poster paint and when dry the intervening areas are cut away with a sharp knife. Pieces of coloured tissue are then glued onto the back of the cardboard. The finished product may also be displayed in a window.

Large stained-glass windows may be undertaken as a group project.

2 Carvings

Blocks of kitchen soap and blocks of plaster of paris may readily be carved without special tools. Both materials are suitable for interpretations of Romanesque imagery.

3 Architectural models

Architecture is the most difficult of the visual arts to study from photographs alone. Making models of buildings—even extremely simple ones which attempt little or no detail—can be a great help in appreciating the concept that buildings are composed essentially of volumes. While medieval architecture is being studied, models of Romanesque and Gothic buildings might be undertaken as a group project. Suitable materials include cardboard, small off-cuts of wood, balsa wood and polystyrene.

For further reading

Larousse Encyclopaedia of Byzantine and Medieval Art (Hamlyn)

Henri Focillon, *The Art of the West,* vol. I Romanesque Art, *and* vol. II Gothic Art (Phaidon)

Kenneth Clark, *Civilisation* (BBC/John Murray)

John Harvey, *The Master Builders—Architecture in the Middle Ages* (Thames and Hudson)

Andrew Martindale, *The Rise of the Artist in the Middle Ages and Early Renaissance* (Thames and Hudson)

John Pope-Hennessy, *Italian Gothic Sculpture* (Phaidon)

Some Important Events		Building and Visual Arts	
962	Otto I, King of Germany crowned Emperor by Pope John xii		
987	Hugh Capet King of France	c. 1000 to 1125–50	Period of great Romanesque building
1016	Canute King of England, Denmark and Norway		
1066	Norman Conquest of England		
		after 1066	Period of Norman building in England
1073	Hildebrand became Pope Gregory VII		
		c. 1075	Santiago de Compostela begun
		1088	Great monastery church at Cluny begun
		1093	Durham Cathedral begun
1095	First Crusade summoned by Pope Urban II		
1099	Godfrey of Buillon captured Jerusalem		
		1104	Vaulting of Durham Cathedral complete— probably first high rib vault in Europe
		early 12th century	Period of Clunaic carving
		1120	Autun Cathedral begun—appearance of first pointed arches in Europe
		1120–32	Carvings of Gislebertus in Autun Cathedral
		1137	St Denis begun Beginning of Gothic style
1147	Second Crusade		
		c. 1150	Chartres Cathedral—carvings in central porch La Belle Verrière
		1163	Notre Dame de Paris begun
1169	Saladin Sultan of Egypt		
1181	Birth of St Francis of Assisi		
1187	Jerusalem taken by Saladin		

	Some Important Events		Building and Visual Arts
1189	Richard Coeur de Lion King of England Third Crusade		
		1194	Chartres Cathedral partially destroyed by fire— rebuilt
		c. 1195	Development of flying buttresses
1215	Signing of Magna Carta		
		c. 1220	Birth of Niccolo Pisano (d. c. 1280)
1225	Birth of St Thomas Aquinas	c. 1225	Labour of the Months—carvings in Amiens Cathedral
1228	Frederick II embarked on Sixth Crusade— Jerusalem retaken		
		c. 1240	Birth of Cimabue (d. 1302)
		c. 1250	Naumburg Cathedral carvings—Eckhart and Uta
		c. 1245	Birth of Giovanni Pisano (d. c. 1317)
1265	Birth of Dante Alighieri	c. 1250– c. 1350	Period of Rayonnant architecture
		c. 1266	Birth of Giotto (d. 1337)
1271	Marco Polo's travels begun		
1304	Birth of Petrarch		
		1305–09	Frescoes in Arena chapel by Giotto
1309	Papal court moved to Avignon		
1348	Outbreak of Black Death		
		c. 1396	Wilton Diptych
1378	The Great Schism—Urban VI in Rome, Clement VII in Avignon		
		c. 1380	Klaus Sluter active (d. 1406)
1381	Peasant revolt in England		
		1395– 1404	Well of Moses by Sluter
		1411–16	Très Riches Heures du Duc de Berry by Limbourg brothers
1417	End of Great Schism		

CHAPTER TWO

Renaissance Art

Europe in the Fifteenth Century

The medieval world, although it holds a certain fascination for us, is still regarded as definitely alien to the one we know. The period which we call the 'Renaissance' on the other hand, we tend to see in quite a different light. Surely, we say, the Renaissance was the very foundation of modern western civilisation, a period of great artists, builders, philosophers, explorers and scientists; a positive, exhilarating period in fact, which saw the emergence of a new and progressive Europe firmly based on rational scientific thinking and capitalist enterprise—and the end of medieval ignorance!

Such a concept possesses several distinct advantages; it is beautifully simple and it presents us with the comforting legend of a 'Golden Age'. Attempts to form a more balanced view of the period unfortunately demand a more complex and contradictory one. Even the term 'Renaissance' (i.e. Rebirth) is open to question; might it not equally apply to the great revival of European civilisation during the eleventh century or to the centuries which gave rise to the Gothic style?

Undoubtedly great advances in art and science were made during the fifteenth and sixteenth centuries; the legend is by no means without foundation. But if the Renaissance was a golden age, it was certainly less than golden for most of those who lived through it.

We have already discussed the great carnage wrought during the mid 1300s by the Black Death. Many areas of Europe remained sadly underpopulated well into the fifteenth century, and the plague remained endemic even into the sixteenth. Localised outbreaks of variable durability and intensity were a constant phenomenon; people had no option but to accept them.

The Triumph of Death. *Engraving from Petrarch's Trionfi, c. 1470–80. (The British Library)*

This book illustration, made in Venice during the 1420s, aptly expresses the widespread feeling of pes-

simistic resignation abroad at the time—those who fall beneath the rumbling cart of Death, far from being the old, the poor or the decrepit, are kings, bishops, knights and merchants all in the prime of life.

The plague was by no means the only agency of destruction at work. Wars too took their toll. The Hundred Years War between England and France dragged on until 1453, leaving France in particular depleted in strength. And, like the plague, the Ottoman Turks remained a constant threat. Constantinople (Byzantium) itself fell to them in 1453 and as the century advanced it seemed that even Rome was not safe.

Conflict was not absent either on the spiritual front. The opening years of the fifteenth century saw the Church still torn by the Great Schism. The Council of Constance deposed and imprisoned the original Pope John XXIII on charges which included simony, murder and sodomy. And the first tremors of dissent were felt within the Church which would lead to an open and irreparable breach early in the sixteenth century.

Although no area of Europe could be described as immune to one or more of these disasters and fears, there were two regions that seemed to flourish. These were the lands of the Duke of Burgundy, which stretched from Mâcon in the south to Amsterdam in the north—and above all, northern Italy.

The Italian Quattrocento

By the beginning of the fifteenth century the Italian city states had coalesced into larger units, each with its own peculiar character and localised culture. Six great states were predominant—the republics of Florence and Venice, the duchies of Milan, Savoy and Ferrara, and the kingdom of Naples. Certain of the minor principalities, particularly Urbino, were extremely important cultural centres however.

The northern regions of Italy seemed particularly impressive to the visitor from north of the Alps. Here were thriving towns at no great distance from one another, busy trade, skilled craftsmen, builders and artists. Warfare, the inevitable result of fierce inter-state rivalries, had been reduced almost to a game left in the hands of professionals—the condottieri. Far from being a sign of decadence, this Italian attitude to warfare was perhaps one of the surest signs of the superiority of civilisation on the peninsula. War was inevitable, how foolish then to allow it to disrupt unduly the lives of those better employed in the government of states, the pursuit of wealth, knowledge and art.

Florence

The very heart of Italian civilisation for the greater part of the Quattrocento (Italian fifteenth century) was

Equestrian statue of the condottiere Gattamelata, *1444–47, by* Donatello. *(Mansell)*

undoubtably the Tuscan city of Florence. To her citizens Florence was the true inheritor of the cultural greatness of ancient Rome; she was the 'moon surrounded by stars'. Florentine scholars, particularly the humanists, applied themselves with great earnestness to the study of Latin and Greek texts. Many ancient texts which had lain dormant for centuries were eagerly sought, read, translated and discussed. Even Florentine banking agents stationed abroad were occasionally required to help unearth such literary treasure as might be found in their locality. Many Florentines travelled to Rome and further afield to collect, to measure and to study—and many outsiders eager to learn made Florence a sort of cultural Mecca.

In theory Florentine government was democratic almost to an absurd degree. In practice the various governments were wholly in the power of one or other of the leading families of the city. Political manipulation is certainly no stranger to our century; the same can hardly be said of the genuine pride in their city which many of these wealthy manipulators felt. The Medici family, who ruled Florence from 1434 to 1494, lavished large sums of money for the general betterment of the city. Members of this great banking family patronised painters, sculptors, architects, poets and scholars. When in 1437 the humanist scholar Niccolo de' Niccoli died and there was danger of his collection of 800 books being dispersed, it was Cosimo de' Medici who came to the rescue and had this valuable collection housed at his own expense. Cosimo's grandson Lorenzo (called 'the Magnificent'), a poet of some talent in his own right, surrounded himself with a number of the brightest intellects of his day.

Lorenzo's patronage of art, philosophy and science bears very little resemblance to the present-day patronage of gigantic oil companies or cigarette manufacturers. He could talk with philosophers and artists as an equal. The painter Botticelli was a close friend. One of Lorenzo's verses even pokes fun at Botticelli's excessive appetite and rather gross figure (so very unlike the graceful figures painted by that artist!)—'And he only regrets that his neck is too short. He'd like to have one like a stork.'

When approaching Florentine art (particularly painting) of the Quattrocento for the first time it is important to keep in mind the background of intellectual fervour which existed in the city. Florentine painting often seems unduly cold, brittle and colourless. To the Florentines painting was often simply another tool with which to measure, weigh and evaluate reality —what we would call a branch of science in fact. The ideas of the humanists prompted painters, sculptors and architects alike to pay particular attention to ancient Roman remains, great and small. While scholars and literati attempted to emulate the great Latin and Greek cultures of the past, the visual artists set themselves the task of creating an art which would have all of the authority and weight of the ancients. The artist was expected to be well informed and to use his intellectual capacities to the full. Gradually his status became less like that of a tradesman and more like that of a philosopher or indeed a scientist. This change in status led to the freeing of art from its purely religious function; it became an isolated entity like philosophy, directing its appeal increasingly to experts. The way was open, towards the end of the Quattrocento, for research into the rules of 'Beauty'. The art historian Lionello Venturi had nicely summed up the situation by stating that while nature had been substituted for God as the goal of art, so human intelligence was also substituted for God as the origin of art.

The Florentine architect and theorist Leon Battista Alberti, writing in the first half of the Quattrocento, aptly described Florence's Cathedral, S. Maria del Fiore, as vast enough to enclose all of the people of Tuscany in its shadow. And the twentieth-century visitor to Florence may still appreciate just what Alberti meant, for the cathedral's great dome still easily dominates the city.

A building less Gothic than S. Maria del Fiore would be difficult to imagine; it rather suggests the massive simplicity of form and weightiness we might associate with certain Romanesque buildings. In fact the Romanesque association is not too far out; the builders of the cathedral found a great deal of their inspiration in the ancient ruins which, in the fourteenth and fifteenth centuries, were still extant in the city of Rome. Much of the construction of the building had

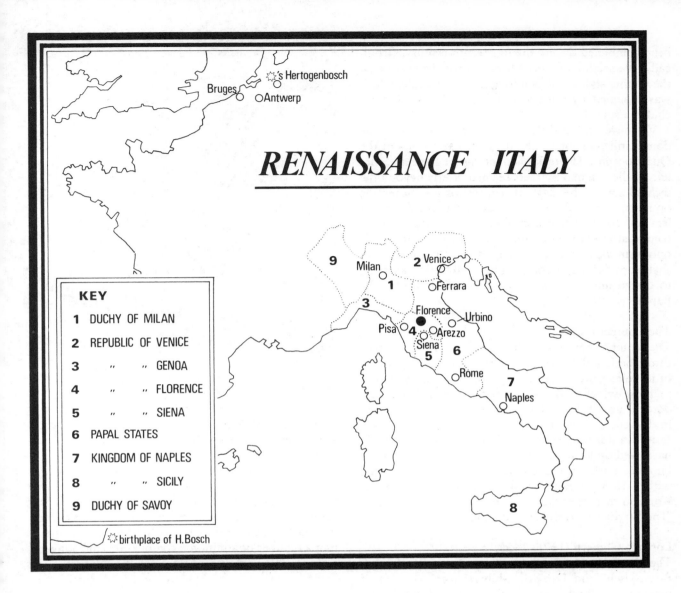

RENAISSANCE ITALY

KEY

1 DUCHY OF MILAN

2 REPUBLIC OF VENICE

3   "   "   GENOA

4   "   "   FLORENCE

5   "   "   SIENA

6 PAPAL STATES

7 KINGDOM OF NAPLES

8   "   "   SICILY

9 DUCHY OF SAVOY

✿ birthplace of H.Bosch

S. Maria del Fiore. *Florence cathedral viewed from the west. (Mansell). Brunelleschi's great dome still seems to dominate the city. The square tower standing on the south side of the façade is the campanile designed by Giotto (c. 1335). Part of the roof of the Baptistry may also be seen in this photograph, bottom right.*

been completed during the fourteenth century. (Ironically, the section of the cathedral most reminiscent of the Gothic style is the bell tower, or campanile, which was designed by Giotto. His original plan even included a spire.)

What was to be the building's crowning glory, the dome, still remained unbuilt in the early years of the Quattrocento. The task of spanning the huge aperture left by the original builders seemed utterly beyond the technology of the day, an expression of Florentine optimism rather than gross miscalculation. No problem was so great that it could not be eventually overcome—at least by Florentines—and as we shall see this optimism was later fully justified. Firstly, though, we shall consider the famous competition to find an artist to design and execute a second set of doors for the Baptistry.

The Competition

The competition was announced in 1401. Artists throughout Italy were invited to come to Florence in order to execute a simple relief panel in bronze similar to those which adorned the first, fourteenth-century door. Vasari tells us that many foreign artists arrived in Florence, eager to win so prestigious—and lucrative—a job for themselves. The field was eventually narrowed down to seven artists—all from Tuscany or Florence itself—and these seven were each presented with a sum of money and instructed to commence work on their specimen panels. The subject was to be 'The Sacrifice of Abraham', the time limit one year.

Lorenzo Ghiberti (1378–1455)

The three Florentine contestants, Donatello, Filippo Brunelleschi and Lorenzo Ghiberti were all men of outstanding ability, as was the Sienese Jacopo della Quercia. As there were thirty-four judges we may well imagine that the merits of each entry gave rise to considerable debate. Eventually the panel submitted by the young goldsmith, Lorenzo Ghiberti, won the day.

This was a complex as well as a competent work. The composition was set in a quatrafoil frame like the reliefs from the earlier door. Although no attempt had been made to render a sense of great depth, Ghiberti nevertheless placed his figures on three clearly differentiated levels. In the foreground (lower left) are two youths deep in conversation, and a donkey. Presumably these young men are servants of Abraham's. In the middle distance are the beautifully articulated figures of Abraham, knife in hand held ready to strike, and Isaac, kneeling upon the sacrificial altar. The modelling of the faces and the nude torseo of Isaac is particularly sensitive and we are reminded that Ghiberti trained as a goldsmith and was thus well used to delicate work. The figure of an angel who hurries to

The Sacrifice of Abraham, *1401, by* Lorenzo Ghiberti. *(National Museum, Florence)*

stay Abraham's hand, and a ram caught in a thicket, are placed at the third level of distance, in the background.

Ghiberti worked for twenty years on the door itself with its twenty-eight panels. During that time his workshop became one of the focal points for artistic activity in the city of Florence. The authorities were obviously pleased with Ghiberti's work as they offered him a number of additional commissions including the task of making the third door for the Baptistry. This commission seems to have occupied Ghiberti for an even longer period than the first and it was not until 1452 that his second door was fitted into place.

Ghiberti's second door was divided into ten large panels, each depicting a story from the Old Testament. Opposite is a reproduction of the 'Story of Jacob and Esau' from the later door. Compare it with the much earlier competition panel. Would you agree that Ghiberti's style had developed a great deal?

The first panel is really a late medieval work groping towards a classical style; the second is completely a work of the Renaissance. The handling of three-dimensional space is probably the element which strikes you most forcibly when you examine the second panel. The arches of the building seem to recede one behind the other and to 'carve out' a deep three dimensional stage for the background figures. This sensation of deep space is clearly emphasised by the lines of the floor tiles and by the fact that the figures and other objects diminish in size the further back in space they are placed.

The Story of Jacob and Esau, *1425–52, by* Lorenzo Ghiberti, *from the Porta del Paradizo, Baptistry, Florence. (Mansell)*

Lorenzo Ghiberti, in common with a number of other artists working in Florence at the time, had discovered how to use 'mathematical perspective'. (We shall discuss the problem of perspective more fully in the second part of this book.) It is sufficient to mention here that this system enabled an artist to create the appearance of a three-dimensional space which was both clear and *measurable.* Many Gothic painters had learned how to create the feeling of depth. This they did purely by intuition, but as the Florentines of the Quattrocento desired clarity almost above all else, only a system like perspective, which enabled the position of each element to be accurately calculated, would satisfy them. The observer's position is also dictated by the perspective scheme—his eye should be positioned directly opposite the 'vanishing point'. This vanishing point may be discovered simply by tracing and extending several of the sloping lines in a composition. With the aid of tracing paper, pencil and ruler it should be an easy matter to do this with the second Ghiberti panel.

Filippo Brunelleschi (1377–1446)

The credit for having invented the perspective system is usually given to Filippo Brunelleschi, another of the contestants for the design of the Baptistry door. He was goldsmith, clockmaker, sculptor, engineer and architect. Along with all of this, Brunelleschi seems to have possessed limitless reserves of energy. After the commission for the Baptistry door had been given to Ghiberti, he and his friend Donatello journeyed to Rome to complete their education. While Donatello's chief interests lay in the field of sculpture, Brunelleschi was fascinated by the buildings. We are told by Vasari that he visited every important building in the city, taking careful measurements and making drawings of architectural details: arches, vaults, capitals, cornices, foundations etc. He and Donatello even engaged in archaeological digs on some of the ancient sites and became known to the locals as 'the treasure seekers'. Both men were certainly seeking treasure of a sort, but not quite the variety imagined by the bemused citizens of Rome.

In 1407 the authorities in charge of construction work on S. Maria del Fiore decided to seek advice from experts regarding the building of the dome. Everyone

Interior of the Pazzi Chapel, *1430–40, by Brunelleschi.*
(Mansell)

seemed in awe of this great project, for even the revered ancients had never solved so difficult a problem. Brunelleschi let it be known however that he was confident of being able to solve the problem. So great was his belief in his own abilities that he consistently refused to furnish a scale model, or any other evidence, to substantiate his claims. Since the authorities refused to take him on trust Brunelleschi suggested a competition open to all comers. Eventually some nineteen models were presented to the authorities along with many outlandish suggestions as to how the structure might be accomplished. (Perhaps the most ludicrous suggestion of all entailed filling the cathedral with earth piled sufficiently high to enable the dome to be built on top. This mountain of earth was to be seeded with coins thus ensuring a willing work force to clear it away.) Brunelleschi, who had lavished much labour on his own model, still refused to display it. Instead he suggested to his fellow architects that whichever of them could succeed in making an egg stand upright upon a marble table should be given the job. It is not recorded whether his sanity was called into question at this stage; suffice to say that all tried and failed. His colleagues' sense of having been led up the garden path may well be imagined when Brunelleschi dented the egg before standing it upright. To their outraged cries of 'We could have done that' he calmly replied that they could build the dome also if they had his model.

Brunelleschi finally signed the contract to build the dome in 1417, and for fourteen years, from 1420 to 1434, he planned, invented, directed and fought until the dome was complete apart from the marble lantern —a building in its own right—on top. As difficulties arose they were tackled and overcome, from engineering problems of scaffolding and lifting machinery to human difficulties: strikes and interference from suspicious officials and jealous rivals. He died before the lantern was complete but not without leaving explicit instructions as to the manner of its completion. He even ensured that sufficient stone was available.

Florentine self-esteem must have received a great boost from the achievements of Filippo Brunelleschi: a modern man had successfully unearthed the secrets of the ancients and had then proceeded, not merely to emulate but to surpass them—'the ancients never dared so to compete with the heavens' . . . His engineering talents, great though they were, represented only one aspect of Brunelleschi's achievements. The style of building which he virtually invented single-handed marked a turning point in architectural style. His beautiful Pazzi chapel is a perfect example. This building, small in scale and composed of simple geometrical forms, has a measured order about it. It was designed as an entity complete in itself to which nothing might be added or taken away without disturbing the overall balance. Such buildings might be termed the architecture of humanism.

Donatello (c. 1386–1466)

Donatello had an impact upon the art of sculpture similar to that of his friend Filippo on architecture. His art reflects a complex, intense and, above all, powerful personality, in which may be detected strong traces of antique, Gothic and contemporary influences. Such was the power of Donatello's personality that these diverse elements were always completely digested and bent to his own will.

The monolithic figure of St George, carved to order for the Florentine guild of armourers, seems to have a classic stillness about his pose. Yet there is a tense alertness in this figure which is typical of Donatello: the possibility of immediate swift action is powerfully suggested. Vasari, when he described the St George as 'a most animated figure', was surely alluding to this quality. This figure of Donatello's, young, alert, proud and ready to take on all comers may be seen as a very apt symbol for the Florence of the 1400s.

The equestrian figure of the condottiere Gattamelata, made for the city of Padua on the order of the Signoria of Venice, demonstrates qualities very similar to the St George, but whereas St George may be presumed to personify certain aspects of Christian virtue, Gattamelata is simply a proud military leader.

After the St George, Donatello's figure of St Mary Magdalen comes as quite a shock. This figure, carved in wood, was made for the Baptistry of Florence cathedral. The ravaged face of the penitent Magdalen, the writhing surface of her ragged dress, her bare

St George, c. *1415, by* Donatello. *From the niche of the Guild of Armourers on the façade of Or S. Michele.* (Mansell)

St Mary Magdalen, c. *1457, by* Donatello. *From the Baptistry, Florence.* (Mansell)

sinewy arms and legs, all add up to a distinctly anti-classical whole. Yet the image is really powerful, almost unbearably so. This is certainly not just a figure made to fulfil an order. It is a work of the deepest emotional commitment.

Donatello's essays in perspective, carried out in bronze relief panels, serve to demonstrate how ultimately conservative and low-keyed Lorenzo Ghiberti's work was. Ghiberti strove for greater harmony in his work, the space he created adding ease to his story telling. Donatello's perspective schemes, on the other hand (as seen in works like the 'Healing of the Wrathful Son' from S. Anthony in Padua), have a note of almost abrasive boldness about them which greatly adds to the drama of his work. The two artists, Ghiberti and Donatello, may be seen as representatives of the two poles of Italian art respectively: the one seeking to gather together all the various elements which make a work of art into a single harmony where no single element obtrudes, the other seeking dramatic effect and a certain grandeur. The first path, as we shall see, was to lead to such giants of the High Renaissance as Raphael, the second to the incomparable Michelangelo.

Masaccio (1401–28)

This age of prodigious achievement in the fields of architecture and sculpture also saw great progress made by Florentine painters. It must be said, however, that the painters still tended to take their cue from the sculptors. Of the painters working in Florence during the first half of the Quattrocento, there is little doubt that the greatest was one Tommaso di Ser Giovanni called Masaccio ('Slovenly Tom') because of his carefree, down-at-heel appearance.

Masaccio's painting called 'The Tribute Money' was one of a series of frescoes painted during the mid 1420s in the Brancacci chapel in Florence. This series of paintings, commissioned by the wealthy silk merchant Felice de Michele Brancacci, was chiefly concerned with scenes from the life of St Peter. 'The Tribute Money' relates the story of how St Peter, on Christ's bidding, catches a fish and draws from its mouth a sum of money sufficient to satisfy the demands of a tax collector. In the centre of the picture we see Christ, who is surrounded by his disciples, giving the order to St Peter. On the extreme left St Peter, who has discarded his cloak, draws the money from the fish's mouth, while on the right we see the defiant saint thrust the sum of money into the hand of the somewhat crestfallen tax collector.

There are many qualities we might notice in this picture, foremost of which is Masaccio's ability to paint wonderfully solid figures. His figures are as weighty and as solidly planted on the ground as those

The Tribute Money, c. *1425–28, by* Masaccio. *Fresco in the Brancacci chapel, S. Maria del Carmine, Florence. (Scala)*

of Giotto, but the awkward, lumpy quality which we often encounter in the work of the earlier artist has been left far behind. Facial expressions, gestures, the sense of objects bathed in light falling from a single source and a very credible landscape setting have all been rendered with considerable skill. The sturdy, aggressive figure of the tax collector who stands with his back to us and facing Christ is a particularly impressive invention. Notice the assurance with which Masaccio has dealt with the various problems of foreshortening posed by this figure, his left hand thrust towards Christ, for instance.

'Slovenly Tom' had studied hard in his trade. His paintings demonstrate how well he had learned the lessons of Giotto and the great sculptors from the Pisani to Donatello and Brunelleschi. Like Donatello, his vision was powerful enough to make something quite new and fresh out of ideas gleaned from others. In its turn Masaccio's work was to prove an inspiration to later generations of artists, and the Brancacci chapel became a school of art for Botticelli, Leonardo, Michelangelo and Raphael among many others. Masaccio admirably continued and extended what Giotto had begun a century earlier. That he should have accomplished so much before he died at the age of twenty-seven is perhaps the most surprising thing about his career.

Paolo Uccello (1397–1475)

In the twentieth century the distinction between the arts (drama, painting, music etc.) on the one hand and science and technology on the other, seems both wide and clear. Such a distinction, which seems so obvious to us, was very blurred indeed during the Quattrocento. We have already seen how, in the case of Brunelleschi, the greatest engineer of the period was also a noted sculptor whose inventions benefited technology and art alike. To a man of Brunelleschi's generation the tasks of carving the figure of a saint, calculating the stresses in the dome of a building or designing a drainage system were simply intriguing problems to be solved. Problems which we would regard as purely technological or mathematical were frequently deemed to fall within the province of the artist. And people who today would undoubtedly be trained as scientists, mathematicians or engineers were, during that period, often apprenticed to painters or sculptors.

The case of the painter Paolo Uccello demonstrates this aspect of Renaissance thinking very well. Paolo was a very talented painter, yet the aspect of his art which interested him most (almost, it seems, to the point of obsession) was an almost exclusively mathematical one: the problem of perspective.

Uccello, it would appear, was quite prepared to endure poverty, the wrath of his wife and the scorn of his friends in the pursuance of his 'obsession'. Donatello, one of his closest friends, was openly contemptuous—'Ah, Paolo, with this perspective of yours, you are losing the substance for the shadow . . . these circles, spirals, squares, and all.'

Much of Uccello's labour was spent on drawings like this one. He delighted in drawing perspective views of the most complex solids, calculating the exact foreshortening of each facet. His paintings have a curiously naive charm; his horses and figures are often reminiscent of clockwork dolls thrashing about on a painted cardboard stage. This impression tends to be accentuated by the arbitrary colour sometimes employed by Uccello; horses might be entirely red—or they might equally well be green. This latter trait in particular was not at all to the taste of later generations and drew from Vasari the priggish comment that 'here he committed an error, for stones ought to look like stones.' Nevertheless it was due to the lifelong researches of men like Uccello that the later generation of the High Renaissance could achieve so much perfection with so little apparent effort.

The painting by Uccello reproduced here was one of a set of three painted for the Medici family. The three pictures commemorate a victory by the Florentines over the Sienese at the Battle of S. Romano. The knight in the centre of the composition on his white charger (and wearing that splendid piece of headgear!) is the Florentine captain Niccolo da Tolentino. Notice how carefully Uccello has strewn the battleground with the debris of war: helmets, lances, shields and even a dead body. The positioning of the broken lances in particular emphasises the depth of the battleground 'stage'.

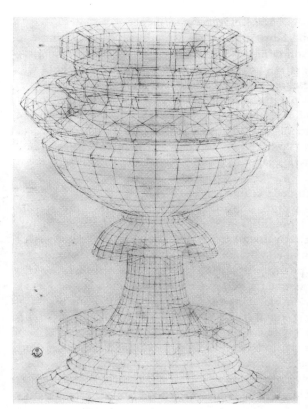

Perspective drawing of a chalice by Paolo Uccello. *(Scala)*

The Battle of S. Romano, c. *1454, by Paolo Uccello. (National Gallery, London). This painting is one of a set of three illustrating the battle in which the Sienese* were defeated by the Florentines in 1432. The set was made for the Medici Palace.

The Spread of Florentine Influence

[38] While Florentine artists were busily assimilating and consolidating the discoveries of the great 'founding generation', the influence of the Florentine school was spreading outwards from that city, especially into various parts of northern Italy. Many Florentine artists, most notably Donatello (cf. his equestrian statue of Gattamelata in Padua) carried their skills and ideas to other cities, while 'foreign' artists in their turn visited Florence eager to learn as much as possible.

Piero della Francesca (c. 1416–92)

The painter Piero della Francesca learned much from the Florentines: a passion for perspective and structural clarity from artists like Uccello, and another for monumentally conceived figures from Masaccio. Yet his painting is not at all like the work of those two Florentine masters. There are several aspects of Piero's work which may readily be appreciated: his beautiful soft colour harmonies and his ability to suggest that his figures are enveloped by a clear crystalline atmosphere and gently bathed in light. His total aloofness is quite another matter; not only do his paintings tell us absolutely nothing about the artist's feelings but his figures display this disconcerting passivity also. All is serenity and detachment, whether the scene depicted is the Baptism of Christ or his Flagellation.

Piero demonstrates a particular approach to art which we shall meet with on several occasions in this book. Here the artist is concerned, not with a display of his own emotions, but rather with the problem of isolating and refining those elements which he regards as most deeply moving in *themselves*. The artist withdraws from the scene completely and allows his work to act upon our sensibilities. With art like this—and we have encountered it before in the portal sculptures of Chartres—we must make a great deal of the effort to establish communication.

In Piero's 'Baptism of Christ' the landscape is a faithful likeness of the kind to be found, even today, in the vicinity of his native Borgo San Sepolcro. The 'River Jordan' is more than likely based on some local stream with its crystal clear surface which so faithfully reflects sky, trees and figures. And that figure of a man in the background, drawing the shirt over his head, is beautifully studied from life. Still, the painting has a quality which quite removes it from time and place.

Piero completed a number of paintings for his birth place, including the 'Baptism', and for neighbouring towns like Arezzo and Monterchi. It is not surprising that he should also have been drawn to the court of Duke Federico da Montefeltro of Urbino, then the most civilised in all of Italy. Duke Federico was a remarkable man, highly cultivated and intelligent, a great lover of literature and painting. Yet the portrait

The Baptism of Christ in the River Jordan, c. *1450, by* Piero della Francesca. *Painted for the Priory of St John the Baptist in Borgo S. Sepolcro. (National Gallery, London)*

(by Justus of Ghent) which he had painted for his library shows him reading a book and fully dressed in armour, for the Duke was one of the finest soldiers of his day. His palace, with its beautifully proportioned interiors, was also a fortress. The court of Urbino served as a sort of finishing school for young men of noble birth. Here they learned to read the classics, to speak quietly, and generally to behave like gentlemen.

Piero worked for Duke Federico from 1469 until he became blind in old age. During this period he also concerned himself with some theoretical works on mathematics, the most important of which was the treatise 'De Prospectiva Pingendi'.

Agony in the Garden *by* Andrea Mantegna. *(National Gallery, London)*

Andrea Mantegna (1431–1506)

This painting depicts one of the best known of all New Testament stories, that of Christ's agony in the Garden of Gethsemane. Christ kneels in agonised prayer, upon a shelf of rock, while some angels, one of whom bears a cross, appear before the Saviour. On the ground beneath, his three disciples sleep, while from the gates of Jerusalem the soldiers, led by Judas, emerge to make their arrest. Yet these elements of the Bible story seem almost incidental in their impact when compared with their powerful landscape setting. The rocks upon which Christ kneels are so clear and hard that we can virtually feel each sharp angle and each fissure, and we can readily imagine walking into the depths of the landscape along that twisting road. First we must step over the rigid forms of the sleeping disciples (who are themselves only marginally less hard and solid than their rocky environment!) and follow the sweeping curve of the road past those frisking rabbits and on

down the slope towards Judas and the soldiers. And we may proceed much further on our imaginary journey; we may climb the slopes which lead to the city nestling so securely beneath those awesome outcrops of rock, pass beneath the walls and turrets and so on into the landscape of undulating hills beyond.

This amazing feat of painting was the work of Andrea Mantegna, an artist whose work seems the very essence of Quattrocento aspirations. His various qualities and accomplishments make a formidable list. From the painting reproduced here you may judge something of his ability to create a tangible world of solid forms and deep tracts of space. His mastery of perspective drawing must also be apparent from this picture; notice the disciple who sleeps with his feet towards us, for instance. Although he always retained a certain grim reserve in his paintings, Mantegna was capable of sensitive portraiture as in the pictures of Ludovico Gonzaga and his family. The treatment of the younger Gonzaga children, one of whom shyly clutches his elder brother's hand, is particularly touching. Mantegna's humanist contemporaries found much to admire in his historical pictures, most of which dealt with the splendours of ancient Rome. He brought a new accuracy to this genre which perfectly paralleled the scientific attitude of humanist scholars in their approach to ancient literature. Armour, helmets, weapons, emblems etc. from ancient Rome were studied with great care, as were Roman buildings.

As a result of this great love for a specifically Roman past, many of Mantegna's religious paintings are not altogether successful—as religious paintings. The cycle of frescoes from the Erimitani Church in Padua (most of these pictures were destroyed in the second World War) which tells the story of St James's trial and martyrdom, is a case in point. Here Mantegna's mastery of space and solid form, wedded to his considerable archaeological knowledge, conjure up such a magnificent historical spectacle that the sufferings of the saint seem almost an afterthought. We are tempted to believe that Mantegna was happiest when painting a subject like the 'Triumph of Caesar' which, of course, is wholly secular.

Northern Realism—Art in Flanders

So far in our survey of the fifteenth century we have considered only the growth of art forms which had originally sprung from Florentine soil. Great as was the Florentine contribution to Renaissance culture that city was by no means the only important centre of artistic growth. North of the Alps, particularly in the city of Bruges, the art of painting was developing along lines quite unlike but no less revolutionary than those in Florence. (In Venice a new and vital branch of Italian painting began to sprout during the second half of the century as we shall see later.)

If there is a single factor common to all European painting during the fifteenth century it is probably the desire to come to grips with the observable world. Painters north and south of the Alps were thus faced with the common problems of making objects look solid and placing those objects in a believable, three-dimensional space. The Italians tackled these problems in a rational, scientific manner; space was laid out carefully according to the dictates of mathematical perspective; colour, light and shade were employed with equal care and precision to give substance to solid forms. The painters of Flanders approached their art from an almost diametrically opposed starting point. Their reconstruction of the world was due far more to painstaking observation than to mathematical calculation (although it should be mentioned that they based their compositions upon geometrical grids or guide lines).

We have already encountered an example of early fifteenth-century Flemish painting in the work of the Limbourg brothers, but even the brilliant accomplishments of those artists hardly prepare us for the achievements of the succeeding generation, least of all for the work of Jan Van Eyck.

Jan Van Eyck (1385/90–1441)

A room bathed in the soft light of northern Europe: the figures of a young man and woman stand facing us solemnly holding hands; on the floor between us and them a little dog and a pair of discarded wooden pattens (for walking in the muddy streets of Bruges).

How shall we approach this painting which seems so simple and yet so complex and private? The more we look, the more questions it seems to pose. Who were these people, why were they so very solemn, why should just one candle burn in their splendid brass chandelier, and what does that curiously ornate inscription above the mirror mean?

We know that Jan Van Eyck painted the picture in 1434: that inscription above the mirror boldly tells us

The Arnolfini Wedding Portrait, *1434,* by Jan Van Eyck. *(National Gallery, London)*

'Johannes De Eyck Fuit Hic 1434'. It was painted for two friends of the artist on the occasion of their marriage; it served a dual purpose: to commemorate the solemn event and also to certify it, for Van Eyck was one of the two witnesses. As to the identity of the newlyweds, they were probably an Italian couple, Giovanni and Giovanna Arnolfini.

In the 1430s Bruges was one of the great commercial centres of Europe and attracted important foreign businessmen like Giovanni Arnolfini. It also attracted artists of outstanding talent, like Jan Van Eyck and his brother Hubert. All of this may help to explain the painting's *raison d'être*, but it hardly begins to explain the apparently miraculous skill with which it has been executed. The artist has powerfully, yet unobtrusively, suggested that real light—the soft light of northern Europe—illuminates the room and its inhabitants. This light of Van Eyck's seems capable of revealing the most microscopic aspects of nature and yet seems to unify everything. How clearly it distinguishes between a myriad of textures, from the hard cold glint of glass and metal to the soft diffuse warmth of fur. These qualities of 'intense realism' are present in all Van Eyck's pictures, from the great religious works like the Ghent altarpiece (painted in collaboration with his brother Hubert) to the small intimate portraits.

Must we regard Van Eyck merely as a talented human camera, devoid of imagination and capable only of slavish imitation? His paintings actually convey the opposite impression; they suggest an artist intoxicated with his world, overwhelmed by the beauty and wonder of every blade of grass and every strand of hair. One is curiously reminded of St Francis of Assisi, that other great man who had 'rediscovered' the everyday world and found it marvellous.

We can also sense that Van Eyck's compositions were anything but arbitrary, and in fact he probably used a geometrical grid to control the placing of his forms. Many of the intimate details which enrich his paintings were not merely fortuitous; he was capable of employing a subtle symbolism. In the Arnolfini portrait the solemn symmetry of the two figures is probably not without significance. The same might be said of the single candle burning in the chandelier, and even the little dog is possibly a symbol of fidelity. We may also learn something if we examine the circular convex mirror placed centrally in the composition. Beside the mirror hangs a rosary and in the frame are set ten roundels depicting scenes from the Passion, both testimonies of piety. In the mirror itself the room may be seen in microcosm—but viewed from the opposite direction so that the two witnesses are visible behind the reflections of the husband and wife. The reflection is a tiny and complete picture within a picture, just as the artist's work is a tiny and complete

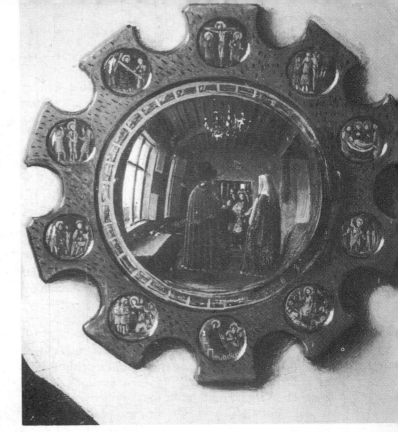

The Arnolfini Wedding Portrait. *Detail of the mirror. The ten roundels depict scenes from Christ's Passion. (National Gallery, London)*

picture within the greater picture of nature.

To compare Italian painting of the same period with that of Van Eyck is perhaps unfair—the Italians were proceeding in a different direction after all—but one is still tempted to comment on how relatively crude is the rendition of light in the work of artists like Masaccio and Uccello. And of course it must be pointed out at this juncture that Van Eyck was using a different type of painting medium to that in common usage throughout Europe. He was the first great artist to grasp the potential of paint mixed with boiled linseed oil.

Van Eyck did not invent oil painting as has often been asserted by historians, including Vasari. He does seem to have brought the method to perfection however, building up his paint surfaces in successive transparent layers which seem to have all the richness of finest enamel, and allow light to be reflected back from the white ground. Oil paint, like enamel or stained glass, is a beautiful material in its own right; this is not really true of tempera (paint mixed with egg) or fresco (paint worked into wet plaster). Both of these latter media tend to produce entirely bland, matt surfaces, and these were the media in general use throughout Europe until the time of Van Eyck. The secrets of oil painting soon spread. The Flemings were the first to fully exploit it, but it did find its way into Italy and even Paolo Uccello used it in his last works.

The accomplishments of the International Gothic style seemed to have been rendered obsolete at a stroke by Van Eyck. In this he is reminiscent of Giotto and, as in the case of the great Italian, the generations which immediately succeeded Van Eyck were not wholly prepared to follow the course which he had pioneered. This is not in any way to detract from the greatness of the northern schools, particularly the Flemish. Artists in France, Germany and the Low Countries produced many pictures of outstanding quality during the early and mid 1400s. Whether their art, and indeed that of Van Eyck himself, should be termed 'Renaissance' or 'Late Medieval' (it was after all the period of the Flamboyant style) I leave to the historians and scholars of the period to argue about.

Rogier Van der Weyden (c. 1399–1464)

Rogier Van der Weyden's 'Pietà' perhaps comes closer to the mainstream of northern European painting in the mid fifteenth century than does the work of Van Eyck. The Virgin kneels at the foot of the cross holding the dead body of Christ. On the right of the composi-

tion a contemplative Dominican—possibly St Dominic himself—stands reading from a book. The figure dressed in black velvet, who piously kneels in prayer on the left, is the layman who commissioned the work (the 'donor') while behind him, dressed in his red cardinal's robes, stands the figure of St Jerome.

Although the background landscape—the wooded slopes, the distant blue hills and the delicately drawn cloud formation—gives the painting a feeling of great depth, the main group of figures has been arranged as if on a very shallow stage. This flatness is emphasised by the very 'frontal' position of the dead Christ and the manner in which the Virgin's cloak spreads itself on the ground behind her. The rhythmic curving forms of drapery and limbs, reminiscent of the International Gothic style, serve to bind the composition together and to further augment this flatness.

Van der Weyden's picture may not have the spatial grandeur and weightiness of his Florentine contemporary Masaccio, nor that almost magical sense of light of Van Eyck, but it speaks with its own very considerable authority. Study the composition. Notice how the

Pietà *by* Rogier Van der Weyden. *(National Gallery, London)*

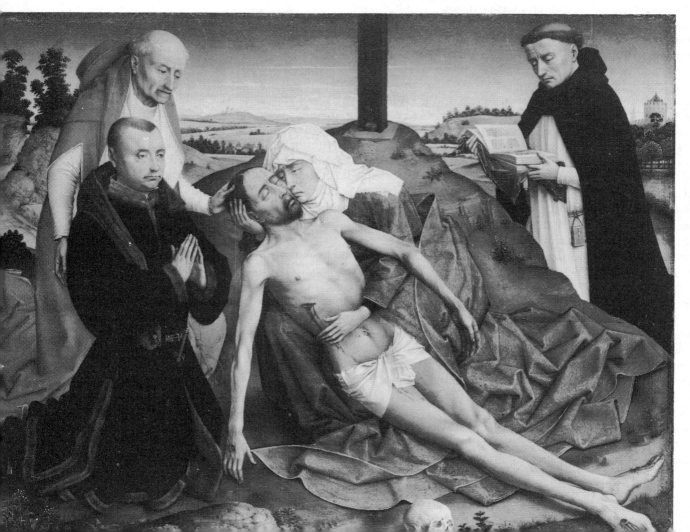

flowing harmony of shapes is sufficiently disturbed by notes of discord to remind us of the tragic nature of the scene: the right arm of Christ which strikes stiffly against the ground and the agitated rucking of the Virgin's cloak.

Now study the faces of each of the characters. How delicately has Van der Weyden depicted the concern on St Jerome's aged face, and the welling grief on the face of the Virgin. And the Donor? Look at his face. Is he really pious or merely some worldly merchant or banker pretending to be so?

Venice

The great cities of Florence and Venice, differing radically from each other in so many respects, were both objects of the intense pride of their respective citizens. In Venice, pride in the state was accorded official status. Great state occasions were celebrated with vast and gorgeous processions and pageants by land and by sea. Here the ordinary citizen might view those living symbols of the state's glory, the Doge and senators, arrayed in robes no less splendid than those worn by Church dignitaries. Such extravaganzas, secular equivalents of the most solemn ceremonies of the Church, helped to reconcile the ordinary citizen to the restrictions which the state placed upon his personal liberty. They were a source of both entertainment and pride, and served as a reminder of the state's overwhelming power and wealth. The contrast with Florence, where government was a far more haphazard affair, is obvious. The Venetian system ensured an internal security found nowhere else in Italy, but it also meant that personal freedom of expression was much slower to develop than in Florence.

Giovanni Bellini (c. 1430–1516)

The first great personality to emerge in Venetian painting was Giovanni Bellini, the founder of a distinctly Venetian school. Giovanni came from a renowned family of painters; both his father, Jacopo, and his elder brother Gentile, having distinguished themselves in that field.

Gentile is remembered chiefly for his minutely observed paintings of great state occasions such as the 'Procession in Piazza S. Marco' (a vast canvas measuring 3·6×7·2 metres) which captures much of the dignity and splendour of the occasion along with the ornate quality of Venetian building. He distinguished himself not only as an artist but also in the role of special envoy to the court of Mohammet II in Constantinople.

Giovanni Bellini's paintings are richly sensuous in their colours. His forms are bathed in light rendered with a skill reminiscent of the Flemish masters. His figures are set in landscapes of meadows and rolling hills whose gentle slopes give rise to outcrops of build-

Agony in the Garden, c. *1460, by Giovanni Bellini.* (*National Gallery, London*)

ings and woods. Distant blue hills blend with the soft greens and oranges of his evening skies. Atmosphere and colour (which were to become basic ingredients of the Venetian school) were never allowed to destroy his strong sense of structure and design; Giovanni's genius lay in his ability to give full expression to all these elements.

His 'Agony in the Garden' makes an interesting contrast with the version by Andrea Mantegna. These two artists, who at first glance appear to have nothing in common apart from the closeness of their ages, were in fact brothers-in-law. The authoritative sense of structure which we find in Giovanni's work owes much to his careful study of the art of his brother-in-law.

Compare the two versions for yourself. They do actually have a number of elements in common: the outcrop of rock and the kneeling figure of Christ recall the Mantegna, as does at least one of the sleeping disciples and also the pathway which twists away into the distance. But the areas of dissimilarity are perhaps more marked: in the Venetian picture the contours of rock are far less harshly obtrusive, the distant hills are softened by the veil of atmosphere and the clouds look as though they were composed of vapour. (Even Mantegna's clouds have a certain stony quality about them!)

So far we have discussed the two pictures only in terms of purely physical qualities. Look at them both again and try to assess them from the point of view of emotional content. Do you think that the criticism levelled at Mantegna as a religious artist is valid here?

The End of the Quattrocento—Prelude to the High Renaissance

Thanks to the efforts made by several popes during the mid 1400s, the city of Rome gradually regained her position as the centre of art and learning in Italy. The humanist cause was taken up by pontiffs like Nicholas V, who founded the Vatican Library, and Paul II, who was a collector of gems and bronzes as well as a restorer of ancient monuments. By the end of the century the centre of creative initiative had begun a definite shift from Florence to Rome. Florentine art had travelled far since the early days of discovery. Techniques which Masaccio and Uccello had striven so hard to master had been virtually perfected, and painters and sculptors felt free to use their impressive resources in a new field of enquiry—the nature of beauty itself.

Botticelli (1444–1510)

The paintings of Sandro Botticelli testify to the perfection of late Quattrocento Florentine painting. His pictures are full of ease and gracefulness yet have that iron core of structure which we identify with Florence. Several drew their inspiration from the legends of a past age quite unmarked by the Christian concept of sin. The dancing figures of his 'Primavera' celebrate an essentially pagan vision of spring, his 'Venus' drifts to land on her shell, his 'Mars' sleeps beside a buzzing wasps' nest while infant satyrs play with the War god's armour and weapons.

Yet even at this period advances were not made without faltering footsteps, for while Rome was re-establishing her pre-eminence Florence was entering a period of crisis and self doubt. During the 1490s the citizens of Florence flocked to the cathedral to hear the words of the Dominican preacher Girolamo Savonarola. The preacher's words lashed out at the life style of the people, their dress, their pastimes, their philosophy, their art. Even the Medici, who had brought him to Florence in the first instance, did not escape his wrath—neither did the papal court of Alexander VI: 'The scandal begins in Rome and runs through the whole clergy; they are worse than Turks and Moors!'

Lorenzo the Magnificent died in 1492, and goaded by the preacher's words, the Florentines drove his successors from the city. Under Savonarola's puritanical influence they indulged themselves in orgies of remorse; processions of penitents marched through the streets to the great bonfires where they burnt their 'vanities'—fine clothes, dices, mirrors, jewellery, false hair, poems and pictures (though fortunately no major works appear to have been damaged).

Savonarola's castigations of contemporary living and his prophesies of doom seemed to give utterance to the Florentine self doubt. Botticelli was one of those artists who 'mended his ways' and returned to Christian subject matter. The Dominican preacher ended his life at the stake in the main square of Florence, condemned as a heretic. The bell which had once summoned the faithful to his sermons was whipped. Savonarola's words had perhaps cut too close to the bone, especially those directed against Rodrigo Borgia—Pope Alexander VI.

The High Renaissance: Leonardo, Michelangelo, Raphael

The summit of achievement in the arts represented by the Renaissance was reached only after a long succession of earlier artists had paved the way to it. And even

Primavera, c. 1478, by Sandro Botticelli. Painted for Lorenzo di Pierfrancesco, cousin of Lorenzo the Magnificent. (Mansell)

then the heights reached by its greatest artists were not long maintained. For a period of twenty years or so all things seemed possible, beauty was measurable, nature could be made to surrender up all her secrets given time and the first of a new race of giants seemed to walk in the world of ordinary mortals. They were a tiny handful, these men whose genius lay at the very centre of the High Renaissance. To their contemporaries they were virtually divine and even to our jaundiced sensibilities their achievements still seem worthy of the deepest respect.

Leonardo da Vinci (1452–1519)

The terms 'artist' 'engineer', 'scientist' or 'philosopher' all seem peculiarly inadequate to describe Leonardo da Vinci; he was all of these and more. His interests included astronomy, biology, anatomy, hydraulics, mechanics, optics, aviation, chemistry and palaeontology along with music, painting and sculpture. It would appear that he set himself the task of understanding everything; the notebooks which he carried everywhere with him were filled with questions to be asked: 'ask Benedetto Portinari how people go on the ice in Flanders', problems to be puzzled over: 'what is sneezing?', observations, both verbal and graphic, on everything under the sun: 'I saw at Milan a thunderbolt strike the Torre della Credenza'. Even the sun did not escape his attentions; he devised a special apparatus which enabled him to watch the total eclipse in 1485 with safety. His breadth of mind was matched by a soaring imagination and an amazing freedom from the prejudices and preconceptions of his day. Although he regarded painting not merely as the most superior of the arts but as the noblest of all human endeavours, he completed comparatively few painted works during his lifetime. It is not difficult to understand why. Painting was to serve as the vessel into which Leonardo could pour all of his discoveries. It was to be the end product, as it were, of all his labours. But how could such a restless mind ever be satisfied with any 'end-product'? Just as one solution was found a dozen other possibilities presented themselves. So we find projects abandoned at an early stage and others suffering from the artist's over zealous research into new techniques. The 'Last Supper', painted on the wall of the refectory of S. Maria della Grazie in Milan, began to decompose even during Leonardo's own lifetime.

The natural son of a Florentine notary, Leonardo served his earliest apprenticeship to the sculptor and painter Andrea Verrocchio. Vasari tells us that the figure of a kneeling angel which he added to his master's 'Baptism of Christ' so impressed Verrocchio that he resolved never to touch paint again. An apocryphal story perhaps but the fact remains that the angel in question is the most accomplished part of the

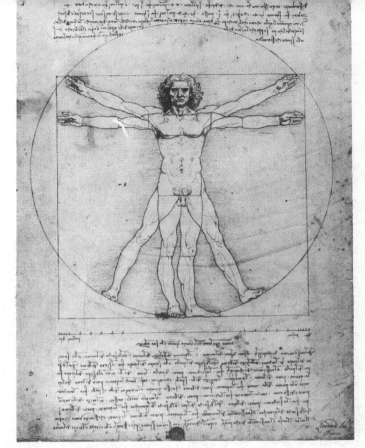

Study in the Proportions of the Human Body, based on Vitruvius, c. *1500, by Leonardo da Vinci. (Mansell)*

painting; Leonardo was obviously a young man to watch. Characteristically the years which followed were not spent merely in perfecting his knowledge of painting and sculpture.

In his letter of introduction to the Duke of Milan he listed a bewildering range of projects in the fields of military and naval engineering which he was prepared to undertake. At the end of his letter he added, almost as an afterthought . . . 'I can carry out sculpture in marble, bronze or clay, and also I can do in painting whatever can be done, as well as any other, be he who he may.'

While in Milan Leonardo invented armoured cars, breech loading guns and mechanical bows capable of hurling flaming projectiles. He designed a diving suit, bridges and forts. And he also found time to paint some pictures, including the 'Virgin of the Rocks' reproduced here, and to work on the gigantic figure of a horse in clay.

In Leonardo's 'Virgin of the Rocks' the landscape of towering rock and distant peaks, and the group of figures (the Virgin, the infants Christ and St John and the angel) although powerfully modelled, are all skilfully unified by the soft, mysterious light which was to become a hallmark of Leonardo's paintings. 'The Virgin of the Rocks' seems like some vivid dream.

The Virgin of the Rocks, *by Leonardo da Vinci. (National Gallery, London). Two versions of this painting exist, one in London (shown here) and one in Paris. It was commissioned in 1483 by the Confraternity of S. Francesco Grande of Milan.*

Those flowers which sprout from the rocks seem so tangible; we can almost feel the pudgy arm with which Jesus supports himself, and the rocks which jut into the sky behind the Virgin seem weighty and solid enough. Yet the picture leaves us unsatisfied, it seeks to vaguely disturb, to leave questions half-forming at the back of our minds. Above all it reminds us of the restlessly questing nature of its creator.

Leonardo's scientific sketches leave an altogether different impression. Here we are in the presence of a mind focused like a powerful microscope on some corner of nature. Storm clouds, rushing eddies of water, tiny plants, the wings of birds, all come in for scrutiny. As does the human machine itself in all its aspects and complexities.

Leonardo spent a busy life in many parts of Italy—Milan, Florence, Rome, Urbino—painting, designing machines and buildings and cramming his notebooks with observations. The last years of his life were spent in France in the service of Francis I. He died on 2 May 1519 at the Chateau de Cloux on the Loire.

Michelangelo Buonarroti (1475–1564)

To his awestruck contemporaries he was the 'Divine Michelangelo', to his friend and biographer Giorgio Vasari he was the special gift of God to Tuscany . . . 'because he had observed that in Tuscany men were more zealous in study and more diligent in labour than the rest of Italy'. (One hardly needs mention that Vasari was also a Tuscan!) Michelangelo's genius differed in almost every respect from that of his great (older) contemporary Leonardo. In contrast to the ever widening horizons of Leonardo's vision, Michelangelo was obsessively single-minded; he has been described as 'passionately narrow'. The art of painting, for instance, which for Leonardo was often too specific, for Michelangelo could never be specific enough: he treated painting as a branch of sculpture, as did many of his Florentine predecessors.

He was born at Caprese, near Florence. He studied painting for a brief period with Domenico Ghirlandaio before entering the Sculpture Academy which Lorenzo the Magnificent had inaugurated in the Medici gardens. Here a pupil of Donatello's, Bertoldo, gave instruction. During this period Michelangelo listened to the sermons of Savonarola, and their influence stayed with him for the remainder of his life.

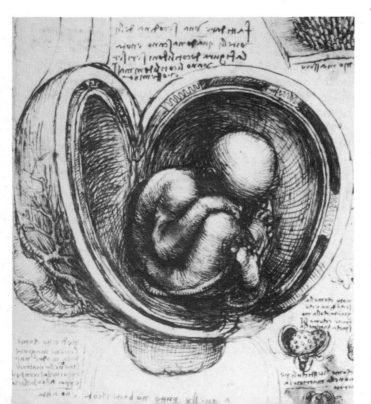

Study of a Child in the Womb *by Leonardo da Vinci. Leonardo claimed to have dissected more than thirty bodies. His anatomical studies tend to be extremely accurate. (Royal Library, Windsor, copyright reserved)*

With the expulsion of the Medici from Florence Michelangelo felt it prudent to leave the city for a time. During a visit to Rome he carved the well-known Pietà which is now in St Peter's. This work—the Virgin with the dead body of Christ—demonstrates his early concern for the 'ideal conception' as opposed to mere representation. Vasari remarks that he had heard several 'dull witted folk' object to the obvious youth of the Virgin, unable to understand that the figure was an expression of her purity rather than an attempt at historical reconstruction.

The period of political idealism which existed for a time in Florence after the Medici expulsion, prompted the return to their home town of both Michelangelo and Leonardo. The gigantic marble figure of David, designed for the Piazza de' Signori, dates from this period, and so too does the commission, given to both artists, to paint frescoes on the walls of the new Great Hall of the Council in the Palazzo Vecchio. These frescoes were to commemorate some great events from Florentine military history. Leonardo chose as his subject an episode in a battle against the Pisans at Anghiari in the valley of the Tiber. Michelangelo also chose an episode from the war with Pisa but his subject was, surprisingly, rather discreditable as it depicted the soldiers of Florence taken by surprise while bathing in the river Arno. The subject, however, gave him ample scope to make use of that motif which was soon to become the vehicle for his greatest statements—the male nude. Neither artist finished the commission. The cartoons (full-scale drawings) for the two paintings were completed and exhibited. Michelangelo's work in particular came as a revelation to contemporary artists. They flocked to see it and later tore it into pieces, so eager was each artist to possess a piece for himself.

In 1503 Michelangelo was summoned to Rome by Pope Julius II—'il pontifice terribile'. The pope was a man driven by a gigantic ambition, both for the Church and for himself. He decided to have one of the largest and most venerable churches in all of Christendom—St Peter's—demolished, and to build a more splendid one in its place. In this new church he wished to have a vast tomb erected in his own memory, and only the finest sculptor of the day was good enough for the job. Michelangelo seems to have received the commission with the greatest enthusiasm. His design for the tomb included a huge figure of Moses, a number of captives representing the various provinces brought to obedience by the pope and also the arts and sciences languishing because of his death. The statue of Julius himself was to be over three metres high. Upon enquiring if the pope desired to be represented holding a book in his left hand Michelangelo was told, 'Put a sword, for of letters I know but little.'

Study for the Cascina Cartoon *by* Michelangelo. *Although the cartoon itself was destroyed, many of Michelangelo's superb preliminary studies still survive. (Fonds Albertina, Vienna)*

For a variety of reasons the tomb, as envisioned, was never completed although it blighted Michelangelo's life for some forty years. He finished the great marble Moses and also, in bronze, the figure of Julius. This latter was later melted down and made into a cannon! Two of the captives were also completed and four more were left unfinished.

The unfinished figures seem uncannily even more powerful than many of Michelangelo's completed works. They seem to be straining all their super-human energies to free themselves from the form of the block of stone which still restrains them. They tell us a great deal about Michelangelo himself and his method of working. He seems to have had the ability to 'see' each figure with amazing clarity before getting to work on the block. His task was simply to cut away superfluous surrounding stone to reveal the figure within. The energy with which the sculptor attacked the stone may still clearly be appreciated when we observe the deeply pitted surfaces left by his chisel.

The second great project which Pope Julius desired Michelangelo to undertake was the painting, in fresco, of the ceiling of the Sistine chapel. This Herculean task was accepted with great reluctance. The scheme for the subjects to be represented was worked out by Michelangelo himself, an unusual procedure for the time; this task was usually left to poets or theologians. More unusual still is the fact that Michelangelo decided to work quite alone on the project and no one, apart from the Pope and one or two privileged individuals, was admitted while work was in progress.

The main themes depicted on the ceiling were in-

The Creation of Adam, *1508–12, by* Michelangelo. *Fresco. Detail of the Sistine Chapel ceiling. (Scala)*

Unfinished Captive *by* Michelangelo. *Originally intended for the tomb of Pope Julius II. (Mansell)*

spired by the Old Testament: from the 'Creation' to the 'Flood'. To these were added figures representing prophets, sibyls and nude youths. All have been placed in an artificial (i.e. a painted) architectural setting. The figure of Adam remains one of the most memorable in all painting. The spark of life has just passed from God to man who, perfect in his beauty, stirs into wakeful life.

How amazing is the contrast between the beautiful, reposeful Adam and this figure painted about a quarter of a century later on the rear wall of the Sistine chapel to represent one of the damned souls from the 'Last Judgment' painted for Pope Clement VII. In this painting the awesome figure of Christ rises from his throne to cast the damned forever from his sight down to hell; the spirit of Savonarola seems to breathe through the entire composition with its writhing masses of tormented humanity.

Michelangelo produced some of the most poignant images of Renaissance man; the David, the nude soldiers from the Cascina cartoon, the newly awakened Adam, are all members of a Titanic race. They combine the attributes of beauty, power, energy and confidence. But Michelangelo's religious vision demanded that he demonstrate the flimsiness even of Titans, before the power of God. He died unable fully to resolve this immense conflict, the impossibility of believing in the greatness of man and of God at one and the same time.

In his very last work, the Rondanini Pietà, he acknowledged the total supremacy of spiritual values. All the immense weight of earlier figures was steadily pared away, leaving an image of deep pathos almost wholly Gothic in conception. It is something of an irony that this last sad work, made by a man in his

Damned Soul *by* Michelangelo. *Fresco. Detail of* The Last Judgement, *1536–41, painted for Clement VII, on the rear wall of the Sistine Chapel. The entire work measures 13·7 by 12·2 metres. (Mansell)*

[49]

eighty-ninth year, unfinished and disunified though it is, should of all Michelangelo's works most deeply impress some of the great sculptors of our day. Speaking of the Pietà Henry Moore has said 'I don't know of any other single work of art by anyone that is more poignant, more moving.'

Raphael Sanzio (1483–1520)

During that period which might be described as Florence's brief Indian Summer, when Leonardo and Michelangelo exhibited their battle cartoons, the city was visited by a young painter from Urbino—Raphael Sanzio. He possessed neither an intellect comparable to Leonardo's nor the dynamic strength of Michelangelo, yet he was destined to achieve what had eluded both of those great men—perfection. Raphael's genius lay in his unerring sense of harmony—he always seemed to know just what elements he must borrow from others to advance his own work, yet he never sank into mere plagiarism. His painting never disturbs, never poses unanswered or unanswerable questions (cf. Leonardo) nor does it ever strive to break through its own boundaries (cf. Michelangelo).

Raphael was born in Urbino where his father, Giovanni, was one of the painters retained by the Duke. He was apprenticed to the painter Perugino whose soft and graceful manner he rapidly mastered, and indeed surpassed. His arrival in Florence brought him into contact with Leonardo and Michelangelo. The researches which he conducted in that city helped him to formulate the ideals of beauty found in so many of his religious paintings.

His Madonnas with pure oval faces, idealised as those of antique statuary, are gracefully posed in pastoral settings with soft blue hills and clear luminous skies. Raphael's calm harmonious treatment is all-pervasive. Even when his subjects suggest violence or suffering—the 'Martyrdom of St Şebastian', or 'St George slaying the Dragon'—no hint of anguish or discord is allowed to disturb the total harmony.

Prompted by his chief architect, Donato Bramante (who was also from Urbino) Pope Julius summoned Raphael to work in the Vatican in 1508. Thus Raphael arrived in Rome at the very time when Michelangelo was about to commence work on the Sistine ceiling. The frescoes which he executed in the Vatican mark the high point of his career ('Parnassus', 'The School of Athens' and 'The Disputa' are among the most important, painted on the walls of the Pope's private library—the Stanza della Segnatura). More important

still they might be regarded as the most perfect flowering of Italian High Renaissance culture. In these frescoes everything is reconciled—the philosophy of the ancients with the ideals of the Church, the world of human endeavour with God and with nature.

Even at first glance 'The School of Athens' suggests the idea of order. Here is perspective perfectly employed to create an architectural setting which is undoubtedly grand but curiously easeful. Any feeling of pomposity or stuffiness is completely eliminated by all that light and air—the place is alive! And there is a curious feeling of order about that crowd of people who argue, gesticulate and draw. Notice how readily they fall into clearly defined groups; that group on the right for instance, who seem so passionately interested in the geometrical drawings being made by the man with the bald head. Notice too how readily your eye tends to stray from this group to the line of figures behind, and how inevitably you are drawn to the centre of the composition. The two figures who stand in the centre are obviously important; we cannot but

The School of Athens, *1509–11, by* Raphael. *Fresco in the Stanza della Segnatura, Rome. (Scala)*

notice them. On the left stands Plato (possibly a portrait of Leonardo), the idealist philosopher who points to heaven; on the right is Aristotle, the disciple of reason. The groups who distribute themselves so harmoniously on both sides of the composition represent various aspects of philosophy, science and mathematics. The man already referred to who bends to draw with the compasses symbolises geometry. This figure is probably a portrait of Bramante, Raphael's mentor, a very appropriate inclusion as the imposing architectural setting for the picture represents his concept for the new St Peter's. Raphael's picture thus gives us, along with its other qualities, a very clear idea of the highest aspirations of his age in the field of architecture.

Raphael's concept of beauty was to leave its mark on European painting up to almost the beginning of our own century, and as we shall see later, not always with the most desirable results. To our own age, groping towards a new identity and in revolt against the ideals of the past, the achievements of Raphael may well seem of little value; our sympathies lie to a far greater extent with Leonardo and Michelangelo. However, although we may find it impossible to actually 'like' Raphael, we may still, by the exercise of a little imagination, appreciate what his achievements meant to his own and succeeding generations.

A Note on Architecture—Bramante

The taste for classical wholeness and basic simplicity of form increased its grip on the minds of the Italian architects of the Cinquecento. (The treatise on architectural principles, written in 25 B.C. by the Roman architect Vitruvius Pollio, was particularly influential.) The Tempietto of S. Pietro in Montorio, which Bramante built in 1503 soon became valued as a model of architectural beauty. This small scale building, basically a drum capped by a dome, had the compactness of design and harmony of proportions which appealed to Bramante's contemporaries. As this building presented no problems of structure, its interest lay purely and simply in its aesthetic content: the manner in which the various elements, already beautifully proportioned in themselves, were combined to form a harmonious whole. The fact that the plan of the Tempietto was based upon the circle (generally regarded as the most perfect geometrical form) greatly added to its appeal.

Buildings built upon a circular or central plan had been constructed by the Romans as the expression of (central) Imperial power (e.g. the Pantheon). To the designers of the High Renaissance the central plan became the most perfect architectural form; it gave expression to their concept of universal harmony and also seemed to symbolise the authority of the Church

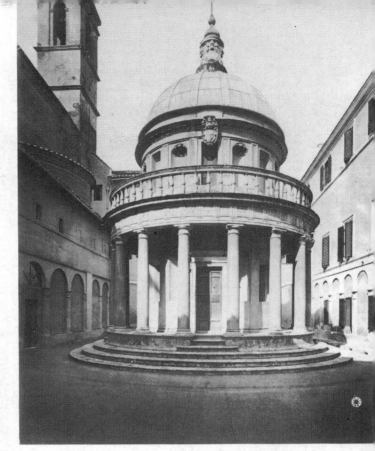

The Tempietto of S. Pietro in Montorio, *1503, by* Bramante. *(Mansell)*

(i.e. authority radiating from a centre, the popes, cardinals, bishops etc.).

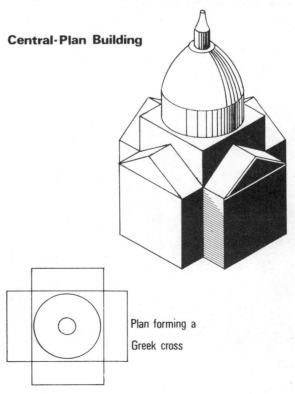

Central-Plan Building

Plan forming a Greek cross

St Peter's, Rome. *The west façade was designed by Carlo Maderna, 1612. Michelangelo's dome is also visible in this photograph. (Camera Press)*

The Villa d'Este *by* Pirro di Ligorio. *(Mansell). Begun in 1550 for Cardinal Ippolito d'Este. The Villa is a fine example of Italian secular architecture from the Mannerist period. The gardens are particularly spectacular, being composed of terraces and great volumes of organised waterfalls and fountains.*

Bramante was the architect chosen by Pope Julius II to design the new St Peter's, and from 1506 until his death in 1514 he worked on that great project. His plan for the building was a powerfully centred concept based on a Greek cross (i.e. having all four arms of equal length) and dominated by a massive central dome (cf. Raphael 'School of Athens').

Building had not progressed very far when Bramante died, and work was not seriously resumed until 1546 when Paul III entrusted Michelangelo, who had already distinguished himself as an architect, with the task of completing the building. Michelangelo, while retaining in essence Bramante's plan, greatly strengthened the original concept.

The Villa Rotonda, c. *1550, by* Andrea Palladio *(1508–80), Vicenza. (Scala). Palladio was one of the most important architects of his time, and among the most influential in the subsequent development of European architecture. He studied the work of Bramante and Raphael but was more deeply indebted to ancient Rome. He described Vitruvius as his master and guide. With his villas he attempted to recreate the Roman villa as he understood it from his reading of Pliny and Vitruvius. The classical temple front was adapted to the façades of his villas because he considered that it created the most suitably dignified entrance. The influence of Palladio's buildings and his publicatons such as the* Quattro Libri dell' Architettura, *1570, reached its climax during the eighteenth century. Palladianism became the dominant style in England from about 1720 to 1760.*

The Decline of Renaissance Values—Mannerism

By the mid 1520s the High Renaissance had passed its peak. With the exception of Venice its decay was rapid, far more so than that of Gothic art which still survived in its late Flamboyant phase in northern Europe. The Renaissance mode was also to experience its own Flamboyant phase, usually referred to as 'Mannerism'.

The exceptionally rapid decline in Renaissance values may be explained in terms of the religious and political traumas of the age which were, it is true, experienced throughout Europe, but which seemed to bear down upon Italy with greater weight than elsewhere. Between 1494 and 1515 Italy had to endure no less than three successive invasions from France. Under Francis I, Leonardo's patron, much of Lombardy was occupied by the French. Interference from Spain, with the resulting defeat of the French, inevitably brought much of the peninsula under the narrow and dogmatic influence of the Spaniards. The infamous 'Sack of Rome' occurred in 1527 when, for a brief period the city was laid waste by the armies of the Holy Roman Emperor, and the Pope imprisoned. And the fact of the Protestant Reformation, with the resultant sundering of the Universal Church, generated its own special doubts in the minds of those generations who still remembered the words of Savonarola.

The art of the Mannerists bears many comparisons with the Flamboyant style. Here too the forms and techniques invented by previous generations were polished, redeveloped and pushed often to the point of parody. The followers of Michelangelo brought into being a race of muscle-bound circus strongmen in gross parody of his Sistine nude athletes. The figures of Leonardo and Raphael reappeared, their limbs and bodies stretched like elastic and their complexions of delf.

Those artistic elements which had once served as tools of clarity were turned on their heads. Space became deeply ambiguous or disturbing, lighting effects were used to break up forms rather than reveal them, colour became shrill and acidic. Artists indulged themselves in feats of virtuosity (Parmigianino's 'Self-portrait in a Convex Mirror' is a notable example).

To dismiss the Mannerist era simply as a period of decline would be far too simple. While it may be maintained that Mannerism does border on the loathsome when it sinks to feeble parody of the art of men like Michelangelo or Leonardo, it included in its ranks artists of real talent: Pontormo, Rosso, Parmigianino, Cellini and Bronzino among them. And not surprisingly, much of the art of these men has a great appeal for our own age.

Italian art, which until this period had little impact north of the Alps, now began to spread its influence

The Madonna with the long neck, c. *1535, by* Parmigianino *(1503–40). (Gabinello Fotografio, Florence). Many of the hallmarks of Mannerism are present in this painting: the elongated proportions of the figures, the polished, delf-like appearance of their flesh, the crowding of the composition to one side, the sudden release into deep space, etc.*

throughout the continent. The different nations were perfectly happy to take from Italy an artistic vocabulary which might so readily be used as a further embellishment of their own Flamboyant style. The transition was smooth and hardly noticeable.

The Venetian School

The Venetian school was the latest to develop in Italy. Perhaps because of this, but possibly also because of Venice's political position, it remained relatively unmarked by the Mannerist upheaval.

The Florentines were never quite happy about Venetian painting: to men like Michelangelo or Vasari it seemed to lack several of the essential ingredients of art, particularly drawing and compositional structure. Coming from a tradition which regarded painting as drawing to which colour and tone had been added, they found it virtually impossible to conceive of an approach which made these elements the very foundation. The Venetians' love of sensuality and their lack of interest in intellectual theorising led them to produce a form of painting rich in colour and tonal harmony and hedonistic in spirit. Two pupils of Giovanni Bellini, Giorgione and Titian, were chiefly responsible for making Venetian painting a force to be reckoned with.

Giorgione (1477–1511)

Giorgio da Castelfranco, called Giorgione, worked wonders during his brief career. He was one of those rare artists who give the impression that they have virtually reinvented their art from scratch.

Notice how completely his figures are an integral part of their setting; their tones merge and fuse with those of the surrounding trees and grass. His 'Concert Champêtre' attempts to evoke some romantic golden age from the distant past. People are shown not as they are, filled with the troubles of this world, but as Giorgione feels they ought be be, at ease with nature and with themselves. He actually makes the nudity of the two ladies seem the most normal thing in the world, and really no more remarkable than the trees or the clouds in the picture.

The freshness of Giorgione's approach, his use of rich sensuous colour, the sense of space which he created by atmospheric perspective (rather than the linear, mathematical variety of the Florentines) all deeply impressed his fellow pupil Tiziano Vecellio— Titian.

Titian (c. 1480–1576)

Giorgione was a young man when he died but his innovations were carried on and developed by Titian during his long lifetime. Although Titian's earliest pictures are virtually indistinguishable from those of Giorgione, as he developed, a sturdier, more down to earth personality emerged. His life-sized portraits of wealthy merchants and aristocrats show us the face of a society still quite confident of its own value. Titian recorded their faces and their gestures with a minimum of personal comment. His business was to please his clients so that he might indulge his painterly instincts for rich colours and textures all the more.

So many of Titian's paintings exude this feeling of

Le Concert Champêtre, c. *1500, by* Giorgione. *(Giraudon)*

the artist's pleasure in the very material of his art, whether he is painting 'Venus and Adonis' or 'Christ and Mary Magdalen'. His later paintings do take on a much deeper gravity however.

'The Crowning with Thorns' is a remarkable example of the kind of painting Titian was capable of in old age. All traces of drawing in the Florentine sense have vanished; these figures which emerge from the semi-darkness, their flesh tones glowing in the harsh lamplight, are composed completely of fluid paint. Notice how inevitably your eyes must follow the thrust of the staves as they batter Christ's head. Titian forces our attention on this vicious act by refusing us any secondary detail to take our minds off the central theme. The architecture is there all right but almost totally lost in shadow. The glowing lamps only serve to add to the harshness of the scene.

The Venetian artists, as we might expect, were by no means unaware of developments in other parts of Italy. Titian had been invited to Rome to work for Paul III. While there he had been 'shown the sights' by Giorgio Vasari and had met Michelangelo. It was perhaps inevitable therefore that eventually the Venetians began to look with some interest at the contorted compositions of the Mannerists, as well as the mighty inventions of Michelangelo. And as often happens with artists, they began to borrow from these sources.

Jacopo Robusti—Tintoretto (1518–94)

A remarkable composition in which all the figures seem to exist in a state of 'free fall'. (Perhaps we are even tempted to ask if the picture has been printed the right way up!) This is the work of Tintoretto, one of

[55]

The Crowning with Thorns, c. *1575, by* Titian. *(Alte Pinakothek, Munich)*

The Origin of the Milky Way, *by* Jacopo Tintoretto. *(National Gallery, London)*

Titian's pupils. It tells a rather complex story taken from Greek mythology. Zeus had begotten an earthly son, Heracles, and wishing immortality for him, he instructed Hermes to put the infant to the breast of his sleeping wife Hera. But the scheme misfired, Hera awoke and leaping from her bed spilled the milk of immortality across the heavens. And the milk became what we know as the 'Milky Way'. The story has been embellished with many intriguing little touches: the canopy of Hera's bed hangs on a cloud, stars shoot from her breast and Zeus, in the form of an eagle with a thunderbolt in his claws, hovers watchfully. Tintoretto has created in this painting a dynamic composition which is concerned above all with conveying the feeling of movement. Notice how powerfully the diagonal from lower right to upper left has been stressed, creating an immediate impression of imbalance, and how the curving form made by the figures of Hermes and the flying putto seems to mesh with the curving form of Hera like two cog wheels (for analysis of this composition see Part II).

'The Origin of the Milky Way' is a tiny painting (1·47 by 1·66 m) by comparison with some which Tintoretto painted for the guild halls, churches and government buildings of his native Venice. (The 'Paradise' which he painted for the Doge's Palace measures over 200 square metres in area!) His compositions were often charged with the kind of excitement found in the best Mannerist works; his colours had something of the quality of Titian and his sturdy drawing bore witness to his admiration for Michelangelo.

Paolo Veronese (1528–88)

Paolo Caliari (called 'Veronese') came from the city of Verona, a dependency of Venice. He shared with the Venetian masters a deep love of rich colour and texture. Like Tintoretto he embarked upon a number of huge compositions which gave full play to his taste for grand occasions: scenes of feasting set in luxurious architectural settings and filled with gorgeously attired personages. Veronese appears to have been an out-and-out hedonist. Unfortunately for him he was living during a period of restraint when the Catholic Church, fired by Spanish ardour, was attempting to make up some of the ground lost during the Reformation. The Council of Trent which terminated after eighteen years, in 1563, laid down certain guide lines for artists to follow: nudity was proscribed in religious art and sacred images were not to be 'painted and adorned with a seductive charm'.

In 1573 Veronese was called before the Tribunal of the Inquisition to explain why he had placed 'buffoons, drunkards, Germans, dwarfs and similar vulgarities' in a painting made for the Convent of SS.

Venice Crowned Queen of the Sea, c. *1576, by* Paolo Veronese. *(Mansell) Ceiling fresco from the Doge's palace, Venice.*

Giovanni e Paolo. He finally satisfied his accusors by changing the title of the picture (a sumptuous banquet) from 'Feast in the House of Simon' to 'Feast in the House of Levi'.

Something of the grandeur of Paolo's work may be grasped from the reproduction of a ceiling painting in the Doge's palace. Can you imagine the effect of looking up at a ceiling like this?

The Mannerism of the Florentine and Roman artists was often tinged deeply by neurosis and even despair. Artists like Tintoretto and Veronese proved that as a style it could be alive and positive, and as we shall see, they pointed the way to many of the major developments in the art of the following centuries.

Postscript: The Northern Genius

Although its influence spread throughout Europe, the Renaissance remained, *in essence,* an Italian phenomenon and a further flowering of Mediterranean culture. The deep-seated Mediterranean desire for clarity and harmony, exemplified by artists like Piero della Francesca and Raphael, found few echoes in northern Europe, and particularly not in Germany. Stated in the broadest terms, the Germanic temperament has acted as the great counterweight to the Mediterranean. Idealised beauty is replaced by intense observation of the particular (cf. Van Eyck), the clear contemplative spirit by the anguish of emotional conflict.

As a postscript to this chapter we shall examine briefly the work of just three northern artists, one Dutch, the others German, in order to make clearer this distinction in temperaments.

Hieronymous Bosch (c. 1450–1516)

In the work of the Dutch painter Hieronymous Bosch the spirit of the Romanesque carvers seemed to live again, but vastly more mature and in possession of a technique both rich and subtle. Rarely, if ever, has an artist probed more deeply into his own subconscious and made greater use of the fearful treasure which lies buried there. The Surrealist artists (q.v.) of our own century owed him much, and it must be admitted that rarely did they even begin to approach the intensity and sheer conviction of his images.

The reproduction which appears here shows the right-hand panel of a triptych by Bosch called 'The Garden of Earthly Delights'. Here the 'external' world of nature, acutely observed and beautifully rendered, meets and is overwhelmed by the 'interior' world of the artist's mind. In the left-hand panel we see a beautiful and dreamlike garden of Eden. Birds, beasts and fish frolic in a pastoral setting; God stands, his hand raised in blessing, with Adam and Eve who are, as yet, unmarked by sin. The central panel shows us the same pastoral landscape, this time swarming with human life; figures frolic with some gigantic birds, gaily ride on the backs of gryphons, horses, camels and bears, and feast on huge strawberries. Here and there the landscape erupts into disturbing 'rock' formations of blue and pink.

With the benighted landscape shown in the right-hand panel we move from dream to nightmare. Bosch shows us here the consequences of human folly. The night sky is made hideous by furnace flares (Bosch came from a region of the Low Countries where real iron foundries were to be seen). The damned souls are tormented in the most elaborate ways: impaled, cast into blood-red lakes, suspended from gigantic musical instruments and consumed by the hideous hybrid monsters which Bosch specialised in creating.

Mere words can hardly do Bosch's images justice. Look carefully at the reproduction for yourself.

The Garden of Earthly Delights, c. *1500, by* Hieronymous Bosch. *(Museo del Prado, Madrid)*

Albrecht Dürer (1471–1528)

[58] Albrecht Dürer was the son of a goldsmith from the city of Nuremberg. A man of wide interests, he was a painter and printmaker and the author of works on aesthetic and mathematical matters. He spent several periods in Italy, and more than any of his northern contemporaries made strenuous efforts to come to grips with the basis of Italian Renaissance aesthetics. Many of his paintings have been broadened and 'Italianised', while his researches into the mathematical proportions of the human body parallel those of Leonardo and other Italian theorists.

It could strongly be argued, however, that Dürer was most convincing when he allowed his deepest instincts full play and was most 'German'. His minutely detailed studies—drawings and watercolours—of plants and animals, and his numerous prints, leave us in no doubt whatsoever that their author was a northern European.

'And power was given unto them over the four parts of the earth, to kill with sword, and with hunger, and with death, and with the beasts of the earth.' How aptly the tangled lines of Dürer's woodcut suit the chilling words of St John the Divine. Look carefully at the reproduction. In what ways is it definitely not a work of the Italian Renaissance?

Matthias Grünewald (c. 1475–1528)

When in the early years of our own century the young German Expressionists (q.v.) attempted to revive the spirit of German art, it was to painters like Matthias Grünewald that they looked with greatest pride.

Grünewald's Crucified Christ, brutalised by intense suffering, writhes in agony on his Cross. Every element of the painting adds to the feeling of torment: the rough unfinished woodwork of the cross, the thorns which sprout like the vicious parody of a halo from Christ's head, the flecks of blood which spatter his body, the feet—twisted and hideous, and finally the writhing of the figures at the foot of the cross. From all of Grünewald's paintings emotion floods in a great wave. He remains the 'Great Expressionist'.

Practical Exercises

By its very nature Renaissance art is probably not particularly suitable as the basis for practical experiments.

Mathematical perspective may however be explored in drawings and paintings (see note on perspective in Part II).

The construction of simple architectural models, already mentioned at the end of the previous chapter, may also prove useful here.

The Four Horsemen of the Apocalypse, *1498, by Albrecht Dürer. From the Apocalypse series of woodcuts. (Mansell)*

For further reading

Larousse Encyclopaedia of Renaissance and Baroque Art (Hamlyn)

Kenneth Clark, *Civilisation* (BBC/John Murray)

Margaret Aston, *The Fifteenth Century—The Prospect of Europe* (Thames & Hudson)

Giorgio Vasari, *The Lives of the most Eminent Architects, Painters and Sculptors of Italy* (Penguin Classics)

Bernard Berenson, *The Italian Painters of the Renaissance* (Phaidon)

Elizabeth Gilmore Holt (ed.) *A Documentary History of Art,* vol. I The Middle Ages and the Renaissance, *and* vol. II Michelangelo and the Mannerists: The Baroque and the Eighteenth Century (Doubleday Anchor Books)

A large variety of books—ranging from slim paperbacks to lavish hardbacks—dealing with the work of individual artists are also available.

Crucifixion, c. *1515, by* Matthias Grünewald. *Panel
from a large folding altarpiece made for the monastery
of the Antonites of Isenheim in Alsace. (Bulloz)*

Some Important Events		Building and Visual Arts
	1377	Birth of Filippo Brunelleschi (d. 1446)
	1378	Birth of Lorenzo Ghiberti (d. 1455)
	1386	Birth of Donatello (d. 1466)
	c. 1390	Birth of Jan Van Eyck (d. 1441)
	1395–1404	Well of Moses by Klaus Sluter
	1397	Birth of Paolo Uccello (d. 1475)
1400 Death of Chaucer	1400	Birth of Rogier Van der Weyden (d. 1464)
	1401	Competition announced for Baptistry door of Florence Cathedral Birth of Masaccio (d. 1428)

	Some Important Events		Building and Visual Arts
1415	Battle of Agincourt	c. 1415	St George by Donatello
		c. 1416	Birth of Piero della Francesca (d. 1492)
		1420–34	Dome of Florence Cathedral built under Brunelleschi's direction
		1426–28	Brancacci chapel
		c. 1430	Birth of Giovanni Bellini (d. 1516)
		1430–40	Pazzi chapel by Brunelleschi
1431	Joan of Arc burned at the stake	1431	Birth of Andrea Mantegna (d. 1506)
		1434	Arnolfini portrait by Jan Van Eyck
		1444	Birth of Sandro Botticelli (d. 1510) Birth of Bramante (d. 1514)
1445	Discovery of Cape Verde by the Portuguese		
c. 1446	Appearance of first printed books. Coster in Haarlem—Gutenberg in Mainz		
		c. 1450	Birth of Hieronymous Bosch (d. 1516)
		1452	Birth of Leonardo da Vinci (d. 1519)
1453	Fall of Constantinople		
		c. 1457	Mary Magdalen by Donatello
1469	Birth of Niccolo Machiavelli (d. 1527)		
		c. 1470/80	Birth of Matthias Grünewald (d. 1528)
		1471	Birth of Albrecht Dürer (d. 1528)
1473	Birth of Copernicus (d. 1543)		
		1475	Birth of Michelangelo (d. 1564)
		c. 1477	Birth of Giorgione (d. 1510)
		c. 1478	Primavera by Botticelli
1479	Gentile Bellini sent to Constantinople as official Venetian envoy		
		1483	Virgin of the Rocks by Leonardo
1485	Henry Tudor victorious at Bosworth		
1486	Diaz rounded Cape of Good Hope		
1492	Crossing of Atlantic by Columbus		
1494	First French invasion of Italy Ending of Medici power in Florence		
1498	Savonarola burnt at the stake Vasco da Gama sailed round Cape of Good Hope to India		
		c. 1500	The Garden of Earthly Delights by Bosch

Some Important Events		Building and Visual Arts
	1501–05	Leonardo and Michelangelo both working in Florence Mona Lisa by Leonardo David by Michelangelo
1503–13 Pontificate of Julius II	1503	Tempietto of S. Pietro in Montori by Bramante
	1508–12	Sistine Chapel ceiling by Michelangelo
	1508	Birth of Palladio (d. 1580)
1509 Henry VIII King of England	1509–11	Stanza della Segnatura frescoes by Raphael
	1510	Isenheim Altarpiece by Grünewald
	c. 1510– c. 1600	Period of Mannerism
	1511	Birth of Giorgio Vasari (d. 1574)
1512 Medici restored to power in Florence		
1513 *The Prince* by Machiavelli		
1517 Martin Luther propounded his theses at Wittenberg		
	1518	Birth of Tintoretto (d. 1594)
1519 Magellan embarks on voyage round the world Cortez entered Mexico city		
1521 Luther at Diet of Worms Loyola wounded at Pamplona		
1527 Sack of Rome		
	1528	Birth of Paolo Veronese (d. 1588)
1530 Invasion of Peru by Pizarro		
	1536–41	Last Judgment by Michelangelo
1539 Foundation of Society of Jesus		
1545/63 Council of Trent		
1547 Ivan the Terrible, Tzar of Russia		
1549 First Jesuit mission to S. America		
1559 Treaty of Catean—beginning of Spanish power in Italy	1550	First edition of Vasari's Lives of the Most Eminent Architects, Painters and Sculptors Villa Rotonda by Palladio
1564 Birth of William Shakespeare (d. 1616)	1564	The Rondanini Pietà—last work of Michelangelo Birth of Galileo (d. 1642)

The Age of Baroque

El Greco (1541–1614)

Philip II, who ruled Spain from 1556 to 1598, was a dour and narrow individual. With grim determination he set about the task of ridding his sprawling domains of heresy, of securing them against enemies in the Atlantic and the Mediterranean, and of demonstrating that Spanish culture could rival that of Italy. The king was very decided in his tastes: his instructions to the architect Herrera regarding the building of his new palace required that it should have 'simplicity of form, severity in the whole, nobility without arrogance, majesty without ostentation'. The palace, part monastery, part mausoleum, with its frontage of grey granite, became known as the 'Escorial' or 'Slag heap'! During the 1570s numerous painters and sculptors, many from Italy, were engaged in the task of decorating the rooms of the Escorial. Among the foreign artists who had arrived to work for the king was a Cretan painter, Domenicos Theotocopoulos.

Domenicos, who was known in Spain simply as 'El Greco'—the 'Greek'—had received his earliest artistic training in his native Crete, then a dependency of Venice, where the highly stylised Byzantine style still survived. In Venice the work of Titian and Tintoretto made a deep impression. The rich colouring and fluid paint handling of these masters were rapidly adopted by the young Greek, but perhaps it is here that the resemblance to them ends. El Greco was soon to demonstrate the power of his own individuality and

Agony in the Garden, c. *1585, by* El Greco. (*National Gallery, London*)

his arrogant contempt for conventions. While in Rome he declared that his own paintings were superior to those of Michelangelo—blasphemy indeed! A visiting friend, Giulio Clovio, found him seated in a room shuttered against the bright spring sunshine for fear that this light would blind the 'other light' within his head.

El Greco's painting was not to the taste of the austere Spanish monarch (whose taste in painting included the work of Bosch and Titian) and although the artist was paid, his work, commissioned for the Escorial church, was not hung there, on Philip's orders. Toledo, city of the mystic St John of the Cross, suited El Greco's temperament perfectly. He settled in that city and there made his greatest paintings, works which seemed to give visual expression to the spiritual fervour of the age of St Ignatius Loyola, St Francis Xavier and St John of the Cross.

The figure of Christ rises from the ground like a flame; about him the landscape forms roll and heave like the waves of some great ocean. Nothing is substantial, clouds and rocks fuse and intermingle, space is wholly ambiguous. How are we to judge just how far away is the group of disciples who sleep restlessly in that egg-shaped hollow? The question is irrelevant, for El Greco was not at all concerned with such matters; painting should strive to express only the spiritual, its function was most properly that of helping men's minds to rise above the gross material stuff of the world. The 'light' inside El Greco's head was to him infinitely to be preferred to the light of the 'real' world. His own painting was superior to that of Michelangelo simply because the great Florentine, by insisting upon the sheer weight and substance of his figures, did not appear to give enough emphasis to the spirit (in fairness to El Greco he did greatly admire Michelangelo's sculpture).

El Greco's overwhelming desire to create a 'spiritual' form of painting brought him, at least in superficial terms, very close to the stylistic flights of the Mannerists. He stretched his figures, sometimes, it seems, to almost twice their normal length, he used light and shade to break up forms and his space is often extremely ambiguous. The resemblance is superficial; El Greco's often extreme modifications of naturalistic proportions carry a weight of conviction and have none of the air of jaded sophistication characteristic of so much Mannerist art. Although he could be an impressive painter of portraits and even landscapes—his 'View of Toledo' is particularly fine—he was by choice a religious painter. Thus his own predilections were very much in tune with the spirit of reform and proselytising zeal to be found throughout the Catholic world, but particularly in Spain.

Many Spanish artists of the period would whole-

St Francis *by* El Greco. *(National Gallery of Ireland)*

St Francis in Meditation, *1639, by* Francisco de Zurbarán *(1598–1664). (National Gallery, London)*

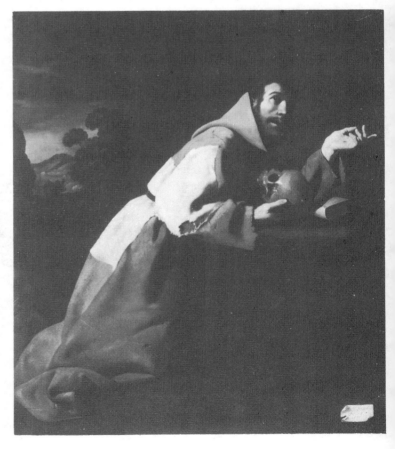

heartedly have shared El Greco's sense of vocation, while not always appreciating his methods. A great deal of Spanish art from the period is a curious mixture of naturalism and 'dramatic piety'. Compare El Greco's depiction of St Francis with that of a younger Spanish contemporary, Francisco de Zurbarán.

Spanish sculpture was often painted in an extremely naturalistic fashion—eyes were made of crystal or glass, wounds of martyred saints and the dead Christ oozed with very authentic looking 'blood'.

This figure, in painted wood, dates from the first quarter of the eighteenth century. Although the subject is 'The Prophet Elias overthrowing the Prophets of Baal' we may well imagine that the message was directed at contemporary heretics.

Elias Overthrowing the Prophets of Baal. *School of Seville, early eighteenth century. (National Gallery of Ireland)*

Painting in Rome—Caravaggio (1573–1610)

The art of Michelangelo Merisi da Caravaggio was no less revolutionary in its own way, than that of El Greco. Caravaggio arrived in Rome during the early 1590s. He found a city which was still very much the cultural centre of Europe, and which had attracted colonies of foreign artists from Spain, France, Germany and the Low Countries. His paintings rapidly attracted the eager—and not so eager—attention of Rome's artistic population. Some hailed them as a fresh departure for the art of painting; to others they were contemptible and degraded. One contemporary commentator, Vincencio Carducho, likened the artist to the Antichrist!

The Supper at Emmaus, c. *1598, by* Caravaggio. *(National Gallery, London)*

Caravaggio's work attracted attention for a number of reasons. His most outstanding virtue—or glaring fault—appears to have lain in his refusal to idealise his figures (as, for instance Raphael and, more particularly, the Mannerists had done). Caravaggio peopled his canvases with figures which looked just like those to be seen in the streets of Rome and thus he appeared to be thumbing his nose at accepted canons of beauty. His version of 'The Supper at Emmaus' demonstrates this, along with other aspects of his approach. The painting takes as its subject the New Testament story which relates how, soon after Christ's execution, three of his disciples met a stranger on the road to Emmaus and invited him to supper, unaware that he was the risen Christ. During the supper 'their eyes were opened, and they knew him; and he vanished out of their sight.'

The figures are obviously drawn from life; the faces of the three disciples are clearly those of simple, working-class folk. (That Christ's disciples were, in fact, drawn from the ranks of the working class seemed hardly relevant to Caravaggio's detractors.) These figures are thrown into powerful relief by the 'spot-light' effect which casts deep shadows behind them. This almost theatrical form of lighting—called 'Tenebrism'—was not exactly new to painting, but Caravaggio gave it a new authority. The same is true of his habit of allowing forms to project violently from the picture plane; in this case two of the figures reach out towards us while the elbow of the figure on the extreme left seems to break through the 'surface' of the canvas. Such projecting forms, while disturbing the classical balance of the composition, also tend to bring the figures closer to us. We can no longer feel that we are looking through a 'magic' window at a scene spread out for our delectation; Caravaggio's figures attempt to thrust forward into our own space.

The short and stormy career of Michelangelo Merisi da Caravaggio was to have a lasting effect upon the course of European painting. His ideas were carried to many European countries by artists returning to their homelands from Rome, and as we shall see later, this was to prove particularly significant for the course painting was to take in the newly formed republic of Holland.

The Carracci

Altogether less revolutionary than either El Greco or Caravaggio were the three Carracci, the brothers Annibale and Ludovico, and their cousin Agostino. The Carracci shared Caravaggio's desire to break with Mannerism, but their attitude to the revered masters of the immediate past was quite the opposite to his. Far from wishing to explore new ground they attempted to borrow from their great predecessors those elements which they considered most worthy: the classical draughtmanship of Michelangelo and Raphael, the colour of the Venetians etc. Behind their essentially eclectic approach lay the assumption that all important discoveries had already been made in painting and that these discoveries could be formalised into a sort of 'grammar'. The school of painting which they founded in Bologna was to be honoured with the title of 'academy'. The way lay open for the establishment of the Academies of Fine Art, those institutions presided over by professors of painting and sculpture, which sought to propagate ad infinitum (or ad nauseam!) the 'correct' approach.

Art in the Seventeenth and Eighteenth Centuries

During the course of the seventeenth and eighteenth centuries the visual arts followed no single coherent path. At least three major trends may be discerned however, and these we shall explore separately.

Following the Council of Trent, strenuous attempts were made to restore painting and sculpture to their pre-Renaissance state. This meant, not revival of Gothic art, but overcoming the intellectual elitism which had crept into the arts in the wake of humanism. Art was to be made accessible to the common man once more: it should attempt to reach him through his senses rather than through his intellect. It must put on a great show capable of captivating the imaginations of the greatest number of people, and its message should be, above all, the glory of the Universal Church. Several artists of genius and large numbers of lesser talents were to emerge during the seventeenth century to fulfil this need. Their art, filled with movement, light and colour and owing much to artists like Tintoretto, Veronese, El Greco and Caravaggio eventually received the label 'Baroque'.

The Baroque style held little appeal for the Protestants of the Low Countries. The Dutch preferred to explore a more down-to-earth path which owed a great deal to the naturalistic subject matter and tenebrist style of Caravaggio. Here too several artists of genius were to emerge along with many lesser talents. This approach, which we shall refer to as 'naturalism', was also to take root in countries as various as Spain, England and France.

The academic approach of the Carracci, which sought to keep alive the ideals of classical art, seems in many ways the least interesting of the three major trends. We can well imagine that this eclectic, 'school-masterish' approach might attract only middle-of-the-road artists. But art is continually full of surprises and the 'classical' or 'academic' approach also produced its men of genius.

Gian Lorenzo Bernini (1598–1680)

A smiling youthful angel stands with arrow held to strike the swooning female figure. She limply submits, with head thrown back and arms falling loosely at her sides. Only her clothing, so vividly alive it seems to fall like cascades of water from shoulders to ankles, gives some clue to the turmoil within. Ecstasy would be a much better term, for the female figure is that of St Teresa of Avila transported by pain and 'infinite sweetness' as the angel pierces her heart with the golden arrow. And this vivid work, far from being executed in fluid oil paint, is cut in hard marble. It is the work of Gian Lorenzo Bernini, one of the supreme masters of the Baroque.

Fate seems to have showered her gifts upon Bernini from the first. While still a child he attracted the attention of Pope Paul V who expressed the hope that the boy would become the Michelangelo of his century, and entrusted him to the care of Cardinal Matteo Barberini. That he should be watched over like some rare and delicate plant in a hot-house did not spoil the young Bernini; it seems rather to have spurred him on to greater efforts. Bernini's biographer Filippo Baldinucci tells us that the cardinal even held a mirror for him so that he might carve his own features on the face of a figure of 'David'.

When in 1623 Cardinal Barberini became Pope Urban VIII, one of his first interviews was with Bernini. Urban told him how great was his good fortune now that his patron had been made Pope, but added . . . 'far greater is ours to have Bernini living during the period of our Pontificate'. The status of the artist had indeed grown by the seventeenth century; even the 'divine' Michelangelo had not received such lavish treatment from his patrons.

As architect of St Peter's, Bernini was faced with the immense task of decorating and unifying the vast interior of that building. The scale of his imagination

The Ecstasy of St Teresa, *1645–52, by* Lorenzo Bernini. *Cornaro chapel, S. Maria della Vittoria, Rome. (Mansell)*

and technical virtuosity were equal to the task. Not only was the interior of the building completely transformed under Bernini's direction but he designed the great curving colonnades which embrace the piazza.

Perhaps the most arresting single feature within the building is the 'baldacchino', the bronze canopy above

The Piazza of St Peter's, Rome. *(Mansell). The colonnade, 1656–67, was designed by* Bernini. *In a drawing he indicated that he regarded it as a symbol of the Mother Church opening her arms to receive the faithful.*

the high altar which rests upon four vast twisting pillars. So great was the amount of metal required for this project that the roof was stripped from one of Rome's most venerable buildings, the Pantheon, so that the work might be completed.

The scope of Bernini's vision seems endless, nor was his work restricted to the ecclesiastical. He designed some spectacular public monuments for the city of Rome. These were conceived as permanent theatrical displays. In the Piazza di Spagna he placed a large stone basin filled with water, in the centre of which a ship appears to float and from whose guns water, instead of flames, gush. For the Piazza della Minerva he carved an elephant bearing an obelisk on its back and for the Piazza Navona the 'Fountain of the Four Rivers'. This work also features an obelisk, but this time it juts from the top of a great hollow rock formation. Water gushes from fissures in the rock into the surrounding basin while from the hollow the half-submerged form of a horse emerges.

The air of theatrical spectacle runs through all Bernini's work. His sheer virtuosity enabled him to create effects at will; cold, hard marble could become soft palpitating flesh or billowing cloth or even fluttering leaves. Light itself might be pressed into service; the overhead lighting for the 'St Teresa' was designed by Bernini so that the group might always be seen to best advantage. The theatre itself claimed some of his energies. We learn from contemporary sources that so extravagant and convincing were some of the illusions which he managed to create on stage that people in the front rows fled in terror.

In the work of Bernini—his architecture, sculpted figures, public monuments, theatrical displays—we find many of the elements which are fundamental to Baroque art; an art which always seems so much larger than life, which seeks to strike with immediate effect, to entertain and to overwhelm. As such it was to become the tool of princes, both spiritual and temporal, for well over a century.

The Piazza Navona *by Giovanni Paolo Panini (1696–1768). (National Gallery of Ireland). Bernini's Fountain of the Four Rivers occupies the centre of the picture. The scene depicted is the preparation for a fete given by the French Ambassador, Cardinal de Polignac, on 30 November 1729, to celebrate the birth of the Dauphin, son of Louis XV. Among the personages portrayed in the picture are Prince Charles Edward Stuart and his brother Henry, later Cardinal of York.*

Fountain of the Four Rivers, *by* Bernini. *Piazza Navona, Rome. (Mansell)*

Peter Paul Rubens (1577–1640)

This painting bears the title 'The Horrors of War'. The imagery of 'war' is not too difficult to find; that splendid armoured figure in the centre of the composition for instance, those ladies in distress, the books trampled underfoot. But where are the horrors? You may well ask. Do those male warriors look really dangerous? And isn't there more than a touch of melodrama in the gestures of the 'ladies in distress'? There is the lady on the left of the composition who throws up her hands and rolls her eyes with such obvious gusto, for instance.

Was the artist totally unaware of what war is really like? This is highly unlikely. He lived during a period which witnessed the destruction of the Spanish Armada, a period of continental war on a large scale (the Thirty Years War) and some of the most vicious religious persecution in European history. Indeed his own parents, who were Protestants, had had to flee from Spanish persecution in Antwerp and had settled in Westphalia where the artist was born.

Peter Paul Rubens was an intelligent, well-read and widely travelled man. We may be sure that he was well aware that war is usually a nasty business leading to genuine horrors. He simply did not choose to express this aspect of reality in his work; he tended to ignore it, in fact. But before dismissing Rubens as a fraud consider how we in the twentieth century have dealt with the same subject in our own great popular art form —the cinema. Remarkably few films about war have been horrific. (This is particularly true of the Holywood variety.) On the contrary, most of them seem to propagate the idea that war is really rather exciting, and far from being frightened, depressed or disgusted, audiences are entertained by them. Although it would be a crude over-simplification to suggest that Rubens,

Horrors of War, by Peter Paul Rubens. (National Gallery, London). The painting is an allegory, so perhaps the text is a little unfair to Rubens.

and the other great Baroque artists, were merely in the entertainment business, it is true to say that their works were made to stimulate the eye rather than the intellect. And Rubens's paintings are usually very stimulating indeed. Once we cease to look for deep 'messages' in his work and view him purely and simply as a creator of spectacle, the orchestrator of a myriad varied forms, colours, tones, all set whirling into vigorous motion, he emerges as one of the most talented and exciting artists Europe has ever produced.

Look at the reproduction of his painting once more but this time forget about its title. The real subject, and this is true of many pictures by Rubens, is energy. So much energy has been generated by this composition that the rectangular shape can no longer contain it; the violent thrust of the forms to the right seems to carry them beyond the boundaries of the picture (for analysis of this composition see Part II). The broad tonal scheme which Rubens has employed adds emphasis to this sideways thrust. The diagonal group of warriors forms a dark band of tone which contrasts sharply with the bright groupings on either side—the roughly circular group of figures placed in the lower right, and the group to the left dominated by the female nude. The rather histrionic figure to the left returns us to another dark area of tone.

Rubens spent his boyhood in Antwerp—after the death of his father, his mother had been reconverted to Catholicism and had returned to that city with her family. In Antwerp he served his apprenticeship as a painter and in 1598 was admitted into the guild. The desire to broaden his understanding of his art led him to Italy where he remained for a number of years. In

Venice he studied the works of Titian, Tintoretto and Veronese, and later, in Rome, Michelangelo, Raphael, Caravaggio and the Carracci. As in the case of all really powerful artistic personalities these diverse influences were thoroughly assimilated and something new emerged. When, at the age of thirty-two, Rubens returned to his native Flanders and was made court painter to Duke Albert and Duchess Isabella (daughter of Philip II) his own style was formed.

Rubens rapidly established himself as the leading artist in Flanders. Demand for his work, from home and abroad, became so great that he established what was virtually a painting factory. Numerous assistants, working from his sketches, carried out many of his projects, the final unifying touches being added by the master himself. He was quite open about his working methods—and his prices!—when corresponding with clients. The list of paintings currently in stock, which he sent to Sir Dudley Carleton in 1618, included, for six hundred florins, 'Leopards, taken from the life, with Satyrs and Nymphs. Original, by my hand, except a most beautiful landscape, done by the hand of a master skilful in that department.' Rubens's working system, although it inevitably led to unevenness of quality, was certainly efficient. The twenty-one vast canvases (each 3·94 by 2·95 metres) ordered for the Luxembourg palace in Paris were completed in under four years, (they relate, in allegorical terms, the history of Marie de' Medici).

Rubens's command of a broad range of subject matter was another aspect of his talent. He was prepared to tackle anything—religious, historical and mythological subjects as well as portraits and landscapes. He was quite capable of producing small, exquisitely painted, and intimate subjects as well as vast dramatic compositions.

The painting called 'Le Chapeau de Paille' shows us the intimate side of Rubens. The sitter—who is not, in fact, wearing a straw hat—may have been his young second wife Helen Fourment, or possibly one of her sisters. Apart from the sensitive treatment of the subject, whoever she may have been, the painting is a superb harmony of colour (red, grey-blue and pearly flesh tint), tone and texture.

The Flemish school produced a number of painters of very considerable talent during the seventeenth century, though none of the stature of Rubens. The best known of these was Anthony Van Dyck, Rubens's most distinguished pupil. He settled in England during the 1630s and became painter to Charles I. The evolving English school of painting was greatly influenced by his work. The compositions of Jacob Jordaens sometimes suggest those of Rubens but the heaviness of his figures and the leaden quality of his colouring only serve to emphasise the greatness of Rubens.

Le Chapeau de Paille, c. *1630, by* Peter Paul Rubens. *(National Gallery, London)*

The Church Triumphant *by* Jacob Jordaens. *(National Gallery of Ireland)*

Baroque Sculpture

[70] Baroque art was dynamic. We have already seen how, in Rubens's 'Horrors of War', the artist hurls his figures against the frame of his picture as though he wished them to break free of the canvas. We feel that the artist wished to eliminate the physical boundaries of his own art form. This tendency is often to be found in Baroque sculpture; groups of figures twist violently in space and often give the impression that they are about to fly apart. The 'Perseus and Andromeda' group by the French sculptor Pierre Puget (1620–94) illustrates this perfectly. The Baroque mode never really took root in France where artistic taste tended far more towards the classical. However it is worth mentioning that Bernini did work for Louis XIV for a short while (although the king did not care for all of the pieces made for him by that sculptor). And it is significant that as a young man Puget studied in Florence and Rome where he was influenced by both Michelangelo and Bernini.

Perseus and Andromeda, *1684, by* Pierre Puget. *(Bulloz). A subject drawn from Greek mythology. Andromeda, the daughter of an Ethiopian king, was chained to a rock as a sacrifice to a sea monster. She was rescued, and later married, by the hero Perseus. The sculpture was commissioned for the gardens of Versailles.*

The Glorification of the Name of Jesus, c. *1675, by* Giovanni Battista Gaulli, *called* Il Baciccia *(1639–1709). Vault of the Gesù, Rome. (Mansell). The composition can no longer be held within the confines of a frame and literally breaks through.*

Baroque Ceilings

Paintings made on ceilings and domes gave Baroque painters full scope to indulge their desires to break out of the bounds normally created by frames. Here they could create the feeling of limitless vistas of sky overhead where billowing clouds and swarms of figures were free to spiral ever upwards to eternity (cf. Paolo Veronese).

...iling fresco glorifying the Barberini family, c. 1635, ...Pietro da Cortona *(1596–1669) Palazzo Barberini,* ...me. (Mansell)

The Eighteenth Century—Rococo Art

The dynamic force of high Baroque art eventually gave way to something more lightweight and frankly decorative. This late Baroque phase emerged quite early in the eighteenth century and affected all the visual arts: architecture, painting, sculpture, furniture, metal work, ceramics etc. Paintings became extremely lighthearted, forms dissolved in atmospheric effects and in colour, and the designers of such things as furniture, ceramics, building interiors, increasingly drew their inspiration from the sinuous forms of shells, seaweed and plants. This style, which was often very similar to the Flamboyant Gothic, was called 'Rococo'.

Rococo commode, mid eighteenth century. A commode was a small side board, usually for holding a chamber pot. (The Wallace Collection, London)

Chelsea porcelain, mid eighteenth century. (Victoria and Albert Museum, London)

La Gamme d'Amour by Antoine Watteau. (National Gallery, London)

THE ROCOCO PAINTERS

Antoine Watteau (1684–1721)

Antoine Watteau was born in Flanders. Although his painting demonstrates none of the dynamism of Rubens he does seem to have inherited something of the earlier artist's gifts for rich colour and tonal effects. His figures, who have usually given themselves to idleness, love and music, languorously disport themselves in Arcadian settings beneath softly tinted skies and gauzy trees. Watteau's art, in common with that of the other painters termed 'Rococo' who were to follow him (François Boucher and Jean Honoré Fragonard were notable examples) was largely escapist.

Giovanni Battista Tiepolo (1696–1770)

Something of the spirit of Tintoretto and Veronese lived on in Venice well into the eighteenth century. The Venetian was the youngest of the Italian schools so it is fitting that it survived later than the others. The pictures of Canaletto and Guardi, filled with Venetian light, record the beauty of Venice's buildings and waterways. The decorations of Giovanni Battista Tiepolo however, more obviously recall the work of the great old masters. His work must inevitably suffer by comparison with theirs; he seems lightweight, sketchy, and even downright anaemic in their company. But perhaps such criticism is ultimately unfair to Tiepolo who was, after all, very much the child of his time, lightweight perhaps, but not without his share of freshness and sparkle.

He enjoyed a considerable reputation both at home and abroad. Among his finest works is the ceiling decoration—with representations of the four corners of the world, Europe, Asia, Africa and America—painted above the vast area of the staircase in the Palace of the prince-bishop at Wurzburg. Tiepolo was to live long enough to witness the decline in the taste for Rococo art. His last years were spent in exile in Madrid.

German Rococo

The massive disruptions which followed in the wake of the Reformation, and the sheer destruction resulting from the campaigns of the Thirty Years' War, halted the course of artistic development in the German states for a good deal of the seventeenth century. Germany's

The Building of the Trojan Horse *by* Giovanni Battista Tiepolo. *(National Gallery, London)*

The Setting of the Sun *by* François Boucher *(1703–70). (The Wallace Collection, London)*

The Swing, *by* Honoré Fragonard *(1732–1806). (The Wallace Collection, London)*

recovery, towards the end of the century, was dramatic; German artists were very quick to adopt the fully formed Baroque style and to mould it to their own vision. The possibilities for seemingly endless development and elaboration, implicit in Rococo decoration, were ideally suited to the northern genius. So it is to Germany that we must look for many of the finest masterpieces of the style. Certainly the eighteenth-century artists most universally admired in modern times have been German, albeit in the field of music

[74] rather than the visual arts. It is worth remembering that some of Europe's greatest musical composers lived during that century, from J. S. Bach and Handel (both of whom were born in 1685) to Mozart (b.1756) and Beethoven (b.1770). It is surely not entirely due to coincidence that the beautifully intricate harmonies of Mozart should evolve so close in time and space to those equally intricate harmonies of colour and form to be found in the Rococo churches of Bavaria and Franconia.

This interior view of the Bavarian Church of Die Wies gives some impression of just how elaborate German Rococo during the mid-1700s could be. Here the decoration—plasterwork and paint—develops at will across walls and ceilings, rendering ambiguous the boundaries between vertical and horizontal. We have the unfortunate tendency to regard decoration as something merely added to prettify a structure—building, utensil, furniture—and therefore as something essentially superficial. Yet the decoration of this church interior, with its sense of overall unity, could hardly be called 'superficial' or 'added' or even 'pretty'. One could not strip this decoration from the walls and ceilings of Die Wies, any more than one could erase the details from a Dürer engraving (q.v.), without destroying the whole. Each decorative form—scroll or leaf or cornice—develops from every other and all seem ultimately to derive from the greater form of the

The Church of Die Wies, *Bavaria. Interior. Built* c. *1750 by* Dominikus Zimmermann *(1685–1766) and painted by his brother* Johann Baptist *(1680–1758). (Hirmer Fotoarchiv, Munich)*

Pulpit by Dominikus Zimmermann. *Church of Die Wies. (Hirmer Fotoarchiv, Munich)*

The Church of Vierzehnheiligen, *Franconia, mid eighteenth century, by* Johann Balthasar Neumann *(1687–1753). (Hirmer Fotoarchiv, Munich)*

building itself. This is further borne out by the fact that the architect of the building, Dominikus Zimmermann, was also responsible for the plasterwork, while his brother, Johann Baptist, did the painting.

The Abbey church of Vierzehnheiligen in Franconia demonstrates a similar approach to decoration. Here the architect was the eminent Johann Balthasar Neumann who was also responsible for the design of the Palace of the prince-bishop at Wurzburg.

THE DEVELOPMENT OF 'REALISM'

The term 'realism' we shall use here merely as a convenient means of grouping together a variety of artists who tended to ignore the Baroque mode, developing instead a more personal vision based, more or less, upon observations made of the contemporary world.

Diego Velasquez (1599–1660)

Philip IV in Brown and Silver *by* Diego Velasquez. *(National Gallery, London)*

Christ in the House of Mary and Martha, c. *1620, by* Diego Velasquez. *(National Gallery, London)*

This picture certainly seems to have drawn most of its inspiration from everyday mundane existence. In a heavily factual manner the artist presents us with the various objects on a kitchen table—earthenware jug, fish, cloves of garlic, eggs etc. The two people in the foreground, the old woman and the young girl, are presented in the same, rather heavy and essentially matter-of-fact way. The lighting in the picture would appear to owe much to Caravaggio; the two figures and a number of the objects on the table are illuminated by a strong light source somewhere 'offstage' to the left. Yet there is very little of Caravaggio's sense of drama in this picture. Such drama as does exist is suggested by two rather anomalous details: that curious 'picture within a picture' in the top right corner and the fact that the two women both appear to

be looking at something on 'our side' of the picture plane.

Does the 'picture within a picture' represent just that, a picture hanging on the wall? This seems unlikely; any picture hanging on such a darkened wall would be almost lost in shadow. Is it an opening in the wall allowing us to see into another room? This seems a better suggestion until we notice that the perspectives of the two 'rooms' are slightly different. All of which suggests a large mirror. Thus we are enabled to see what it is that so interests the two women.

The subject of the picture is 'Christ in the House of Martha and Mary', the artist Diego Velasquez. This painting was made when Velasquez was still in his early twenties and before his mature style had formed. Still, it tells us a good deal about him. He was no religious painter (in El Greco's sense); the figures of Christ and his two listeners don't quite fit into the composition and leave us with the feeling that they were merely a pretext. The two women, on the other hand, along with the objects on the table, seem to have been painted with a certain amount of relish.

Velasquez was soon to lose the rather heavy touch noticeable in this picture, but he was to remain a painter of observable reality. His genius lay in his remarkable ability to transform the sensation of light from the observable world into small dabs of colour and tone. His method of painting, which became extremely sensitive as he developed, was not at all like that of Van Eyck and can perhaps best be compared to that of the Impressionists (q.v.) over two centuries later.

He was very fortunate in that his talents were recognised by the Spanish King, Philip IV who made him court painter in 1623. Although he travelled to Italy on two occasions, his life was mostly the sheltered existence of the courtier. He painted pictures of the royal family and their retainers, and looked after the royal collection of pictures.

With paintings like 'The Surrender of Breda' (a scene drawn from recent military history) and 'The Maids of Honour' (a portrait group of the Infanta Margarita and her entourage, and including a self portrait, brush in hand) Velasquez proved that he was capable of handling large compositions involving complex problems both of lighting and of space. His many portraits, of the king, Pope Innocent X, various court dwarfs, are always quietly impressive. His occasional ventures into the realms of mythology or religion were not quite so happy for his genius lay in dealing with what the eyes could see. In many ways he is the antithesis of El Greco.

The Dutch School

Seventeenth-century Dutch society left an exceptionally thorough visual record of its existence. The influence of the Protestant faith led to the rejection of religious imagery; the main source of artistic patronage, thoroughly in keeping with the spirit of this new republic, passed to the new rulers—the middle-class merchants and bankers. These Dutch burghers, whose hard-headed enterprise rapidly made Holland one of the richest and economically most active countries in the world, had their feet securely on the ground. They asked of art only that it should faithfully record the world as they knew it. On the walls of their houses they wished to see likenesses of themselves drinking, listening to music or simply sitting and chatting to each other, views of the landscapes which they knew so well and which they had wrested with such difficulty from the Spanish, views of the sea, so important to the economic life of Holland, views of their city streets and buildings, and images of things which they owned or simply liked—a prize bull or a pile of fruit.

To meet these various demands with greater efficiency, painters began to specialise to a greater degree than anywhere else in Europe: some of them painted animals, others night scenes, while sea-scapes, interiors, portraits etc. were all subjects for specialisation.

Craftsmanship was meticulous; subjects were often rendered with a precise impartiality which serves to remind us that seventeenth-century Holland was also one of the great centuries of scientific research in Europe; one might mention the fields of optics and cartography in particular.

So far we have imagined a school of painters com-

Still Life *by* Pieter Claesz. *(National Gallery of Ireland)*

The Village School *by* Jan Steen *(1626–79). (National Gallery of Ireland)*

mendably efficient and workmanlike, understandably in reaction against the philosophy as well as the dramatic excesses of the Baroque. We might easily imagine that individualism could flourish in such a social climate, so liberal by the standards of other European states, but we might also be tempted to conclude that real genius, on a level with that of El Greco, Bernini or Rubens, was equally unlikely. Such an assumption would almost be correct, if it were not for the emergence of Rembrandt Van Rijn.

Banquet of the Officers of the Civic Guard of St George, Haarlem, *1627 by* Frans Hals (c. *1580–1666). (Frans Halsmuseum). Hals brought a new spontaneity to the art of painting, applying his pigment in a single opaque layer—alla prima—instead of the traditional series of transparent layers over a monochrome foundation. This rapid method enabled him to give full rein to his natural virtuosity, to capture fleeting facial expressions and effects of light. Hals was one of the most popular portrait artists of his age, but nevertheless he ended his days in receipt of charity from his native Haarlem.*

Winter: The Heylige Weghts Gate at Amsterdam *by* J. A. Beerstraten. *(National Gallery of Ireland)*

Portrait of the Painter in Old Age, c. *1665, by* Rembrandt Van Rijn. *(National Gallery of Ireland)*

Rembrandt Van Rijn (1606–69)

This is hardly a 'beautiful' picture in the usually accepted sense of that word. The subject is an old man in his sixties. He stands with hands clasped together glaring rather sourly out at the world. His form is almost lost in shadow; only his head is clearly illuminated. The artist obviously wishes us to concentrate our attention on the face, to 'confront' the sitter eye to eye.

He seems to return our gaze in a most uncanny fashion, this old man. Is he really sour, or defiant, or

arrogant perhaps? What can we learn about him merely by studying his face? He is certainly defiant; the steady, almost hypnotic gaze indicates that he is by no means defeated. But sour, or arrogant? Not really. Try covering the left side (his right) of the face with a piece of paper and look carefully at the side which remains exposed. Here the shadows reveal more—the drooping eyelids, the cluster of wrinkles beneath the eye—and the face takes on the unmistakable expression of deep sadness. The face, which was probably never particularly attractive, is that of a man who has apparently suffered a good deal during his life but who still seems capable of bearing his lot stoically.

Rembrandt Van Rijn painted this amazingly frank picture of himself a few years before his death. Fortune had dealt capriciously with him. Once he was rich and famous, a celebrated artist patronised even by princes, happily married and the respected master of a flourishing school for painters in Holland's greatest city, Amsterdam. Now he was old and poor, his two wives had died, his pictures no longer pleased. Rembrandt seems to acknowledge all of that, the good and the evil, in this self-portrait. (And he had yet to witness the death of his only son, Titus.)

Success came early to Rembrandt. He arrived in Amsterdam, from Leyden, in his mid-twenties and rapidly established a reputation for himself in the big city as a portrait painter of great talent. The group portrait which he painted for the Amsterdam guild of surgeons soon after his arrival was initially responsible for this early recognition. This painting vividly portrayed the eminent anatomist Dr Tulp, complete with partially dissected corpse, lecturing to a group of guild members. Within a few short years Rembrandt had married Saskia Van Ulenburch, who brought him a handsome dowry. The couple lived in great style; Rembrandt bought a large house which he stocked with expensive works of art. Important commissions continued to arrive, including one from Prince Frederik Henry of Orange for a series of paintings depicting the Passion of Christ. The self-portraits which he painted during these early years of success and happiness contrast markedly with the one we have discussed; we see him dressed as a gay cavalier boisterously raising a glass of beer, or posing self-consciously as an 'Oriental', complete with turban.

Rembrandt was a unique figure within the Dutch school for a number of reasons. Far from specialising, in the manner of his contemporaries, his talents ranged over a wide field and included portraits (individuals and groups), religious, historical, mythological and contemporary subjects, still life and landscapes. His sheer virtuosity and daring in the use of oil paint and copper-plate etching was unrivalled, even by Frans Hals. Nor was his ability to convey a powerful sense of

Head of an Old Man *by* Rembrandt Van Rijn. *(National Gallery of Ireland)*

Christ Preaching the Forgiveness of Sins *by* Rembrandt Van Rijn. *Etching. (British Museum)*

solidity matched by any other member of the Dutch school, and indeed Rembrandt has very few superiors in this field, in all of European painting. It was his use of art as an instrument of psychological probing which really set him apart however. In his portraits, particularly in later ones, he managed to isolate and record not merely the likeness of some individual seen at a particular time and place, but in an uncanny fashion also to suggest all of the diverse pressures which had gone into the moulding of the visage under scrutiny. Like Leonardo, Rembrandt looked at everything, but unlike the great Florentine he brought the immense warmth of his own personality to bear on almost everything he painted or drew; he rarely remained detached. Some of the great figures of literature—Shakespeare or Dostoevsky, perhaps—spring to mind rather than other visual artists. Like them Rembrandt was not unduly concerned with aesthetic theories; 'art' and 'life' had no hard and fast line separating them and one cannot consider the artist without also considering the man.

With Baroque art we have seen the triumph of sweeping generalisation, with Rembrandt we encounter the triumph of the individual, made possible by the gradual maturing of the Protestant ethic. Protestantism preached the doctrine of personal responsibility; the world, and ultimately God, must be approached separately by each individual. Doctrinal formulas must therefore take second place or be virtually ignored. This approach is particularly noticeable in the portraits, but also in the religious and mythological works. Rembrandt was extremely fond of religious themes, drawn from both the Old and the New Testaments. His treatment of such subjects, however, has a freshness of approach which suggests that they are being depicted for the first time. The lives of biblical personages are intimately related to, and reconstructed in the light of, the artist's own experience of life. Even the beautifully observed but apparently trivial anecdotal details so often to be found in his compositions serve to make the stories from the Scriptures that much more alive, and are anything but irreverent. A dog scratches himself while the infant Christ is being presented in the Temple, a child idly draws in the dust with a finger while Christ preaches the forgiveness of sins, and two children who play with a wreath of wild flowers are oblivious to the words of John the Baptist. The Council of Trent would hardly have approved.

Although Rembrandt was a great individualist he borrowed from a wide range of artistic sources. Whereas he probably never left Holland, his activities as a collector and dealer in paintings and prints made him familiar with the Italian and Flemish schools (he owned a painting by Rubens). Most of his borrowings were thoroughly digested and may be discovered in his work only with difficulty. His dramatic use of light and shade, his tenebrism, obviously owes a great deal to Caravaggio however. Among Caravaggio's followers in Rome were certain Dutch artists, most notably

Gerrit Van Honthorst, who carried many of the Italian master's ideas back to Holland with them.

Jan Vermeer of Delft (1632–75)

Rembrandt represents one extreme in Dutch painting, Jan Vermeer of Delft another. Vermeer's art, with only a handful of exceptions, consists entirely of views of the interior of his own house. Of the artist himself we know nothing except the barest outline of his life.

He was the son of a tavern keeper and art dealer. He inherited his father's house and tavern on the market square in Delft where he lived for most of his life. He appears to have made his living as a dealer and valuer of paintings; there exists no record of his ever having sold one of his own pictures.

Lady and Gentleman at the Virginals, c. *1662, by* Jan Vermeer. *(The Royal Collection, copyright reserved)*

No two of Vermeer's pictures are exactly alike but many of them are composed of elements so similar that we are strongly reminded of a musician playing a series of variations on the one theme. The rectangular forms of paintings, maps, mirrors and virginals recur as do the diamond patterns of floor tiles, the leaded windows, upholstered chairs, heavily patterned table cloths, and of course the human beings. All of these elements from everyday life appear casual and yet uncannily ordered. Nothing is out of place, no element obtrudes; the harmony of verticals, horizontals, diagonals and curves has a kind of completeness which recalls the humanist ideal requiring the harmony of a work of art to be such that no element may be added or removed. If Vermeer's painting invokes the harmony of the great humanist painters like Piero della Francesca, so too in another sense does he recall Van Eyck. Vermeer was also—some would say above all—a master of light. Like Van Eyck he was remarkably sensitive to every nuance of light, and it is light which ultimately completes the harmony of his pictures. Advances in the field of optical instruments in his native Holland probably aided his researches. It seems likely that he viewed his subjects with the aid of a camera obscura.

The human beings who inhabit Vermeer's interiors, reading letters, practising on the virginals or lute, drinking wine, we feel are of no more importance to the painter than the other 'stage props'. They are there merely because people are to be found in rooms, as are tables, maps and floor tiles. We might well imagine that when these human 'props' are no longer required, the master is left quite alone in his empty house to contemplate the next variation on the theme. It comes as something of a shock to learn that he was married and had eleven children!

Towards the end of the seventeenth century the Dutch school lost most of its vigour and Holland ceased to be one of the creative centres of Europe. A number of important 'realist' artists did emerge during the century of the Rococo style, of whom only the Spaniard, Francisco Goya, might be compared in stature to Velasquez or Rembrandt. We have already mentioned the Venetians, Canaletto and Guardi, whose work was certainly 'realist' and we shall consider the career of Goya at the beginning of the next chapter.

'REALIST' PAINTING IN FRANCE AND ENGLAND

Jean-Baptiste-Siméon Chardin (1699–1779)

The paintings of Jean-Baptiste Chardin are strongly reminiscent of certain aspects of the Dutch school. His subjects are drawn from some of the most banal aspects of everyday existence; a young governess patiently instructs her pupil, kitchen maids busy themselves amid pots and pans, a youth builds a house of cards, a cat finds itself upon a table laden with fish. Often Chardin restricts himself to the inanimate paraphernalia of everyday existence, to the jugs, bottles, napkins and coppers of the kitchen. His paintings, which appear so spontaneous are, in fact, nothing of the kind. They are the result of the most painstaking

The Scullery Maid, *1739, by* Jean-Baptiste-Simeon Chardin. *(Hunterian Museum, University of Glasgow)*

application of the French sense of order and good taste. The colour schemes, rich browns and creams and slate blues, occasionally 'spiced' with touches of pure colour, are immaculate. So too is Chardin's sense of structure; his carefully modelled figures have a satisfyingly weighty quality about them, which distinguishes them from the 'confections' of the Rococo painters, yet they never become leaden.

Look at Chardin's 'Scullery Maid'. A young serving girl with a rather distracted, or perhaps bored, expression on her face works in the poorly lit basement of her employers. How carefully Chardin balances his large, simplified forms; the simple cylinders of the girl's skirt and of the metal vessels and the tub are assembled almost in the way an architect organises the masses of a building.

Chardin put a great deal of effort and skill into each of his disarmingly simple pictures; indeed it is a tribute to his skill that he makes it all look so easy.

William Hogarth (1697–1764)

The painter from London, William Hogarth, was a 'realist' of a very different kind. Although he had very little of the superb taste and sense of structure of Chardin, his biting, satirical approach affords us a humorous and frequently irreverent view of his contemporaries. His best known paintings were conceived in series—'Harlot's Progress', 'Rake's Progress', 'Marriage à la Mode' and the 'Election Series'—each picture in a series telling part of a story rather like the chapters of a novel.

Chairing the Candidate, c. *1755, by* William Hogarth. *(Sir John Soane's Museum, London)*

'Chairing the Candidate' is taken from the Election Series, painted quite late in Hogarth's career. Amid scenes of mayhem and to the accompaniment of fiddle music, the successfully elected parliamentary candidate, fat, bewigged and, one suspects, none too bright, is raised in triumph by his supporters. Is the fat sow who rushes through this happy throng and sweeps a lady off her feet, meant to be a comment on the porcine girth—and intelligence—of the candidate or is she merely there to add to the general confusion? And there is plenty of that. In the centre of the picture, with his back turned to us, the one-legged proprietor of a performing bear and monkey aims a vicious blow at a second man, with his cudgel. This man, equally eager to get in a blow with his flail, has so far succeeded only in stunning one of the bearers who is obviously in danger of releasing his grip on the pole supporting the chair. The performing bear, meanwhile, is helping himself to the contents of a barrel strapped to the side of a donkey, much to the owner's annoyance. All of this is too much for the unfortunate lady who looks down on the scene from the right. She collapses into the arms of a negro servant while a bottle of smelling salts is thrust beneath her nostrils to revive her. And what are those two negro boys, with blue ribbons in their hair, up to? They, at least, seem to derive great pleasure from the proceedings.

Joseph Wright of Derby (1734–97)

Joseph Wright's painting 'Experiment with an Airpump' presents us with an altogether different view of eighteenth-century England. Wright was very conscious of those forces which were soon to thrust England into the Industrial Revolution; his paintings reflect the growing interest in scientific experiment and technological advance. 'Experiment with an Airpump' is painted very skilfully in a tenebrist style reminiscent of the Dutch school. The scientist or 'natural philosopher' who conducts the experiment obviously has something of the showman about him; he wishes to impress the company no less than to advance the frontiers of knowledge. His experiment apparently seeks to prove that air breathing creatures, in this case

Experiment with an Airpump, *1768, by* Joseph Wright *of Derby. (Tate Gallery, London)*

a bird, perish when the supply of air is withdrawn. The unfortunate bird's fate is anticipated in a variety of ways; the two girls are upset, the boy on the left, almost lost in shadow, seems fascinated. The man who comforts the two girls—their father?—seems to be explaining that sometimes it is necessary to cause suffering in the sacred interests of science, for who knows what rewards await mankind as the result of such experiments? Who knows indeed? Perhaps these very words are passing through the mind of that rather thoughtful-looking man who sits to the right of the two girls.

Among Joseph Wright's patrons was Richard Arkwright of Preston whose spinning frame (1770) was one of those inventions which marked the beginning of mass production. Wright painted Arkwright's portrait, and also a picture of his great bleak mill.

CLASSICISM

Art in France during the seventeenth century

In its broadest sense 'classical' art denotes any art —painting, sculpture, architecture, poetry etc.—in which the principles of order and clarity are predominant. Classical artists have tended to look to the fountainhead of these concepts, Ancient Greece and to a lesser extent Ancient Rome. We have already seen how the ideals of the Renaissance, essentially classical in inspiration, gave way first to Mannerism and eventually to the distinctly anti-classical Baroque and 'realist' movements. We have also noted the attempt of the Carracci to construct a bulwark—in their academy—against the steadily rising anti-classical tide, and to them must be accorded at least some of the credit for the amazing success of classicism in painting, sculpture and architecture during the seventeenth century. It is to France, and to a lesser extent to England, that we must look for this classical revival.

Georges de la Tour (1593–1652)

The figure of Mary Magdalene sits before a table; on her knee she holds a skull, while her intense gaze seems fixed upon the wooden cross and the scourge which lie in front of her upon the table. These objects, the cross, the skull and the scourge, are symbols of her penitence, while the tall, bright flame burning in the glass of oil is surely a symbol of divine truth. This flame, apart from its symbolic value, serves as the sole source of illumination in the picture. We may immediately be reminded of Rembrandt, or indeed Caravaggio, both of whom used a similar 'spotlight' effect to intensify their images. Yet there is something about this figure which is not at all like the work of those artists. She sits, static and immovable, more like a piece of sculpture than a

human being, and the clear light, far from causing her form to fit softly into the background, creates such hard-edged shadows that she seems composed of rigid blocks.

We know remarkably little about the artist who composed this monumental figure. His name was Georges de la Tour and he appears to have spent most of his working life in Lunéville, a town in the independent duchy of Lorraine. During the early decades of the seventeenth century Lorraine was one of the most important centres of French painting, producing several masters of great significance. Painters from the region tended to spend at least the early part of their careers in Italy, and it is likely, though by no means certain, that Georges de la Tour was in Rome during his early twenties. This would, of course, neatly account for his obviously Caravaggesque lighting effects. But he could never be accused of extravagance; his compositions were made with the greatest deference to harmony, his figures tend to have a static quality reminiscent more of Vermeer or even Piero della Francesca than Caravaggio. He used tenebrist lighting in the service of clarity and monumentality of form rather than for its inherent dramatic quality.

Many of his subjects, like the 'Penitent Magdalene',

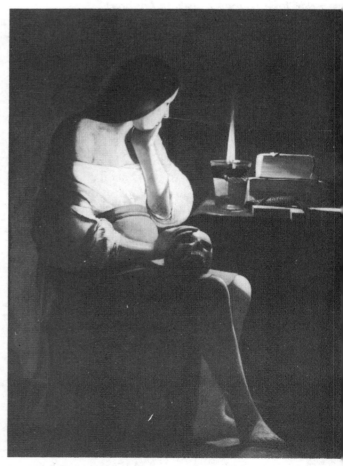

La Madeleine à la Veilleuse, c. *1635, by* Georges de la Tour. *(Louvre Museum, Paris)*

are imbued with a strong feeling of Counter-Reformation piety. He was, however, quite capable of painting contemporary life, as works like 'The Dice Players' and the remarkable 'Hurdy-Gurdy Player' testify! Should we call him a 'classical' or a 'realist' painter? A question like this merely serves to demonstrate how thoroughly arbitrary most labels are. Georges de la Tour was both 'classical' and 'realist' as was Jan Vermeer of Delft; it is simply a matter of convenience to discuss these two artists under two separate headings.

Nicolas Poussin (1594–1665)

Shortly after the young Bernini had been so warmly received by the newly elected Pope Urban VIII, a painter from Normandy, Nicolas Poussin, settled in Rome. With the exception of one brief intermission (spent in Paris working for Louis XIII) Poussin was destined to live and work in Rome until his death in 1665. The contrast between the two artists, Bernini and Poussin, was very marked. Bernini, the great virtuoso, was the artist par excellence of public spectacle; his work appealed to the widest possible public. Poussin, essentially a painter of easel pictures, appealed to a very narrow public; his art was directed only towards those of the most discerning taste, to a small group of intellectuals and connoisseurs. Yet in the work of this great man—so deeply intelligent, so hard working, so passionately single-minded—the spirit of the High Renaissance seemed, for a time, to live again in the Baroque Age. It is obviously no easy task to write convincingly about such an artist in so short a space. Before looking at any of his paintings we shall briefly consider his approach to the task of making a picture.

As there was a literary basis for almost all of Poussin's compositions, he began by carefully researching his subject matter. This might entail reading some section from Plutarch, Ovid or Livy or, in the case of religious subjects, some story from the Bible. Then some rapid sketches in pen were made, with areas of shadow freely brushed in, setting down his first concepts. The next step entailed the construction of a number of wax figures, 30 cm. or so in height, based on the figures in the sketch. These Poussin placed on a model stage where he could move them about until he arrived at what seemed to him a satisfactory grouping. He might then provide his model stage with a 'backdrop', a sheet of paper upon which the landscape or architectural setting for the piece had been sketched. The lighting for this ensemble could also be varied by means of movable slats on both sides of the stage. Sometimes larger models of individual figures were made; such figures allowed for greater refinement in anatomical details and they could also be draped.

When all of these details had been sorted out, Poussin began work on the actual canvas. No element of his painting was left to chance; the very style of the painting, the colours and tones, all had their precise part to play. He was very impressed by the idea of 'Modes', a concept derived from ancient musical composition, whereby different classes of theme were treated in the manner most suited to them. Thus the Dorian mode was developed for the treatment of grave, heroic themes, the Phrygian for violent themes, and the Ionic for festive themes etc. Poussin carefully explained the concept of modes in a letter written in 1647 to a patron who did not fully appreciate the artist's approach. In the letter he remarked, by way of illustrating his own application of the concept, 'I hope . . . to paint a subject in this Phrygian mode. The subject of frightful wars lends itself to this manner.'

Poussin's deeply contemplative turn of mind (he is often likened to his great contemporary Descartes), the literary basis of his art and the fact that many of his figures were borrowed from earlier artists, by no means entailed his rejection of nature. His numerous landscape sketches, made in pen and wash, display a keenness of observation and a freedom of handling worthy of one of the Impressionists. And a contemporary of Poussin's has recorded, 'I have seen him bringing back in his handkerchief moss, flowers and similar objects which he wanted to paint accurately, from nature.'

Nature, however, he viewed as a sort of metal-bearing ore; it was the artist's strict duty to select and to refine, and to discard the dross. He was openly contemptuous of Caravaggio—'this man was invented in order to kill painting'—and of the 'realist' approach generally—'those who choose base subjects find refuge in them because of the feebleness of their talent'.

As he grew older Poussin's personal philosophy grew deeper and indeed stricter; his leanings towards the philosophy of the Stoics became more marked while his reverence for nature approached a form of pantheism.

Poussin is at his most light-hearted with scenes like this one. A group of revellers dance with gay abandon

Bacchanalian Revel before a Term of Pan, c. *1635, by* Nicolas Poussin. (*National Gallery, London*)

Entombment, c. *1655, by* Nicolas Poussin. *(National Gallery of Ireland)*

before a garlanded statue of the god Pan. The colours are light and airy, the rhythmic movement of limbs —thrusting legs and twining arms—all pervasive. The painting is so filled with fluid movement, the composition so strongly marked by the diagonal forms of the central tree-trunks, that we must inevitably be reminded of the Baroque. And Baroque elements there certainly are, but how carefully contained. All this frenetic movement is carefully turned back into the picture space before it can strike against the frame and upset the integrity of the composition (for analysis of composition see Part II).

The 'Entombment', painted quite late in Poussin's career, conveys a very different impression from that of the 'Bacchanal'. This is a stark and rigid composition, dominated by the powerful vertical form of the Virgin Mary and the horizontal form of the dead Christ. The pictures are painted in a heavily sculptural manner; the very colours of the picture have a leaden quality, apart from the 'electric' blue of the Virgin's cloak and smouldering scarlet of the garment beneath Christ's head.

Claude Gellée (Le Lorrain, 1600–82)

Claude Gellée was another painter from Lorraine (he is usually referred to as 'Le Lorrain'). Like Poussin he spent most of his life in Rome. The two painters had certain characteristics in common—their love of antiquity, their love of order, their rejection of Baroque excesses—but there existed certain fundamental differences between them. Claude was no intellectual; his feeling for the past seems to have been imbibed directly from the pastoral beauty of the Roman Campagna with its sprinkling of antique ruins, rather than from literature. Although his paintings frequently had biblical or classical titles, they are all essentially landscapes in which the human figures play a relatively minor role. Claude's figures were sometimes painted for him, by other artists.

This landscape is typical of many that Claude painted. He frequently employed the compositional device of placing a dominant mass of foliage slightly off-centre, carefully balancing it with other landscape elements on the other side of the picture. The feeling of deep space is greatly enhanced by his sensitive use of light and atmospheric perspective. Claude's foliage masses are never merely silhouettes, they always reveal an innate 'sculptural' sense, an aspect of his work which often seemed to escape his many imitators. To many of his admirers it was his imaginative use of light which seemed most impressive. In certain of his paintings the sun itself is placed near the centre of the composition, and buildings, trees, ships, clouds and people seem bathed in a cone of light.

The Academies—France
During the seventeenth century the concept of an Academy of the arts spread to France where it took firm root. In 1648 the 'Academy of Sculpture and Painting' was founded, and in 1663 it received royal recognition from Louis XIV. One of the founders of the Academy was the painter Charles Le Brun who rose to artistic pre-eminence in France due to the good offices of his patron, the powerful minister Colbert. Le Brun, who was a prolific artist and a keen student of Italian painting (particularly Raphael) and Nicolas Poussin, firmly advocated the classical line. Along with other leading academicians he delivered discourses and published learned papers, particularly on the subject of 'the passions' (i.e. the various emotions—anger, fear, sorrow, joy etc.) and their relationship to facial expression and bodily gesture. The figure compositions of Poussin, where facial expressions and gestures were all calculated to a nicety, were an obvious field for academic research. Le Brun delivered a lecture on the suitability of each expression in the 'Israelites gathering Manna' for instance. His book, published after his death, 'A Method of Learning to Draw the Passions as Proposed in a Lecture on Expression, in General and in Particular', which was illustrated by the author, was widely read and translated.

But Le Brun himself was not another Poussin; he had neither the intellect nor the artistic ability. Ironically, his own painting tended towards a rather insipid Baroque style. These inconsistencies were reflected in the Academy itself; official homage was paid to the cerebral 'Poussinist' approach with its insistence upon the primacy of drawing over colour, but in practice a more sensual form of painting (ultimately derived from Rubens) in which colour played an important role, gradually gained a foothold. By the beginning of the eighteenth century this lighter form of painting, so perfectly exemplified by Watteau (who was received into the Academy in 1717), had established itself.

Hagar and the Angel, *by* Claude le Lorrain. *(National Gallery, London)*

During most of the eighteenth century French painting tended to be lighthearted and decorative. The small, portable easel painting became fashionable, collectors increased in number, giving rise, in 1737, to the establishment of the 'Salons', or large annual exhibitions. The Salons, in their turn, gave rise to a new breed of popular writer—the 'art-critic'.

England
The academic spirit also found its way to England during the eighteenth century. Joshua Reynolds helped to found the Royal Academy in 1768. As president of the Academy, Reynolds delivered fifteen Discourses, outlining the theory of an artist's education, the characteristics of various artists and schools, and his concept of the 'grand style'. Reynolds felt that a young artist could best approach nature by submitting himself to the study, not of nature, but of the art of the 'great masters'. Although he insisted that such study should be analytical rather than slavish, the consequences of ideals like this were ultimately not very happy. In countries like England and France (where the academies eventually gained what was virtually a stranglehold during the nineteenth century) too many students of art were to have what spark of originality they possessed ground out of them through long hours

spent making immaculate—and slavish!—drawings from plastercasts of antique statuary.

Postcript—A note on Architecture

Rather more impressive than the paintings of Le Brun and his colleagues was the architecture built for Louis XIV, the 'Sun King'. The great palaces—the Louvre, Versailles—built for Louis, were conceived as expressions of kingly authority in keeping with the ideals of that monarch. They were grand and impressive in a manner altogether more severe than the current Baroque style. Bernini had, in fact, been asked to submit designs for the east façade of the Louvre but these were rejected and the project was undertaken by a French architect, Claude Perrault.

The palace and gardens of Versailles were conceived as a 'total' work of art: luxurious interiors, ceilings painted by Le Brun, huge imposing apartments faced with marble, gardens laid out in the 'French' style (i.e. where the various elements of nature, trees, lawns, lakes etc. are laid out according to a rigid architectural plan).

The Louvre, *east façade and colonnade, 1667–78, by* Claude Perrault *and* Louis le Vau, *from drawings by* François d'Orbay. *Bernini's designs for this façade were rejected. (Louvre Museum, Paris)*

England

English architecture seems to have passed from a Gothic to a classical style without any clearly defined period of transition. Inigo Jones, who designed the Banqueting House in Whitehall had travelled in Italy where the buildings of Palladio (q.v.) had deeply impressed him. Sir Christopher Wren, to whom fell the task of rebuilding much of the city of London after the Great Fire of 1666, rebuilt St Paul's cathedral in a style strongly reminiscent of St Peter's in Rome.

By the eighteenth-century Palladianism had virtually become the national style in England. The neo-

---

The Palace of Versailles. *(Camera Press). The Pool of the Swiss is in the foreground. Versailles evolved over a period of several generations; it was begun in 1624 during the reign of Louis XIII, and considerably extended and modified during the reign of Louis XIV.*

The Banqueting House, Whitehall, *1619, by* Inigo Jones *(1573–1652). (Camera Press). Jones visited Italy on several occasions and made a special study of the work of Palladio. All of his most important work was done for the Crown.*

Hellenic architecture of Robert Adam (1728–92) marks the climax of this road to classicism.

St Paul's Cathedral, *1673–1710, by* Sir Christopher Wren *(1632–1723). (Camera Press). Wren's aim was to build a Protestant St Peter's in London. He also undertook the task of rebuilding fifty-one other churches in London after the great fire of 1666.*

Osterley Park House, *Middlesex, 1761, by* Robert Adam *(1728-89). (Camera Press)*

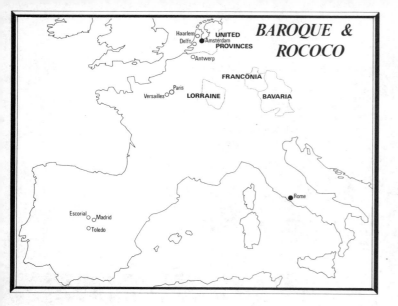

BAROQUE & ROCOCO

based on a vertical axis, (*b*) packed composition, (*c*) simplified outlines of figures, (*d*) flattened space, (*e*) proportions of figures distorted for dramatic effect and to aid cohesion of composition, (*f*) figures linked by strong linear rhythms.

2 Rembrandt

The great Dutch artist used chiaroscuro (light and shade) for dramatic effect, and also to simplify his composition. His method might be explored in the art class as follows: make a large figure composition (this might be based on a series of studies drawn from life) in pencil or pen. Superimpose a chiaroscuro scheme borrowed from a Rembrandt painting. Use a wash of ink or water colour. When the wash has dried add any necessary details without disturbing the tone scheme.

Practical exercises

The art of the seventeenth and eighteenth centuries, like that of the Renaissance period, does not serve ideally as the basis for art class experiment. There are, however, at least two notable exceptions.

1 El Greco

The study of El Greco's painting might suggest an approach to figure composition. The following pictorial elements could be stressed: (*a*) composition

For further reading

Larousse Encyclopaedia of Renaissance and Baroque Art (Hamlyn)

Kenneth Clarke, *Civilisation* (BBC/John Murray)

Elizabeth Gilmore Holt, *A Documentary History of Art*, Volume II (Doubleday Anchor)

Germain Bazin, *Baroque and Rococo* (Thames and Hudson)

Michael Levey, *Rococo to Revolution: major trends in 18th Century painting* (Thames and Hudson)

	Some Important Events		Building and Visual Arts
		1541	Birth of El Greco (d.1614)
1567	Netherlands in revolt against Spain		
		1573	Birth of Caravaggio (d. 1610) Birth of Inigo Jones (d. 1652)
		1577	Birth of P. P. Rubens (d. 1640)
		1580	Birth of Frans Hals (d. 1666)
1584	Sir Walter Raleigh—expedition to Virginia		
		1585	Academy founded in Bologna by the Carracci.
1588	Defeat of the Spanish Armada		
		1593	Birth of Georges de la Tour (d. 1652)
		1594	Birth of Nicolas Poussin (d. 1665)
1596	Birth of R. Descartes (d. 1650)		
		1598	Birth of G. L. Bernini (d. 1680)
		1599	Birth of Velasquez (d. 1660)
		1600	Birth of Claude Gellée (d. 1682)
1603	Death of Elizabeth I James I King of England		

Some Important Events		Building and Visual Arts	
		1606	Birth of Rembrandt (d. 1669)
1609	Dutch Independence Galileo—first astronomical telescope		
1618	Beginning of Thirty Years War		
1620	Mayflower expedition First negro slaves landed in Jamestown	1620	Birth of Pierre Puget (d. 1694)
1622	Birth of Molière (d. 1673)	1622	Rubens begins work on 'The Life of Marie de Medici' series
1623	Birth of Pascal (d. 1662)		
		1624	Work begun on Versailles Palace
1625	Circulation of the blood discovered—Harvey	1624–1633	Baldachino by Bernini
		1632	Birth of Vermeer (d. 1675) Birth of Christopher Wren (d. 1723)
		1634	Velasquez—Surrender of Breda
1636	Descartes—*Discours de la Méthode*		
1637	Creation of Venetian opera by Monteverdi		
1639	Birth of Racine (d. 1699)		
1642	Birth of Newton	1642	Rembrandt—Night Watch
1643	Louis XIV King of France		
		1645–1652	Bernini—Ecstasy of St Teresa
1648	Treaty of Westphalia	1648	Academy founded in France
1649	Execution of Charles I of England—The Commonwealth		
		1656	Velasquez—The Maids of Honour
		1663	Royal recognition granted to the Academy by Louis XIV
		1665	Bernini invited to design the east façade of the Louvre
1666	Great Fire of London		
1672	Assassination of the de Witt brothers		
		1673–1710	St Paul's, London
		1684	Birth of Antoine Watteau (d. 1721)
1685	Birth of J. S. Bach, and Handel		
1686	Law of Gravity—Newton		
1690	Battle of the Boyne		
		1697	Birth of William Hogarth (d. 1764)
		1699	Birth of J. B. S. Chardin (d. 1779)
		1728	Birth of Robert Adam (d. 1789) Influence of Palladian architecture increasingly felt in England

	Some Important Events		Building and Visual Arts
1742	Handel's Messiah first performed in Dublin		
		c. 1750	Church of Die Wies
		c. 1755	Hogarth—Election series
1755	Dr Johnson's Dictionary		
1756	Birth of Mozart		
		1759	William Chambers—Treatise on Civil Architecture
c. 1760	James Watt—first steam engine		
1760	George III King of England		
		1767–75	John Wood—Royal Crescent, Bath
		1768	Royal Academy founded in England Joseph Wright—Experiment with an air pump
1769	Birth of Napoleon		
1770	Birth of Beethoven Arkwright's spinning frame		
1776	American Declaration of Independence		
		1779	First cast iron bridge built at Coalbrookdale, Shropshire
1789	Storming of the Bastille		

CHAPTER FOUR

The Nineteenth Century

The Oath of the Horatii, *1784, by* Jacques-Louis David. *(Louvre Museum, Paris)*

Jacques-Louis David (1748–1825)

In the Salon of 1785 one painting in particular was hailed as a great success. It seemed, by its austerity of colour and its starkness of design to be the perfect antidote to the Rococo style. Jacques-Louis David's picture 'The Oath of the Horatii' was painted in a grimly undecorative manner; the figures were taut and muscular, the architectural setting uncompromisingly plain. And the subject—the three warrior brothers stoutly swearing to lay down their lives for the Roman republic—seemed to many of David's contemporaries wholly in keeping with their own aspirations. For France was on the brink of revolution; within a few short years the old order would be swept away—the Bastille would be stormed, the King and Queen would die, mobs would march to the strains of La Marseillaise, and many heads would fall to the guillotine.

David himself was a staunch republican. He was, in fact, one of those Deputies who voted for the King's execution in 1793. His paintings, although inspired by antiquity—particularly republican Rome—were quite consciously works of political propaganda. Contemporary subject matter he considered, in the main, to be beneath contempt. Occasionally his republican sentiments overcame his artistic prejudices, as when, for example, he made a preparatory drawing for a picture to commemorate the famous Tennis Court Oath and, when Marat was stabbed to death in his bath, David recorded his 'martyrdom' in a painting which is still curiously moving. His portraits too are clearly stamped by his 'Roman' austerity; gone are the lavish furnishings, the wigs and the frills which are so often the hall-mark of the eighteenth-century fashionable portraiture.

While the French Revolution was in full flood David had virtually dictatorial powers over the arts. His fortunes seemed to wane however, when, after Robespierre's death, he was thrown into prison. His conversion to Bonapartism and his acceptance of the post of 'Premier peintre de l'Empereur' comes therefore as something of a surprise. From Napoleon he received a commission for four large compositions including a painting of the Coronation of the Emperor and the Empress Josephine. On the day of the Coronation (3 December 1804) David was provided with a suitable position in Notre Dame from which to observe and sketch the proceedings. The finished painting (6·10 by 9·31 m) which shows Napoleon about to place the crown on Josephine's head, was put on public display in the Salon of 1808.

David was by no means an isolated figure in his total rejection of the Rococo manner and in returning to the classical past for inspiration. In many European countries, including Germany, England and Italy, painters, sculptors and architects were moving in a similar direction. The result was the international 'neo-Classical' movement which was to exert a considerable, if not always healthy, influence on artistic thinking during the first half of the nineteenth century. Neo-Classicism, like every other artistic movement, was the product of a number of forces. It may be seen as an inevitable reaction against the 'frothiness' of the Rococo style, but it received a great deal of impetus from the renewed vigour of archaeological research during the eighteenth and nineteenth centuries, which brought to light a number of important discoveries in sites such as Herculaneum and Pompeii, and in Greece itself. But the austerities of the neo-Classical style were by no means to everyone's taste. During the early decades of the nineteenth century the movement had at least one major opponent, and as the century advanced it was finally submerged by an increasing number and diversity of opposing artistic forces.

Francisco Goya (1746–1828)

On 2 May 1808 the streets of Madrid echoed to the sounds of vicious conflict. The populace had risen against their French occupiers only to be speedily and

The Execution of the Rebels on 3rd May, 1808, *by* Francisco Goya. *(Museo del Prado, Madrid)*

ruthlessly crushed by Murat's North African Cavalry. Reprisals followed on 3 May. Throughout that day and well into the night, the firing squads did their brutal work. Such things happened in wars and are soon relegated to the pages of history books or else forgotten altogether. But the memory of these events in May of 1808 lives on, not because they are particularly significant to the long narrative of human conflict, but because they were observed and recorded by a very remarkable witness. His name was Francisco Goya, fashionable portrait painter, Director of the Academy of San Fernando, and First Painter to the Spanish Court. From the windows of his apartment in the Puerto del Sol he watched Murat's Mamelukes ride through the streets below cutting down his fellow countrymen with their sweeping sabres. He saw and remembered. Some six years later, when peace had been restored to Spain, he painted 'The Citizens of Madrid fighting Murat's Cavalry in the Puerto del Sol, May 2nd, 1808' and 'The Executions of the Third of May'.

Although its title would appear to tie it down to a particular date and a particular place, the 'Third of May' has a timeless quality about it. The soldiers who comprise the firing squad are seen as an anonymous mass; their faces are turned away from us, their weapons are raised in unison. They are a killer machine, impersonal, efficient and ruthless. And the people about to die, their faces masks of fear or defiance, are the people who suffer and die in all modern wars, citizens who find themselves caught up in a surging tide of events only half understood and not of their own making. (We have seen their faces and their gestures so often in the pages of our newspapers and on our TV screens—from Vietnam, Cambodia, Biafra, Bangladesh.) What a particularly memorable image Goya has created with that man whose shirt gleams brightly in the lantern light, whose arms stretch out as though crucified. What was he doing two or three days ago—minding his shop, mending shoes, drinking with his friends, playing with his children perhaps?

This is not the kind of painting we might expect from the director of an Academy, or from a court painter for that matter. But nothing about Francisco Goya, the artist or the man, was simple. He was a mass of contradictions. Was it simply patriotism which drove him to paint those two pictures? If so it is odd that he should also have painted portraits of King Joseph Bonaparte and his generals, thus making himself a collaborator of sorts with the enemy. Goya himself would probably have maintained that, as an artist, it was his business to remain above politics and matters of nationality; he must remain quite free of such matters in order to observe and comment as he

The Sleep of Reason Produces Monsters, *by* Francisco Goya. *A plate from* Los Caprichos, *first published in 1799. (British Museum)*

saw fit. So from his hand we have a bewildering variety of work, asserting by its very variety a degree of freedom virtually unknown to previous artists. There are paintings filled with the carefree sweetness of the Rococo style (showing the influence of Tiepolo and made as studies for tapestries), and superbly painted portraits of the great beauties of the day: the singer Lorenza Correa and Dona Isabel Cobos y Porcel among many others. There are paintings of the Royal Family, and of the great men of the land like the Queen's favourite, the minister Godoy. But these were all works by Goya the public artist. The private Goya could be a satirist of unrivalled ferocity, a realist of unflinching honesty and finally an explorer of the subconscious comparable, in terms of sheer conviction, if not in style, to Bosch himself.

With a series of etchings which he called 'Los Caprichos' (Caprices) Goya lashed out at the follies of contemporary Spanish society. With mordant wit he attacked the institution of marriage, the fickleness of women, the greed of the clergy, the incompetence of doctors and the parasitic nature of the aristocracy. Only his royal connections prevented him from falling foul of the Inquisition, which was still a power in the land. Nevertheless, he was forced to withdraw 'Los Caprichos' from sale and only avoided having his copper plates destroyed by presenting them to the King. His series of etchings called 'The Disasters of

You who cannot go on, *by Francisco Goya. (British Museum). One of the most inflammatory plates from* Los Caprichos: *two peasants bear the weight of two well-fed donkeys—the aristocracy and the clergy. The ideals of the French Revolution had obviously left a deep impression on Goya, and one can easily understand why the Inquisition should wish to take action against him.*

War' were a further exploration of man's inhumanity to man. Here there are remarkably few heroes and very many victims: dead bodies, mutilated and stripped naked, are impaled on a tree, a soldier views with obvious satisfaction the result of his handiwork—a corpse hanging by the neck, children weep for their dead parents, a woman desperately claws the face of a ravishing soldier.

In 1792 Goya suffered a severe illness which left him stone deaf for the remainder of his life. This deafness facilitated his detachment and was at least partially responsible for turning his vision inwards. During the last decade of his life his painting took on a truly nightmarish aspect. This is particularly true of the murals which he painted on the walls at his own house, the 'Black Paintings'. These pictures seem to represent a desperate attempt of Goya's to rid his own mind of all the horrors which had accumulated and festered there. They were a sort of exorcism! A coven of witches congeals and writhes before the goat-headed figure of Satan; old men, with skull-like heads slobber over their soup, and Saturn, gigantic and horrible, devours the body of his own son.

The artist as a 'law unto himself' (independent of all social ties and free to choose his own subjects and his own methods of execution), was a new phenomenon only hinted at in earlier times by artists as various as Rembrandt and Leonardo. As a concept it grew in strength during the nineteenth century, challenging the entrenched values of neo-Classicism. It found expression in literature, painting and music, and became known as 'Romanticism'.

Jean Auguste Dominique Ingres (1780–1867) and neo-Classicism

The most powerful upholder of the primacy of neo-Classicism in France during the first half of the nineteenth century was undoubtedly David's pupil J. A. D. Ingres. Ingres preached a severe doctrine: painters must subject their art to the discipline of line. He declared 'a thing well enough drawn is always well enough painted'. Before the great masters of the past, Raphael of course, but also the painters of the Florentine Quattrocento, Giotto, and the Greeks, he prostrated himself with humility. He was 'not an innovator'. It is hardly surprising that he regarded the art of Rubens with loathing, refusing to allow his pupils even to look at the work of the great Fleming as they passed through the Louvre to view 'more wholesome fare'. Nor did he look with favour on the Romantic movement.

Many of Ingres's paintings were dry and pedantic. Yet he was an artist of considerable power, and certain of his pictures reveal a vitality and even a sensuality which undoubtedly break the bounds of his own self-imposed ideological straitjacket. His fascination for

The Turkish Bath, *1863, by J. A. D. Ingres. (Louvre Museum, Paris)*

the mysterious Middle East spanned most of his long career. He painted a number of pictures in which languorous harem girls recline and stretch with feline sensuousness, culminating in his great 'Turkish Bath' painted when the artist was well into his seventies. This painting was delivered to Prince Napoleon in 1859, but it was too much for the prince's wife, the Princess Clothilde, and Ingres was forced to take it back.

He was also a superb portrait painter. Some of his portraits must rank among the finest in all of French art. His portrait of the publisher M. Bertin is strikingly monumental but filled with the suggestion of the sitter's energy. This painting seems to epitomise the nineteenth-century ideal of masculine strength. By contrast, many of his female portraits are lyrical and full of fluid movement; the early oval portrait of Madame Riviere is a good example.

The Academy School, the Ecole des Beaux Arts, was the most influential disseminator of artistic doctrine during the nineteenth century, and the doctrine which it sought to perpetuate was basically that of Ingres. This institution became part of a 'closed circle' outside of which any artist would find it virtually impossible to make a living. It was largely composed of a number of studios, each presided over by an artist of distinction. To these studios the young aspirant artists came to draw from the cast (i.e. from plaster-casts of antique sculpture) and from the life (i.e. from the living human model, male and female). Originality was positively discouraged and the students were not encouraged to look to nature or the world around them for inspiration. Style was what mattered, the dry and highly polished style of M. Ingres. That master was capable of breathing life into it; in the hands of most of those who passed through the Ecole des Beaux Arts it became utterly lifeless. Very few of the students rebelled, they soon realised that their future financial security rested upon their readiness to accept and apply all that their teachers had to offer. These same teachers were likely to be members of the Salon jury, theirs was the power to accept or reject submitted works. Then there were prizes to be awarded; a first class medal could make an artist's name overnight! Members of the Salon juries could always be relied upon to 'do something' for a favoured pupil. Failure to exhibit at the Salon almost certainly ruled out the possibility of selling one's work. So it paid to conform, to play the game strictly by the rules. A few bribes dropped here and there to ensure a good position in the exhibition would certainly help, and if one were fortunate enough to number a journalist or two among one's friends so much the better. Favourable mention in the press could do a lot for an unknown artist.

To be fair to him, Ingres clearly saw the evils of this system and for a period of some twenty years, while at the height of his fame, he refused to exhibit his own paintings in the Salon. 'The Salon' he said 'stifles and corrupts the feeling for the great, the beautiful; artists are driven there by the attractions of profit, the desire to get themselves noticed at any price.' The Salon was merely a shop window; it dragged the work of art down to the level of common kitchen utensils. Ingres could afford to stand aloof from the system, his name had been made and he had more than enough customers. He seemed unwilling, or else felt unable, to do anything to bring about a reform however.

For a time the neo-Classical style—in painting, sculpture and architecture—seemed to triumph throughout Western Europe. Imitation Greek or Roman buildings sprang up in many of Europe's great cities; the gods and goddesses of antiquity abounded in both marble and paint. Furniture, interior decoration and even the hairstyles and dresses of the ladies affected the antique manner. But very few of the neo-Classical artists ever approached the genius of either David or Ingres. These two artists remained the greatest exponents of the style.

Arc de Triomphe de l'Etoile, *1806–36. (Camera Press)*

Neo-Classical art, with its immaculate, unruffled surfaces, seemed to take little or no account of the deep-seated tension of the age as, for instance, the art of Francisco Goya had done. And Goya was by no means alone; throughout Europe an increasing

Orestes Pursued by the Furies, *1793, by* John Flaxman. *Flaxman's line drawings were studied by artists all over Europe.*

number of men and women of talent and sensibility turned their backs on the established and revered conventions of the age. Greece and Rome were all very well, Raphael was wonderful, but there were other sources of inspiration, other gods to follow. There was 'Nature', for instance, and 'liberty', and a newly discovered 'golden age' which was soon to supplant classical antiquity. classical antiquity. This latter was the 'Middle Ages', despised since the Renaissance as a period of darkness and ignorance.

We have seen it happen before several times in the course of European history; the hard 'shell' of the established social order, with all its trappings—its religious and political ideals, its art, its customs—had once again become too tight. It must be burst asunder. Violence, of course, was inevitable: real, and idealised in the form of art. Europe had to suffer her fair share of real violence with revolutions and wars of independence—in France, Spain, Greece, Poland and Flanders —and as a result of the Imperialist adventures of Napoleon Bonaparte. Painters, writers and musicians celebrated the violence of nature and of men. Their life styles often become inseparable from their art, and the artist, along with his art, became an object of awe and veneration and the raw material of legend. We have only to think of the deaf Beethoven, pacing his room like a caged lion, shouting at the top of his voice, or of the dashing Lord Byron giving his life in the sacred causes of Greek independence, or Joseph Turner lashed to the mast of a ship so that he might observe the raging storm which threatened to engulf the vessel and himself. These men, Beethoven, Byron, Turner, were among the great prophets of Romanticism, a movement so powerful that its effects were to be felt throughout the nineteenth century and well into our own.

Eugène Delacroix (1798–1863) and French Romanticism

Eugène Delacroix accepted the label 'Romantic' with a certain amount of reluctance; nevertheless he declared 'If by Romanticism is meant the free manifestation of one's personal impressions I am a Romantic'. Not that he rejected the art of the past; like Ingres he admired Raphael. But Rubens was, above all, his idol. In many of Delacroix's paintings, especially the battles and hunting scenes, Rubens seemed to live again. Like the Flemish master Delacroix loved violence and movement for their own sake, and he also shared something of Rubens's mastery of colour.

He found little in contemporary France to fire his imagination, but looked instead to literature—particularly to the works of English writers like Shakespeare, Walter Scott and Byron—and to North Africa for many of his subjects. Certain contemporary events did appeal to him, however, most notably the struggle for independence from the Turkish Empire by the Greek people. The war of independence, which resulted eventually in the foundation of modern Greece, was a bloody affair, with atrocities committed by both sides. In April 1822 the Turks massacred several thousand of the inhabitants of the Greek Island of Scios (Khios). During the following year Delacroix set to work on a series of studies for a large painting of the event which he intended to submit to the Salon. The studies alone cost him eights months of labour, but the painting was completed in time for submission to the 1824 Salon, due to open on 16 August of that year. The painting was accepted with a certain amount of reluctance. Delacroix himself was not too pleased with his own handiwork either. Somehow the surface of the painting seemed flat and dead. His apparent failure was brought home to him even more forcefully when he encountered some paintings by the Englishman John Constable (q.v.) purely by accident. Constable's paintings fascinated him, for the English artist had managed to create painted surfaces which seemed fresh and alive. Constable had discovered a secret which certain painters of the past—the Venetians, El Greco, and Goya—had also stumbled upon, namely that when an area of colour is built up of a number of unmixed colours placed side by side on the canvas, maximum luminosity is achieved. Later Delacroix was to write, 'Constable says that the masterly green of his meadows comes from its being composed of many different greens placed in juxtaposition, not mixed . . . They merge naturally at a certain desired distance as a result of the sympathetic law which has associated them. This gives the colours more depth and freshness.' This was all very well, but what was he to do about his own picture? The Salon was due to open in four days and the paintings had already been hung. But there was still

Massacre at Scios, *1824, by* Eugène Delacroix. *(Louvre Museum, Paris)*

in 1824. When, in July 1830, the citizens of Paris proved that the spark of revolution was not yet dead and took to the barricades, Delacroix applauded their actions. The reactionary regime of Charles X was successfully toppled and the event was commemorated in another great allegory 'Liberty on the Barricades'. The new monarchy of Louis Philippe was favourably disposed towards Delacroix. Early in 1832 he accompanied Count Charles de Mornay on a special mission to the Sultan of Morocco on behalf of the new French king. Although the mission only lasted for a few months it left a very deep impression on him; his memory and sketch books became stocked with images which he was to return to repeatedly throughout his life. Morocco supplied him with the raw materials for some of his finest pictures. Although he exhibited his work at the Salon, Delacroix had little time for the officially approved art of his time. Of the students in the Ecole des Beaux Arts he dryly remarked 'They are taught the beautiful as one teaches algebra'. His prestige was great, however, and during the mid-1800s it seemed that the French art world was split into two warring factions—the followers of Ingres and those of Delacroix.

time! He begged permission of the Salon committee to work further on his picture, and, as a special favour he was allowed to remove it from the wall of the exhibition hall and was even provided with a room in which to work. Considering that Delacroix worked in a manner which was officially disapproved of this may seem surprising. He had influential friends in high places, however, and it was rumoured that he was the natural son of Tallyrand! When the Salon was officially opened Delacroix's 'Massacre at Scios' was revealed, still quite wet, but transformed by a new brilliance. Delacroix had learned a lesson he was never to forget.

The painting itself depicts a group of islanders dejected and helpless, waiting for death. The Turkish cavalry man who draws his sabre with studied coldness, will ensure that they have not long to wait. The poet Baudelaire, who was a great admirer of Delacroix's art, described the 'Massacre' as a 'hymn of terror composed in honour of doom and hopeless grief'. Compare it with others in this book which deal with a similar theme: Rubens's 'Horrors of War', Goya's 'May 3rd' and then Picasso's 'Guernica'. Which do you feel is the most effective in dealing with the theme of man's inhumanity to man?

Delacroix returned to the theme of Greek independence several years later with his allegorical 'Greece expiring on the Ruins of Missolonghi'. It was at Missolonghi that his much admired Lord Byron had died

Arab Horses Fighting in a Stable, *1860, by* E. Delacroix. *(Louvre Museum, Paris)*

The art of the French Romantics, both painters and sculptors, might be termed 'neo-Baroque'. As with Delacroix, their work shows a love of movement and violence. Delacroix's friend Théodore Géricault (1791–1824) had a great passion for horses, which he expressed with great force in pictures like 'The Race of Barbary Horses', 'The Epsom Derby' and 'Officer of the Chasseurs Charging'. Géricault also made studies of the effects of poverty in contemporary London, and a remarkable series of portraits of the insane. Horses were to prove his undoing, as he died while still a young man after sustaining a fall from his horse.

Auguste Préault, with works like 'The Slaughter', 'Famine' and 'Destruction', carried the Romantic taste for violence and sudden death into the realms of sculpture. So too did François Rude, whose monumental relief 'The Departure of the Volunteers in 1792' was placed on the side of the Arc de Triomphe de l'Etoile. Perhaps the most original of the French Romantic sculptors was Antoine Barye (1796–1875) who found most of the raw material for his art in the Natural History Museum and the Zoological gardens. Barye's sculptures are mostly of wild beasts engaged in violent combat: an elephant crushes a tiger, a greyhound rends a hare, a lion and a great serpent do battle. It was not until the latter half of the nineteenth century that the greatest French Romantic sculptor emerged. His name was Auguste Rodin, who was, very briefly, a student of Barye's. We shall deal with Rodin's career later in this chapter.

The Romantic Movement in England

'In art there are two modes by which men aim at distinction. In the one, by a careful application of what others have accomplished, the artist imitates their works, or selects and combines their various beauties; in the other, he seeks excellence at its primitive source, nature. In the first, he forms a style upon the study of pictures, and produces either imitative or eclectic art: in the second, by a close observation of nature, he discovers qualities existing in her which have never been portrayed before, and thus forms a style which is original.'

Thus the painter John Constable, writing in 1830, summed up the differences between his approach to art and that of the academies, and in so doing neatly put his finger on one of the chief sources of Romantic inspiration. Nature has been with us for a long time, so the Romantics certainly didn't discover it, although they often behaved as though they had. The important point is that they were the first generation to be so acutely aware of Nature in all her aspects. The men of the Renaissance saw in nature something to be probed, understood and ultimately bent to the will of mankind; the Romantics, on the other hand, were conscious only of forces vast and fathomless, capable of moulding a great mountain range or a tiny celandine. Nature was a deity, impersonal and indifferent to the aspirations of mankind. She was the ultimate source of all beauty and all wisdom; men might only approach her in order to marvel at her vastness and her power. For a time England became one of the centres for the new 'religion' of nature. Her poets, Wordsworth, Shelley,

Lion and Serpent, c. *1850, by* Antoine Barye. *(National Museum of Ireland)*

Keats, Coleridge, turning their backs on past modes, celebrated the many faces of nature with a new freshness. And many of England's painters were to do exactly the same in their own art.

John Constable (1776–1837)

When one of John Constable's patrons, Sir George Beaumont, suggested to the artist that the prevailing tone of a painting should be based on the colour of an old Cremona violin, he was simply expressing the common prejudice of his time. Constable's reply, however, was to fetch such an instrument and lay it on the lawn of his patron's house. The message was obvious —grass is green, look!

Constable himself spent a great deal of his life simply looking, often with brush in hand. Throughout his life he turned out large quantities of sketches in oil paint, made, of course, out in the fields. These were acutely observed slices of nature, often with the time of day and the prevailing weather conditions noted on the back. However, he did not consider such sketches as finished works worthy of exhibition. The large paintings, his 'six-footers', made for the Royal Academy's annual exhibition, for instance, were always carefully composed in his studio.

Constable was not merely an eye, mindlessly recording whatever was in front of him like a camera. His 'scientific' application of colour which sought to parallel, rather than to slavishly imitate, the sparkle of nature, was duly noted by Delacroix as we have already seen. Nor was he unaware or unappreciative of the great art of the past. He had a deep admiration for Claude Lorrain and Jacob Van Ruysdael, but was not content, like so many of his fashionable colleagues, merely to imitate the manner of those masters. Sir George Beaumont owned the painting by Claude al-

Cloud Study *by* John Constable. *(National Gallery of Ireland)*

ready reproduced in this book. Constable made sketches from it and even used a similar compositional balance in several of his landscapes.

Ultimately the landscapes of his native Suffolk, particularly a section of the Stour Valley, meant far more to him than the work of any artist. 'Willows, old rotten banks, slimy posts and brickwork. I love such things,' he declared, and proceeded to make them the central theme of his art, often to the consternation of his contemporaries. To the gentleman who suggested to him that one of his paintings, exhibited at the annual Academy exhibition, was merely a picture of a house

and ought, therefore, to be placed in the Architectural room, he replied rather testily that it was 'a picture of a summer morning, including a house'.

'The Haywain' was one of those pictures by Constable which so impressed Delacroix and led him to alter his 'Massacre at Scios'. It is a rather difficult picture for a twentieth-century person to appreciate in that it seems almost too obvious. Once again our sight has been blunted—by over-exposure to photographic images and also to the innumerable pastiches of Constable's 'Naturalness' which have clogged so many exhibitions for the past century or so. But we cannot hold Constable responsible for all that. If we wish to appreciate his work we may do so only by an act of imagination, by seeing him in the context of his own age. Then he emerges as a revolutionary, albeit a quiet one, similar in so many ways to his great contemporary William Wordsworth.

Joseph Mallord William Turner (1775–1851)

When we consider that the straightforward, down-to-earth John Constable met with a lack of comprehension, it is difficult to imagine how the painting opposite, first exhibited in the 1840s, was greeted by the public. It was called 'Snowstorm—Steamboat off a Harbour's Mouth'. But where was the steamboat, or the harbour? Surely the picture was quite senseless, just another of Mr Turner's little jokes? Mr Turner was not joking, of course, and he must have grown used to the good-humoured scorn from critics and public which tended to greet his contributions to the Royal Academy exhibitions. And although these contributions tended to grow ever more incomprehensible

The Haywain, *1821, by* John Constable. *(National Gallery, London)*

Snowstorm: Steamboat off a Harbour's Mouth, *1841,*
by Joseph Turner. *(Tate Gallery, London)*

as Turner grew older, the Academy could not refuse to exhibit them as Turner was an academician of long standing. Unlike his close contemporary Constable, he had achieved considerable success, both financial and in terms of recognition, very early in his career. His watercolours of scenic views, often made in series like the 'Picturesque views of England and Wales' and the 'Rivers of France', were engraved commercially and sold in large quantities, bringing the artist substantial financial gain. His larger oil paintings in the 'grand manner'—'Aeneas with Sibyl' or 'Hannibal Crossing the Alps'—which often amounted to little more than extremely clever pastiches of earlier artists like Claude, also ensured his early success with the Royal Academy. In fact he was made a full academician in 1802 at the age of twenty-seven. Here again we may observe a marked contrast with Constable who had to wait until he was fifty-three years of age before a similar honour was bestowed upon him.

Turner's travels on the continent were instrumental in ridding his art of eclecticism. The grandeur of the Alps helped his growing awareness of nature as a vast, pitilessly destructive force and of the insignificance of mankind. The dazzling light of Italy, particularly in Venice, helped him to see that his genius lay in the exploration of light and colour. As his concern for light and colour developed, so his statements of clearly discernible forms diminished and eventually disappeared altogether beneath atmospheric haze. He produced many thousands of watercolours, and this technique, which entails constructing a picture in delicate, wholly transparent washes, influenced his application of oil paint and augmented the luminous, ethereal quality of his later pictures.

The violence of nature fascinated him—storms on land or sea, avalanches and great fires. How puny man and all his works seemed before these manifestations of nature in her moods of destructive excess. In response to this vision Turner developed an art of controlled violence which seems perfectly to accord with that of certain of his great contemporaries: with the

Beethoven of the fifth and seventh symphonies and the Emperor Concerto, and with the Shelley of 'Ode to the West Wind':

> Thou on whose stream, 'mid the steep sky's commotion,
> Loose clouds like earth's decaying leaves are shed,
> Shook from the tangled boughs of heaven and ocean,
> Angels of rain and lightning! there are spread
> On the blue surface of thine airy surge,
> Like the bright hair uplifted from the head of some fierce Maenad,

A lady, Mrs Simon, has recorded how, while on a train journey in 1842, the gentleman sitting opposite to her held his head out of the window for eight or nine minutes. Outside it was raining torrentially and, as might be expected, when he regained his seat, his head and shoulders were streaming with water. She was to learn this eccentric gentleman's identity the following year while visiting the Royal Academy exhibition. He was J. M. W. Turner R.A., whose painting 'Rain, Steam and Speed' celebrated his train journey through the rainstorm. A similar, rather more dramatic story lies behind the painting of 'Snowstorm—Steamboat off a Harbour's Mouth'. Turner was on board the paddle-steamer which seems, in his painting, to lie at the very heart of the vortex. The other passengers were all below deck, the hatches had been securely battened down, and Turner was tied to the ship's mast so that he might experience the fury of the storm to the full. It must have been an extremely frightening experience, and was very nearly his last. In his painting he attempted to distil and clarify his impressions which presumably were very confused and disjointed at the time. This is not at all like Constable's 'realism'. The tonal scheme which Turner has imposed on sea and sky, with its alternating bands of light and dark, is quite as artificial as that used by Rubens in his 'Horrors of War'. The effect which Turner achieved, however, far from recalling Rubens, seems to anticipate certain aspects of twentieth-century art, that of the Expressionists and the Futurists (q.v.)

John Martin (1789–1853)

Whereas neither Constable nor Turner were unduly concerned about popular acclaim, the painter from Northumberland, John Martin, seemed to thrive on it. More than any of his contemporaries 'Mad' Martin, as he was called, brought Romantic imagery before the English public. And for a time they were entranced by his work. In 1821 when his monumental version of 'Balshazzar's Feast' was placed on public display in The British Institution in Pall Mall, the picture had to be railed off to protect it from the crush. Martin specialised in the epic, drawing his subject matter from ancient history and the Bible. As with so many Romantic artists, the underlying theme of his work was usually violence—'The Fall of Babylon', 'The Destruction of Herculaneum and Pompeii', 'The Seventh Plague of Egypt'—the list of epic disasters seems endless. To John Ruskin, the foremost English theorist of the arts during the nineteenth century (and the great champion of Turner) Martin's work was merely cheap

The Great Day of His Wrath, c. *1820, by* John Martin. *(Tate Gallery, London)*

commercialism with as much thought behind it as a mass-produced coal-scuttle. The opinion of posterity would appear to agree with that of Ruskin, although Martin's reputation is at present undergoing some revision. He did have a genuine visionary gift, although many of his works teeter perilously close to bathos, and in a painting like 'The Great Day of his Wrath', he demonstrates at least some of the power of Turner. In any case the work of Mad Martin does demonstrate that Romanticism was not merely the prerogative of a small handful of intellectuals and eccentrics; it also had its appeal for the man in the street.

The Gothic Revival

The Romantic movement brought in its wake a taste for the Middle Ages. The great Gothic buildings of Europe had been in existence for so long that nobody seemed to notice them any more. They seemed to be almost a part of nature, like mountains or forests. And while people began to discover the beauty of nature and to appreciate the mountains and forests, so too they began to look at the Gothic buildings with new interest. Gothic buildings which had, for a variety of reasons, fallen into disrepair, like St Denis and Rouen, were restored, and work was resumed on some which had never been completed by their original builders, like Cologne Cathedral. This widespread interest in the buildings of the Middle Ages led inevitably to the neo-Gothic style, which bears roughly the same relationship to genuine Gothic as neo-Classicism does to the architecture of ancient Greece or Rome. In Bavaria, for instance, several neo-Gothic 'fairytale' castles were built with clusters of turrets and pinnacles. In London the Palace of Westminster, which was destroyed by fire in 1834 (Turner recorded the scene of conflagration in one of his paintings), was rebuilt in the late English Gothic style called 'Perpendicular'.

The Pre-Raphaelite Brotherhood

The newly discovered 'golden age' was eventually to leave its mark on nineteenth-century painting. In 1848 three young artists, William Holman Hunt (1827–1910), John Everett Millais (1829–96) and Dante Gabriel Rossetti (1828–82) founded the Pre-Raphaelite Brotherhood. This title was, in effect, a manifesto of sorts, and declared to the world their rejection of the ideals of the High Renaissance (and therefore of the academies) and their desire to return to a world which, at least in their opinion, was purer and more spiritual. In reaction against the idealised images of the academies they embraced the particular; some of their paintings might be described as obsessively detailed. They often used rich pure colours and high tonalities as opposed to the more conservative colour schemes advocated by the academic painters.

Subjects were often drawn from Medieval or biblical sources. Holman Hunt actually travelled to the Holy Land to paint some of his biblical scenes—the 'Scapegoat' painted in 1854 is an example—with scrupulously accurate local scenery. They were virtually responsible for the invention of a particular female type, wistful (sometimes to the point of anaemia!) with long delicate neck, hair flowing in ample auburn cascades across the shoulders, and dressed in loose, almost shapeless garments. It is just such a Pre-Raphaelite lady who gazes so soulfully at us from D. G. Rossetti's 'Astarte Syriaca'. Rossetti, who was the son of an Italian political refugee, lived an amicably eccentric existence among his collection of antiques and curios which included a four-poster bed draped in heavy seventeenth-century curtains. Although his works were often marred by defective technique and a vision which often bordered on the insipid, he did manage to produce some of the most revolutionary pictures of his time. This is particularly true of his 'Dantis Amor' which was painted in a curiously flat, heraldic manner recalling a medieval banner or shield.

Astarte Syriaca, *1877, by* Dante Gabriel Rossetti. *(City Art Gallery, Manchester)*

Realism—Reaction against Romanticism and neo-Classicism

'One has come to realise that the people are the source of intelligence and inspiration.'

George Sand (1841)

'Realism is a barbarous style where art is debased and degraded.'

Delécluze (1850)

Gustave Courbet (1819–77)

1855 was the year of the great 'Exposition Universelle' in Paris. The Exposition was a vast affair; the section devoted to the arts was to put on public display no less than five thousand pictures. These were to include the works of foreign artists as well as the greatest of the contemporary French. The two leaders of the rival artistic factions were fairly evenly represented: Ingres submitted forty pictures and a number of drawings while Delacroix submitted thirty-five pictures representing the various stages of his development. This latter idea was quite new to the nineteenth century as retrospective exhibitions of an artist's work, or indeed 'one-man' shows, now so common, were virtually unheard of.

On a site in the Place de l'Alma, near the exhibition hall, a new pavilion had been erected. Outside, a placard boldly proclaimed 'Realism by Gustave Courbet—Exhibition of forty of his works'. Courbet was a positive individual, a man of action. Since the jury of the Exposition Universelle had insulted him by turning down several of his pictures he resolved to set up his own exhibition hall. Courbet's one-man show was not exactly a roaring success. Delacroix strolled down to the Place de l'Alma to have a look. He stayed for an hour and was quite alone during that time. And the great man was impressed: Courbet had talent.

There was nothing particularly strange, or even objectionable in most of Courbet's work. He did take an occasional swipe at the clergy it is true, but most of his work consisted of landscapes, painted with something of Constable's directness and freshness, portraits, often of himself and scenes drawn from everyday life in the country: men breaking stones for road mending or a village funeral. Courbet simply called himself a 'Realist', but to the bourgeois society of his day all of this smacked too readily of Socialism, the new-fangled threat to private property, the integrity of the state and common decency. To make matters worse Courbet made no secret of the fact that he *was* a Socialist. Even his pronouncements on painting had something of the flavour of a political manifesto about them. 'I hold that painting is an art which is essentially concrete and can only consist in representing real and existing things,' he said, thus dismissing all of neo-Classicism and almost all Romanticism in no uncertain terms. This was the artist who boasted that he would paint an angel only after he had seen one, and who, some years later, was to set up a teaching studio to rival those of the Ecole des Beaux Arts. In this studio Courbet made mockery of that sacred academic institution, the life class, by having a bull or a horse chained to the wall for his pupils to draw.

There was something which disturbed ordinary decent folk about the large compositions which Courbet seemed so fond of. Large canvases should only be reserved for 'important subjects' of course, never for a subject so coarse and commonplace as a village funeral. There was something derisory in Courbet's insistence on the depiction of peasants and other members of the lower orders on so grand a scale.

The Funeral at Ornans, *1850, by* Gustave Courbet. (*Louvre Museum, Paris*)

The Wood Sawyers, c. *1850, by* Jean François Millet.
(Victoria and Albert Museum, London)

The fears of the French middle classes are understandable; increasing industrialisation had brought in its wake increasing upheaval and unrest, not just in France but throughout Western Europe. The new concept of 'progress' had given rise to dreams and aspirations more potent than those engendered by either neo-Classicism or Romanticism. This same 'progress' had already created a new class of human being, restless and growing numerically all the time—the proletariat. Gustave Courbet was simply one of a number of artists to acknowledge the new social climate in their work: Realism was moving with the tide of history.

Jean François Millet (1814–75)

Jean François Millet drew his inspiration continually from the toil and hardship of the peasants. They were his people, and he wished to show in his art that the lives of these humble, uncomplaining country folk had something of the heroic about them. His figures, loose-limbed and brawny, their faces made vacant by a lifetime of toil, saw timber, sow, glean and hoe and, as the angelus bell rings out across the fields, bow their heads in prayer. Millet's paintings and drawings are often impressive. His 'Wood Sawyers' for instance, powerfully evokes the sheer animal energy of the two men so deeply engrossed in their task. The figure on the right, with his bulging calf muscles and his solid, tightly knit body, has become a symbol of energy worthy of one of the Romantics. The influence of Romanticism was difficult to shake off entirely, and it must be admitted that very few of Millet's works are

completely free of it. Millet shows us only one side of the peasant, his fortitude in the face of a lifetime of hard work, his energy and his simple piety. 'His peasants are pedants who have too high an opinion of themselves', said Baudelaire. 'Instead of simply distilling the natural poetry of his subject, M. Millet wants to add something at any price.' Perhaps Baudelaire was expecting too much; after all, Delacroix was only sixteen years older than Millet. In any case the achievement of breaking free of the Romantic influence and 'simply distilling the natural poetry' etc. was to lie with a later generation.

Honoré Daumier (1808–79)

Louis Philippe, the 'bourgeois' monarch, wished his regime to be a tolerant one, but tolerance can go too far! The drawing of the king which appeared in an edition of the satirical journal *La Caricature* in 1832 had certainly overstepped the limits; his Majesty was represented as Gargantua, vast and obese, gobbling up the nation's wealth and excreting favours to his toadies. The artist, Honoré Daumier, son of a Marseilles glazier and then in his early twenties, was given a six months prison sentence. The young satirist remained quite unrepentant. To a friend he wrote from prison, 'Well, here I am at Pélagie, a charming place though not everyone enjoys it. I enjoy it, however, if only to be contrary.' Despite his term spent behind bars Daumier continued to be one of the regime's most articulate and mordant critics. When *La Caricature* was suppressed he went to work for *Charivari*. He was to remain with that journal for most of his working life, producing thousands of drawings for publication and developing into one of the world's great social satirists. Although his satire could develop a cutting edge approaching that of Goya, it is essentially good-humoured, and when, for instance, he pokes fun at the posturing of the lawyers and judges of the Palais de Justice, it is gentle and rarely tinged with real malice. A number of his drawings wittily commented on the art world of his day. One, titled 'Battle of the Schools: Classical Idealism v. Realism', which was published in *Charivari*, shows a gangling and bespectacled nude gentleman wearing a Roman helmet and using his palette as a shield (the figure was based on one by J. L. David) confronting a little tough wearing clogs and a top hat who brandishes a paint brush instead of a sword. Some of Daumier's political satires are still quite relevant today; one such depicts a politician smiling at his own image reflected in a mirror and is titled 'Rehearsing a smile for the Electors'.

La Blanchisseuse, *1862, by* Honoré Daumier. *(Louvre Museum, Paris)*

It was not generally known by his contemporaries that Daumier was both a painter and sculptor of great power. As he could make a living from his satirical drawings he could afford to paint entirely to please himself. He developed an extremely broad and fluid style. His subjects ranged from the Romanticism of the Don Quixote series to the Realism of works like 'La Blanchisseuse' reproduced here. Daumier's washer-woman is both monumental and dignified. Slowly she mounts the steps which lead down to the Seine, her bundle of washing slung beneath her powerful arm. The other great arm reaches down with some tenderness to assist the child at her side. The background of buildings and sky is brushed in with broad sweeping strokes. Presumably Daumier witnessed just such a scene very frequently, as he lived for a time on the quai d'Anjou. His sculpture, mostly works of caricature related to his satirical drawings, shares with his painting an amazing freedom of execution held in check by a superb overall control.

It was Balzac who said of him, 'This young joker has Michelangelo under the skin.'

Edouard Manet (1832–83)

It was the Emperor, Napoleon III himself, who decided that, since so many paintings had been rejected by the Salon jury of 1863, a special showing of the works found unacceptable should be arranged. The people could judge for themselves whether the jury had been unjust or not. The 'Salon des Refusés' was therefore hurriedly organised. And it proved to be a great popular success—in a sense. The exhibition afforded the public an unprecedented opportunity to jeer and to mock and generally to show their distaste for the new wave of subversive daubers whose only wish was to drag the name of French art in the mud. Most of this public vilification seems to have been reserved for a picture by Edouard Manet; his 'Déjeuner sur l'Herbe' shocked the good people of Paris to the roots.

The painting by Manet depicted a naked woman. Nothing new in that whatsoever; each year saw a new crop of nudes in the Salon—Venuses, harem girls, nymphs and allegorical figures of many descriptions. And of course, the great J. A. D. Ingres was a master of the nude. Manet's young lady is not a nymph or a Venus however, for she is sitting in a forest glade in the company of two young men dressed in modern clothes. The men seem thoroughly engrossed in conversation and pay little heed to the girl who gazes abstractedly out of the picture; on the ground beside her lie the untidy remains of a picnic, while in the background another young woman, clothed this time, washes her feet in a stream. How could one explain such a subject? The title was of very little help, derisory in all probability; safer to assume that something scandalous

was being perpetrated. And the manner in which the painting was executed made no appeal to the public or the critics. It seemed to lack the evenness of lighting and careful modelling of the figures which everyone had come to expect. So even Manet's attempt to bathe his scene in 'real' out-of-door light, as opposed to the contrived, even lighting of the studio, was interpreted as subversive.

The English critic, P. G. Hamerton, did notice that there were certain similarities between Manet's picture and Giorgione's 'Fête Champêtre' (q.v.). He was very generously prepared to pardon the 'doubtful morality' of Giorgione's picture 'for the sake of its fine colour'. But as for Manet, —'some wretched Frenchman has translated this [the Fête Champêtre] into modern French realism . . . with the horrible modern French costume instead of the graceful Venetian one'. Hamerton concluded that 'there are other pictures of the same class, which lead to the inference that the nude, when painted by vulgar men, is inevitably indecent'. Dante Gabriel Rossetti had no doubts about his feelings towards the Manet either, 'simple putrescence and decomposition', he sniffed.

This villain Manet was to perpetrate still more obscenity. In the Salon of 1865 his 'Olympia' was revealed to the public gaze: another nude, this time reclining on a bed and attended by a negro maid who presents her with a large bunch of flowers. Again the girl is not a nymph or a Venus, or even the inmate of a harem; she is simply a girl without her clothes lying on a bed. The critics were just as vitriolic. 'What is this odalisque with yellow belly?' asked Jules Claretie. 'A degraded model picked up I don't know where, and representing Olympia.' One of the most popular paintings in the Salon also happened to be a nude. This was Cabanel's 'Venus'. It was thought to be 'not in the least bit indecent' and was bought by the Emperor.

Birth of Venus, *by* A. Cabanel. *(Louvre Museum, Paris). This painting won considerable acclaim when shown at the 1865 Salon. Compare it with Manet's* Déjeuner. *Do you consider either indecent?*

Unlike Courbet, Edouard Manet was not a rebel by nature; the very opposite in fact. He wished whole-heartedly for official recognition. Studying the works of the Old Masters with great attention and borrowing freely from them, he didn't see himself as an artistic innovator. His 'Déjeuner sur l'Herbe' was, in fact, a conscious attempt to update Giorgione, a sort of homage to the Venetian master's Fête Champêtre. The group comprising the two men and the girl had been 'borrowed' straight from Raphael. The subject had no sinister undertones, Manet had simply depicted two artists with their models enjoying a break from work.

The 'Olympia' might also be regarded as a tribute to the Old Masters; Manet wished to extend the tradition of reclining nudes which extended back through Ingres, Goya and Velasquez to Titian and Giorgione. The simplified and flattened tonal areas, which Manet handled with such remarkable delicacy in the 'Olympia', also owed a great deal to his study of the Spanish masters, particularly Velasquez and Goya. He was a traditionalist and an eclectic, his notoriety was a constant source of surprise and pain to him. He was an innovator only in one important sense—he regarded the act of painting itself, i.e. the assembling of areas of tone and colour and texture on a flat surface, as more important than subject matter, which he regarded merely as a necessary pretext for painting. In itself this may seem of little importance, but to certain of Manet's younger contemporaries it came as something of a revelation. The way now seemed open for the art of painting to achieve the kind of freedom enjoyed only by music.

The Impressionists

Manet and his friends and admirers were frequently to be found in the Café Guerbois, at the beginning of the avenue de Clichy. Here they sat, drank coffee, and talked endlessly about painting. Manet himself was hardly the most charismatic of leaders, but his paintings did seem to the young painters and writers who paid court to him to point the way forward. It seemed to go that one important step beyond the Realists, whose work was also known and admired by the group. Gradually, as the result of endless discussion, certain principles were thrashed out: painters must leave the cloistered atmosphere of the studio and paint out of doors, subject matter was of no importance, the study of natural lighting effects was almost everything.

Then came disruption, before these ideas could be fully explored and developed. On 15 July, 1870 the streets of Paris rang to the cries of 'A Berlin!' and 'Vive la guerre!' France was at war with Prussia.

Manet stayed in Paris as an officer in the National Guard, while his friend Edgar Degas served in an artillery battery. Other members of the group left Paris for a time. Paul Cézanne simply returned home to the south and continued painting. Camille Pissarro, Alfred Sisley and Claude Monet went to London. That city, with its great looming buildings and its persistent fogs, which filtered and softened the light continually, enthralled the French painters. They sent some of their pictures to the Royal Academy, but were turned down. They did have the opportunity to discover the paintings of Constable and Turner in the National Gallery however. Pissarro seems to have been impressed; Monet, on the other hand, is reported to have remarked, 'This brown thing—is this your Turner?' which would seem to indicate that he was not.

Returning to France after the war, the group reassembled. They held their first exhibition together in 1874, in the studio of a photographer called Nadar. It was anything but a success. The Parisian public, still smarting from the humiliating defeat at the hands of the Prussians, and further shaken by the rise and fall of the Paris Commune, had less time than ever before for artistic innovation. During the period of the Commune, Gustave Courbet had risen to a position of prominence as 'Curator of Fine Arts'; at that time the French Academy in Rome, the Ecole des Beaux Arts and the medals distributed at the Salons had all been abolished. The good people of Paris had had enough of such anarchy.

The group did emerge from the 1874 exhibition with a name. One of the exhibits, a vaguely defined atmospheric piece by Claude Monet, was titled 'Impression—Sunrise'. A deriding critic referred to the entire group as 'Impressionists'. The name was to stick and Impressionism, after a hard struggle, was to gain a firm foothold in France, and ultimately to spread throughout Europe.

Claude Monet (1840–1926)

Claude Monet, the most radical and forthright of the Impressionists, rapidly assumed leadership of the group. For the art of the past he had no time whatsoever. The study of natural light was his great passion and it was largely due to his experiments that the Impressionist painters developed a method of painting sensitive enough to record even its most fleeting effects. Black and brown were banned from the palette. Lines were deemed quite unnecessary. Only the colours of the spectrum, red, orange, yellow, green, blue and violet, along with white, were those required. Painting became purely a matter of turning the rays of coloured light which struck the retina of the painter's eye into dabs of paint on the canvas. The paint itself was applied in strokes of pure colour modified as little as possible on the palette. The real 'mixing' was done by the eye of the beholder. This method called 'optical mixing' had already been strongly hinted at in the

Waterloo Bridge, *1900, by* Claude Monet. *(National Gallery, London).* **[107]** *One of a series painted between 1899 and 1904 in London.*

Les Parapluies, *1881, by* Auguste Renoir. *(National Gallery, London)*

work of Constable and Delacroix; the Impressionists put it onto what was virtually a scientific footing and made it almost the be-all and end-all of their art.

For Monet, objects merely existed to receive and transmit light. He was just as happy painting a haystack as a cathedral or a human being. He maintained that the subject changed when the light changed, and to prove his point he painted a number of subjects in series, working throughout the day and changing his canvas as the light changed. His series of Haystacks and the views of Rouen Cathedral were painted during the 1890s and at the turn of the century he returned to London and there painted a series of the river Thames and Waterloo Bridge. He remained an Impressionist throughout his career, and during the early decades of the twentieth century he produced some of his largest and most uncompromisingly Impressionistic works: the water-lily gardens with their flickering, suffused colours and almost total lack of forms.

Auguste Renoir (1841-1919)

Auguste Renoir worked closely with Monet for a number of years and helped to evolve the Impressionist method. There were certain important differences between the two artists however. While Monet was passionately narrow in following the dictates of his own vision, Renoir was far more open to influence and development. Nor did he share Monet's detachment from subject matter; Renoir liked his fellow human creatures and made no secret of the fact. His output includes many portraits and subjects drawn from everyday middle-class life: boating parties, dances, bathers, etc. He painted many superb nudes which recall the lighthearted, carefree art of Boucher and Fragonard, as well as the sensuality of Rubens.

A growing disenchantment with the increasing formlessness of Impressionism was intensified by ex-

posure to Renaissance art during an Italian trip. He resolved to revise his approach and, without losing touch with the atmospheric nuances of Impressionism he reintroduced solid and firmly constructed figures into his paintings. 'Les Parapluies' is probably one of the most successful of his later pictures. It is beautifully composed yet retains the air of spontaneity and freshness which is one of the lasting virtues of Impressionism.

His last years were marred by arthritis which badly crippled his hands. He managed to continue his painting however, developing a late style of great breadth and vigour. He even took up sculpture, albeit by proxy—another sculptor carried out the actual modelling under his direction—during the last years of his life.

Edgar Degas (1834–1917)

'Try indeed, to make M. Degas see reason,' scoffed the critic Albert Wolff. 'Tell him that in art there are certain qualities called drawing, colour, execution, control and he will laugh in your face and treat you as a reactionary.' It is difficult to recall any artist of the nineteenth century *less* in need of instruction in drawing, colour, execution and control than Edgar Degas. The most richly gifted of all of the artists who exhibited with the Impressionists, he excelled in all these fields. Manet had first encountered him in the Louvre busily copying an 'Infanta' by Velasquez. Degas was engraving straight onto a copper plate; 'You're not afraid?' enquired Manet, obviously impressed by such skill, 'I should never dare engrave like that without a preliminary sketch.' He was soon to join Manet's circle at the Café Guerbois and became an active participant in debates. He agreed with Manet and the rest that the painter must now seek his inspiration from everyday subjects, although he had begun his career in the hope of becoming a 'history painter' in the tradition of Ingres and David. He was also impressed by the experiments in light and colour which were being pursued by the group but refused to take seriously the suggestion that the painter must, henceforward, forsake the studio for the streets and fields, and jokingly suggested that gendarmes should be specially employed to shoot down the easels of outdoor painters. Nor would he give way on the matter of lines; here he was in complete agreement with Ingres, an artist whom he continued to venerate throughout his career. He had once actually met Ingres and the great man had told him, 'Draw lines, young man, many lines, from memory or from nature.' Degas was later to describe himself as a 'colourist in line.'

Degas chose his subjects from those readily to hand in contemporary Paris: race meetings, scenes in cafés, milliners' shops and the theatre—particularly ballet. He also composed many bathroom scenes, having a bathtub set up in his studio and requiring his models to sponge and towel themselves while he observed and

Two Dancers *by* Edgar Degas. *Pastel. An apparently casual little picture, but Degas insisted that his art was anything but spontaneous. (National Gallery of Ireland)*

drew. A servant was usually ready with fresh hot water whenever the baths grew cold! He liked to give the impression that his compositions were haphazard slices of life, as spontaneous as a snap-shot (Degas was a keen photographer). His bathing models were to be depicted as though viewed through a keyhole. Frequently, in his pictures figures are cut in half by the frame, sometimes only the arm of a figure may protrude into the composition. In fact, Degas' compositions were as carefully and as consciously calculated as those of Poussin had been.

His chosen medium was pastel rather than the more usual oil paint, which he grew to dislike. With pastels he could give full rein to his remarkable skills as a draughtsman and his equally remarkable abilities as a colourist. Thus he could be true to his two great artistic idols, Ingres and Delacroix, at the same time. He was also a superb sculptor, vividly modelling in clay the same subjects which appeared in his pictures: race-horses, dancers, bathing women. After his death over a hundred such works in clay were discovered in his studio, many of them irreparably damaged, broken and crumbling to dust.

Although he was a thoroughly 'modern' artist, Degas' relationship with his own age was very much one of love mixed with hate. He detested all of the newfangled inventions which daily made life more complex, and had no use for the telephone and the motorcar when they appeared. 'Two centuries ago I would have painted Susannah taking a bath,' he remarked with deeply felt bitterness, 'Today, I paint only women in their tubs.'

Auguste Rodin (1840–1917)

'For the artist . . . all is beautiful in nature, because his eyes, boldly accepting all truth shown outwardly, read the inner truth as in an open book. That which is ugly is that which is false and artificial.' The sculptor Auguste Rodin might have been speaking for all of his Impressionist contemporaries. He had a great deal in common with them and has frequently been regarded as the great exponent of Impressionism in sculpture. He must also be regarded as the greatest Romantic sculptor however.

His career was a curious mixture of acclaim—even the state recognised his genius—and controversy; many of his major works got him into some sort of trouble. Early in his career he found himself accused of imposture, of casting one of his figures from the living model. This was the 'Age of Bronze' (1877), a figure which Rodin made soon after a trip to Italy where he had seen, and had been deeply impressed by, the works of Donatello and Michelangelo. This figure, with its tautly modelled surfaces, owed much to Donatello, but more perhaps to Rodin's own penetrating observation of every nuance of muscle and sinew, and his unsurpassed ability in rendering the feeling of living, moving flesh in clay. The grossly unjust accusation caused many influential voices to be raised in his support, and eventually, by way of recompense, the figure was bought by the state. The commission which he received shortly afterwards, a door for the future Museum of Decorative Arts, was also probably a gesture of reconciliation.

As the theme for the door he chose the 'Gate of Hell', a subject derived from the poet Dante. The task was to occupy his energies and his imagination for over twenty years and gave rise to many of his most impressive inventions, including the justly famous 'Thinker'. The 'Gate of Hell', over six metres in height and containing nearly two hundred figures, is one of the supreme works of Romantic sculpture.

The group of 'Burghers' which he made for the town of Calais, is also deeply Romantic in spirit. A figure to commemorate Eustache de St Pierre, the Burgher whose unhappy task it had once been to surrender the key of the town to the English king, was originally all that was required; Rodin added five more figures and composed a loosly knit, though emotionally charged, group.

Along with the large commissioned pieces Rodin produced many portraits—'Baudelaire', 'Shaw';

The Age of Bronze, *1877, by* Auguste Rodin. *Rodin was accused of casting this figure from a live model. (National Gallery of Ireland)*

A detail of the Burghers of Calais *Group, 1884–6, by* Rodin. *(Camera Press). The group was unveiled in Calais in 1895 after ten years of negotiation between the artist and the municipal council.*

figures drawn from mythology or the Bible—'John the Baptist', 'Polyphemus'; allegorical subjects—'The Eternal Idol', 'The Cathedral'; and some 'Impressionistic' fragments such as 'The Flying Figure'. Although a great deal of his work might be termed Romantic —certain figures, like the 'Balzac' are closer to Expressionism (q.v.)—his working methods were perfectly in tune with those of the Impressionist painters. He hired a number of models, and these were required to move freely about his studio, nude, so that he could observe their every gesture and also accustom himself to the human form as a matter of everyday experience. As his models moved about him Rodin drew and modelled in clay with great rapidity. When he noticed a pose which particularly pleased him the model was required to hold the position until a rapid sketch in clay could be made. Rodin's working method was very much at variance with that practised by almost all of his contemporaries in the field of sculpture. The usual method was to start with a preconceived idea and to pose the model carefully on a pedestal.

The Post-Impressionists

The Impressionists brought a new and much needed vitality to the art of painting. Their influence spread rapidly, and inevitably their original concepts suffered change and adaptation to a variety of needs. The artists termed 'Post-Impressionist' held widely divergent views on art; the term is merely one of historical convenience.

Georges Seurat (1859–91) and neo-Impressionism

Temperamentally Georges Seurat had more in common with certain of the great austere artists of the past—Piero della Francesca, Jan Vermeer and Georges de la Tour—than with Monet or Renoir. His mind was clear and incisive, his ambition to create an art worthy of, and perfectly in tune with, the new age of science and technology. Such an art must itself be clear and precise and firmly based in scientific method. While still a student Seurat had studied a number of scientific works dealing with colour, particularly the writings of Michel Chevreul, a theorist who had also influenced the Impressionists and led to their use of optical mixing. Seurat also adopted optical mixing but in a way wholly at variance with the intuitive approach of Monet, Renoir or Pissarro. Optical mixing was, for Seurat, a method of gaining the maximum control over his colour rather than a means of capturing fugitive light effects.

He applied his colour to the canvas in carefully placed and uniformly sized dots, the exact amount of each colour required having been calculated beforehand. Even the size of the dots depended on the size of the canvas! All other elements in the painting

were likewise calculated, horizontals, verticals, diagonals, curves, etc. The result was a harmonious whole—Seurat equated art with harmony—in which each and every detail played its precise and preordained part. The painting had become an analogue of the machine.

In 1885 Camille Pissarro met Seurat. He was impressed by the younger man's art and invited him to submit some work to the forthcoming Impressionist exhibition—the eighth and, as it transpired, the last the group were to hold together. Seurat was not exactly made welcome. Monet left in disgust—'the select group had become an uncritical rabble, ready to admit anyone into its ranks!' Renoir and Sisley also withdrew. For his part Pissarro began to adopt Seurat's 'scientific Impressionism' which, he believed, had superseded the 'Romantic Impressionism' of the original group.

The painting submitted by Seurat was called 'A Sunday Afternoon on the Island of La Grande Jatte'. It was a large canvas, measuring approximately two metres by three. He had depicted a number of people strolling or reclining in the afternoon sunshine on an island in the Seine, near Paris. It was a typical Impressionist subject, in fact. Seurat's obvious desire to render a feeling of light and air was not out of keeping with the ideals of Impressionism either. But the deliberate clarity of his forms with their crisp, clean contours, the carefully modelled volumes of trees and human figures, and the general feeling of calculation about the whole picture, were all totally alien to Impressionism.

The style of painting evolved by Seurat and his associates, Signac, Cross, Luce and Angrand, was called 'Pointillism' ('Point' being French for 'dot'). Seurat himself preferred the term 'Divisionism' and to make matters more confusing still, the practitioners of Pointillism or Divisionism are usually referred to as 'neo-Impressionists'.

Seurat died in 1891, still a young man. He left behind him a number of large canvases like the 'Grande Jatte', each one solving a different problem. Along with these he had produced a number of small, perfectly harmonious pictures, many of them painted on the Channel coast, a number of sketches in oil paint, far more Impressionistic than his finished works, and finally a series of remarkable drawings made in black chalk, which explore the problems of pure tone.

Paul Signac assumed leadership of the neo-Impressionists after Seurat's untimely death. His book, 'From Delacroix to neo-Impressionism' records the theories of the movement.

Sunday Afternoon on the Island of La Grande Jatte, *1884–6, by* Georges Seurat. *(The Art Institute of Chicago)*

Paul Gauguin (1848–1903)

When he first met Camille Pissarro, Paul Gauguin was a successful stock-broker. He was also an amateur artist, a 'Sunday painter'. Pissarro, as ever, was very helpful; he introduced the Sunday painter to the theories of Impressionism, assuring him that only inept artists might properly be called amateurs. Gauguin bought Impressionist paintings and learned how to paint. He learned quickly; soon he was exhibiting with the Impressionists. In 1883 he gave up his job in order to devote his energies full time to painting.

Gauguin was restless, and he possessed immense reserves of energy. He grew tired of Impressionism, and also perhaps, tired of being merely one of a group. The ideas of the neo-Impressionists, the 'little green chemists' as he called them, did not really appeal to him either. His restlessness drove him away from Paris, to Panama and Martinique, where the brilliant light and the blazing colours of the foliage impressed him. It was while staying in Brittany however, that he discovered his true path, and incidentally became the revered leader of a new group of artists.

Vision after the Sermon, *1888, by* Paul Gauguin. *(National Galleries of Scotland)*

Gauguin painted 'The Vision after the Sermon' in 1888. Both in terms of treatment and subject matter this painting was decidedly at variance with the ideals of Impressionism. It is Sunday morning; a group of Breton women wearing their best bonnets leave church. In his sermon the priest had related a story from the Old Testament, of how Jacob had wrestled with an angel. The women experience a vision; Jacob and the angel appear before them. The picture is composed in large and almost flat areas of colour, and each form is carefully delineated (the term 'Cloissonism' has been used to describe this form of painting). Very little attempt is made to model the forms, to give them a feeling of weight and volume, there is no attempt to render naturalistic light and shade, and the area representing the ground is a pure vibrant red.

How had Gauguin arrived at this remarkable result? Several aspects of the painting are reminiscent of medieval painting and stained glass: the flattened forms, the use of arbitrary colours, the lack of perspective. And it is true that Gauguin had been impressed by the medieval glass which he had seen. In common with a number of artists of the period he was beginning to look at Gothic art with keen interest, and also at the wood-block prints from Japan which had recently been made available in Europe. But it was thanks to a painter called Emile Bernard, rather than to any Gothic or Japanese influences, that Gauguin was able to make what amounted to the greatest breakthrough in his career.

The two artists had met at Pont-Aven in Brittany. At Pont-Aven Bernard had made a painting of a group of Breton women seen against a flat green background. The areas of colour were simplified and flattened, and lines were used extensively to define the forms with maximum clarity. Gauguin was sufficiently impressed to acquire the painting and also to borrow from Bernard the very paints he had used. The result was 'The Vision after the Sermon' painted in the style which Bernard had invented. Emile Bernard was undoubtedly an artist of talent, but Gauguin was an artist of genius, and it was he who gave depth and vitality to the new style, which Bernard called 'Synthetism'. And it was largely because of Gauguin's charismatic personality that the new style spread to a number of other artists. Inevitably Gauguin was credited with the invention of Synthetism (or Cloissonism) much to Bernard's chagrin. Fate is often both unkind and unfair!

Gauguin's decision to quit Europe, and his departure for Tahiti in 1891 are all well-known facts and have contributed much to the artist's almost legendary status. His dream of discovering a paradise on Earth proved to be a bitter disappointment, the islands of the South Seas had long since been tainted by Western civilisation. He managed to paint some of the finest pictures of his career however, and in them to create the paradise which he never discovered in fact. He died in miserable circumstances in 1903. Ironically, his fame was already growing in Europe, particularly among artists.

Vincent Van Gogh (1853–90)

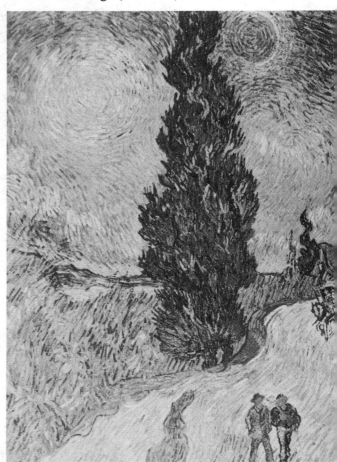

Road with Cypress Trees, *1890, by* Vincent Van Gogh. *(Rijksmuseum Kröller-Müller)*

The subject of this picture could hardly be more commonplace: a country road meandering through wheat fields, the tall spires of cypress trees, two farm labourers—first cousins of Millet's peasants—a small horse-drawn carriage clopping along, the summer sun low in the sky. It all sounds so peaceful, so drowsy almost. But it is not a scene of peace and tranquillity which the Dutchman, Vincent Van Gogh has painted. The world which he shows us has taken on a wholly unexpected and alarming aspect; the road rushes to meet us like a cascading stream, the cypress trees rise from the earth like a great column of flame, and the sky with its sun and moon and evening star writhes with agonised life. We are looking at this simple rural scene through the eyes of a visionary. But the nineteenth century, with its underlying philosophy of crass materialism was not an era conducive to visionaries. Van Gogh, in following his vision with unrelenting singlemindedness risked both his sanity and his life. And he was to forfeit both; he had already spent some time in the asylum of St Remy, and within two months of painting this picture he was to die by his own hand, aged only thirty-seven.

Van Gogh's career was a curiously chequered one. His first real contact with the art of painting seems to have come through a job with the Paris firm of picture dealers, Goupils. Turning abruptly from selling sentimental genre pictures he sought fulfilment in the first great passion of his life—religion. With a fervour which was later to typify his approach to painting he gave himself totally to the task of ministering to the mine workers and their families in one of the grimmest regions spawned by the Industrial Revolution—the Borinage in Belgium. Another abrupt turn and he was devoting all his energies to art.

His earliest paintings and drawings are strongly Realist in flavour, pictures of poor farm labourers and weavers, and painted in sombre colours. He arrived in Paris in 1886 to join his brother Theo, the mainstay of his life. In Paris the combined influence of Impressionist paintings and Japanese prints led to a radical alteration of style. His colours became light and gay, and for a time his work was Impressionistic. He made the acquaintance of artists like Seurat, whose Divisionist technique he dabbled with for a time, and Gauguin, whose work also impressed him. His move to Arles, in the South of France, led to the final transformation of his art into a vehicle capable of recording the fluctuating tides of his emotions, from ecstasy to deep despair. Like Gauguin he had taken what was necessary from Impressionism and had gone his own way.

With what other artists may we compare Van Gogh, if any? With El Greco perhaps, an artist who was fortunate enough to have been born during an era sympathetic to his personal vision, and of course, with the great northern artists like Grünewald. Van Gogh's art, although it matured under the bright sun of southern France, belongs essentially to the northern tradition, and not the least of his achievements was to breathe new life into that tradition.

Paul Cézanne (1839–1906)

The ageing Cézanne to his young friend Emile Bernard: 'To achieve progress nature alone counts and the eye is trained by contact with her.' His letters to Bernard, written during the early 1900s, repeatedly return to the same piece of sage advice—look at nature. The advice of an Impressionist, one might imagine. After all, Paul Cézanne, accompanied by his friend Emile Zola, was one of the original group who

sat at Manet's feet in the Café Guerbois, and he had participated in the very first group exhibition. But Cézanne had been an Impressionist—a painter of light —for only a brief few years. His mature paintings have a character quite unlike that of Monet or Pissarro. Not alone does he rank with those artists termed 'Post-Impressionists', he was very probably the greatest of them and, so far as the development of art during the first half of the present century is concerned, undoubtedly the most influential of them. One should also add that he was the most complex of the great Post-Impressionists and therefore the most difficult to introduce briefly.

His earliest paintings reveal two aspects of his personality: his extremely Romantic nature and his unusual clumsiness. These early paintings, with titles like 'The Rape' and 'The Temptation of St Anthony' were theatrical and rather lurid pastiches of Delacroix and Daumier. With their heavy colours and awkward, unshapely forms, they reveal an artist lacking the ability to work from memory or imitate the mannerisms of others. Cézanne possessed absolutely none of the gifts which gave the art of Degas and Seurat its apparently effortless elegance.

With Camille Pissarro he learned to lighten his palette and to work directly from nature. Although for a time he became an Impressionist, his work never took on the ephemeral airiness of Monet or Renoir. His approach was blunt and direct, and both the critics and many of his fellow artists simply dismissed him as a clumsy oaf, all thumbs.

As his own personal convictions began to crystallise so he moved away from Impressionism. He wanted 'to make of Impressionism something solid like the art of the museums' and 'to do Poussin over again from nature'. In other words his ambition was to create an art of total harmony while still remaining true to nature. And this is more or less what he managed to achieve—thanks to a massive effort of the will which overcame all his shortcomings—in the landscapes, still lifes and portraits made from the early 1880s to the time of his death in 1906.

What do we discover in a mature work by Cézanne? Truth to nature usually; only when he attempted to work from his imagination, as in his large figure compositions, did his painting look rather stiff and contrived. Before nature, whether landscapes or still lifes, he was superb. His use of colour was remarkable. Cézanne's colour exists on several levels; his blues and greens and oranges form beautiful harmonies, but they also do much more. Colour is employed as one of the basic structural elements in his paintings; each touch of pigment helps to 'build' the three-dimensional and often weighty forms, as well as describing their local colour.

Mont S. Victoire, c. *1885, by* Paul Cézanne. *(Courtauld Institute Galleries, London)*

Still life with Cupid, c. *1893, by* Paul Cézanne. *(Courtauld Institute Galleries, London)*

Cézanne was therefore 'modelling' with colour, as opposed to the traditional method of modelling with light and shade. Colour used in this way need not be 'diluted' with the dark tones required in traditional modelling; it could remain pure and fresh.

Cézanne's composition also exists on several levels; his forms relate to each other both in terms of flat design and also as design in depth (see Part II for diagrams). Look at the reproduction of a landscape by Cézanne. The main motif is Mont Sainte-Victoire near his home in Aix-en-Provence, and one of his favourite subjects. Notice how beautifully the picture works as flat design, how the rhythmic arabesques formed by the branches in the upper third fit in with the rising shape of the mountain, and what a pleasing, taut shape the trunk of the tree on the left makes. Even in this small black and white reproduction something of Cézanne's command of space comes across also; the great plain, dotted with trees and buildings, stretches back into space, the horizontals gradually accommodating themselves to the rigid vertical surfaces of the mountain.

Cézanne was a tireless and relentless worker; his great self-imposed task that of distilling directly from nature those timeless and monumental elements which he had found in the work of the great masters of the past. His method entailed looking long and hard at his subject, 'dismantling' it piece by piece, discarding non-essentials, noting essentials, and finally reassembling what he had noted on his canvas. Nature had first to be analysed, then sifted, then translated into touches of colour and lines on the surface of a canvas. And each touch of colour had to be descriptive, structural and decorative at one and the same time. That Cézanne could keep so many apparently disparate elements in his mind simultaneously and not lose track of any of them while he worked, points to a side of his character which we have not, as yet, mentioned: his truly phenomenal powers of concentration.

And there is yet more to Cézanne: his apparently intuitive rejection of traditional perspective with its single point of view for instance. By showing several views of an object in one composite view—the front and both sides of a building or the profile and the mouth of a jar—he felt that he was making a 'truer' description of the object. This concept was not new to painting however; it was common practice during the Middle Ages. Likewise he reversed the process of atmospheric perspective in many of his landscapes. A range of distant mountains far from being indistinct and blurred in outline, might be clarified and enlarged.

Cézanne is not the easiest artist to appreciate fully; however some understanding of his achievements is necessary in order to make sense of the development of painting in Europe during the first few decades of the twentieth century.

The Eiffel Tower *by Gustave Eiffel (1832–1923). (Camera Press). Eiffel was one of the greatest of the engineer-architects of the second half of the nineteenth century. His celebrated cast iron tower, built in the centre of Paris, for the International Exhibition of 1889, remained the world's tallest building until the erection of the Empire State Building, New York, during the 1930s. Along with Joseph Paxton's Crystal Palace, built in 1850–51, the Eiffel Tower was one of the first truly modern buildings.*

The Menai Suspension Bridge, *Anglesea, 1819–26, by* Thomas Telford (1757–1834). (Radio Times Hulton Picture Library). *New engineering techniques—particularly in the use of cast iron and steel—began to exert a definite influence on the architecture of the nineteenth century. New techniques gradually led to new forms, and there was a growing desire among architects to escape from the syndrome which saw in architecture only a means of imitating the forms of the past.*

Symbolism and Art Nouveau

[116] We have already seen how the materialistic ethos of nineteenth-century European culture had alienated a number of artists; some, like the Pre-Raphaelites, looked to an earlier and 'purer' era for inspiration, while others, like Van Gogh and Gauguin, felt that physical escape from the urban environment was necessary.

This feeling of alienation—of disenchantment with the new industrial age—seems to have been experienced by many artists throughout Europe. It helps to explain why, during the closing decades of the century a number of them—poets, painters and sculptors—in countries as various as France, Germany, England and Russia, rejected realist subject matter and turned instead to the exotic and the bizarre. The term 'Symbolist' is usually given to such writers and artists. Their number included artists of genius—Verlaine, Rimbaud, Baudelaire and Mallarmé among the poets, Gustave Moreau and Edvard Munch among the painters—and many of lesser note. Their styles varied from ultra-conservative to extremely experimental.

In fact we have already examined in some detail the work of a French artist who was, at least for a time, regarded as one of the leading Symbolist painters. This was Paul Gauguin. A painting like his 'Vision after the Sermon' is an excellent example of Symbolist art.

Edvard Munch (1863–1944)

Writing in 1889, the Norwegian painter Edvard Munch expressed his contempt for a type of subject matter which had gained considerable popularity during the closing decades of the century: a rather cosy and anecdotal form of Realism. 'No longer shall I paint interiors', he declared, 'and people reading, and women knitting.' His purpose was altogether more serious: 'I shall paint living people, who breathe and feel and suffer and love . . . People will understand the sacredness of it and take off their hats as though they were in church.' The last part of his statement notwithstanding, we may begin to appreciate something of what Munch meant by looking at the reproduction of his 'Cry'. A girl (?) stands upon a bridge; her body writhes in torment, her two hands are clapped to the sides of her head. Everything about the head implies suffering: its simplified form quite obviously suggests a skull, while the eyes are wide and staring and the mouth opens to give vent to a cry of agony. But the pain which this girl feels has been transmitted to the entire landscape; everything seems to reverberate with it. Munch has attempted to create an intense image of suffering—acute depression or nervous breakdown—which would strike home its message as directly and powerfully as possible. And more, he has attempted to demonstrate what it is like to experience a despair so great that madness is only around the corner. The world itself has become warped and twisted by the girl's pain, just as, in reality, the world may appear to take on a grim and threatening aspect, or even to decompose, in the eyes of a sufferer from certain types of acute depression.

Although most of Munch's pictures are not quite so grim as 'The Cry', there is a deep pessimism underlying his work. Symbols of death and illness recur frequently. In several paintings the essentially transitory nature of human existence is insisted upon. His 'Dance of Life', painted in 1900, shows, on the left, a young woman glowing with health and dressed in white (a colour symbolising purity and innocence). In the centre of the picture she dances with a number of partners and already the fresh bloom has faded from her face. Finally we see her on the right, old and alone and dressed in black, the colour of death. We are presented with an altogether different view of womanhood in a picture called 'The Vampire'. Here the woman is the destroyer of man; he submits meekly while she drinks his life blood. This particularly unflattering view of the female is also to be found in the plays of Munch's friend August Strindberg (cf. *The Father*).

The Cry, *1895, by* Edvard Munch. *Lithograph.*

Few of the other Symbolist artists achieved Munch's sheer concentration, but many shared his melancholic view of life. Generally, Symbolist art tends to range from the wistfully sad to the distinctly depressive. It is also of significance that Munch worked for a number of years in Germany where his art struck a deep chord with certain young painters who were engaged in reviving the spirit of German art which had lain fallow for so long. These were the Expressionists, whose work we shall discuss in the course of the following chapter.

Aubrey Beardsley (1872–98)

The English artist Aubrey Beardsley died in 1898 of tuberculosis. His artistic career had spanned just five years. Yet during that period, in which he had engaged in a frantic race against encroaching disease and impending death, he managed to create not only a large body of work but also a highly distinctive style. And more than almost any other artist he managed to capture in his work a certain flavour so characteristic of the 'gay nineties'—a taste for the decadent, the bizarre, the perverse, and a hyper-refined aesthetic sensibility. In fact, Beardsley's art, and much of the Symbolist art of the nineties, might be regarded as a form of Mannerism.

Beardsley was essentially an illustrator, his chosen medium pen and ink. His prestige in this field was already growing when, in 1894, he was asked to produce a series of illustrations for Oscar Wilde's play *Salomé.* The resulting publication excited a great deal of interest. Beardsley's drawings were a tour de force; elegant arabesques of line contrasted markedly with areas of dense black and intricate texture. But this was far more than highly accomplished decoration; the images themselves—from the sensual to the downright grotesque, with a strong hint of perversion—must have seemed to the late Victorian public very risqué indeed.

This mixture of elegance and scarcely veiled sensuality may readily be judged from the reproduction; Salomé kisses the severed head of John the Baptist while his dripping blood merges with the decorative scheme of arabesques.

The art of Beardsley and Munch, while it had many characteristics in common with the work of other Symbolist artists, is also linked with another international movement. This was known as Art Nouveau in France and England, and Jugendstil in German-speaking countries. Art Nouveau primarily manifested itself in what we tend to term 'design' or 'commercial art', although it had very close links with some of the painting and sculpture of the 1880s and nineties. Art Nouveau designs—whether they were in furniture, jewellery, architecture, posters or table ware—gave great emphasis to flowing arabesques and to colour.

The Kiss *by* Aubrey Beardsley. *One of the sixteen illustrations for Oscar Wilde's play Salomé which was first published in England in 1894.*

Beardsley's drawing, and to a lesser extent Munch's lithograph, demonstrate the first of these characteristics.

The various centres of Art Nouveau were widespread and included Glasgow, Munich, Vienna, Paris and Brussels. In these centres designers in many fields gave themselves over to the all-pervasive curve. And significantly, many painters and sculptors turned their talents to applied design. In Paris, the painter Henri Toulouse Lautrec—usually regarded as a post-Impressionist—produced a number of justly celebrated commercial posters, for instance. These posters, while they certainly relate directly to his painting, tend to be more experimental, and elements implicit in the paintings are boldly stated in poster form. One might mention the figures reduced to decorative silhouettes and the almost total neutralisation of three-dimensional space.

One of the most important aspects of Art Nouveau design lies in this very principle whereby artists were made aware of the purely abstract possibilities inherent in their work and afforded the opportunity to explore fully such opportunities. It must be seen therefore as one of the main bridges between the art of the late nineteenth century and the slightly later abstract art of the twentieth.

Poster for Jane Avril *by* Henri Toulouse-Lautrec. *Lithograph. (Victoria and Albert Museum, London). Lautrec discovered the dancer Jane Avril working as a chorus girl at the Moulin Rouge. He helped launch her on a successful solo career and depicted her many times in drawings, lithographs, posters, etc.*

Practical exercises
The art of the late nineteenth century suggests a number of practical ideas for the art class.

1 Impressionism and Pointillism
Using only spectrum colours, a painting might be built up of broken strokes (as with Monet or Renoir) or more carefully, of dots (as with Seurat). Work from observation, colour photographs or sketches.

2 Van Gogh's vivid use of rhythmic brush strokes might suggest an approach for painting. Use a medium which lends itself to impasto painting, e.g. tempera, oil, molten wax.

3 Gauguin
The flat, simplified forms and resonant colour harmonies of Paul Gauguin might suggest an approach for painting. Look again at some medieval art.

4 Art Nouveau
The study of Art Nouveau is particularly useful as a basis for the design of numerous crafts including (*a*) lino cuts, (*b*) ceramics, (*c*) posters, (*d*) wood carvings, (*e*) wall hangings, (*f*) stage sets.

For further reading
Larousse Encyclopaedia of Modern Art (Hamlyn)
Marcel Brion, *Art of the Romantic Era* (Thames and Hudson)
Timothy Hilton, *The Pre-Raphaelites* (Thames and Hudson)
Edward Lucie-Smith, *Symbolist Art* (Thames and Hudson)
Phoebe Pool, *Impressionism* (Thames and Hudson)
Germain Bazin, *Impressionist paintings in the Louvre* (Thames and Hudson)

Japanese print, eighteenth century. Japanese woodblock prints exerted a great influence on European artists during the late nineteenth century, including Van Gogh, Degas and Toulouse-Lautrec.

Some Important Events		Building and Visual Arts
	1746	Birth of F. Goya (d. 1828)
	1748	Birth of J. L. David (d. 1825)
	1755	Birth of J. Flaxman (d. 1826)
1770 Birth of W. Wordsworth (d. 1850)		
1775 Birth of Jane Austen (d. 1817)	1775	Birth of J. M. W. Turner (d. 1851)
	1776	Birth of J. Constable (d. 1837)
	1780	Birth of J. A. D. Ingres (d. 1867)
	1784	David—Oath of the Horatii
1792 France declared a republic		
1793 Louis XVI executed	1793	David—Death of Marat
	1796	Birth of A. L. Barye (d. 1875)
	1798	Birth of E. Delacroix (d. 1863)
1799–1815 Period of Napoleonic Wars	1799	Goya—Los Caprichos published
1805 Battle of Trafalgar	1805	David—Coronation of Napoleon.
1808 Faust by Goethe	1808	Birth of H. Daumier (d. 1879)
1809 Birth of Charles Darwin (d. 1882)		
1810 Birth of F. Chopin (d. 1849)		
1814 Louis XVIII on French throne	1814	Goya—Executions of 3rd May Birth of J. F. Millet (d. 1875)
1818 Mary Shelley—Frankenstein		
1819 Keats—'Ode to a Nightingale'	1819	Birth of G. Courbet (d. 1877) Goya—The Black paintings
	1821	Constable—The Haywain
1822 Niepce—first successful permanent photograph Greek independence proclaimed Birth of Louis Pasteur		
1824 Beethoven—9th Symphony Charles X on French throne	1824	Cologne Cathedral—work resumed Delacroix—Massacre at Scios
1825 First railway—Stockton to Darlington		
	1828	Birth of D. G. Rossetti (d. 1882)
1830 Revolution in France	1830	Birth of C. Pissarro (d. 1903)
	1832	Birth of E. Manet (d. 1883)
	1834	Birth of E. Degas (d. 1917)
1837 Queen Victoria on British throne		
1839 Dickens—Oliver Twist Development of daguerreotype	1839	Birth of P. Cézanne (d. 1906)
1840 Birth of E. Zola (d. 1902)	1840	Birth of C. Monet (d. 1926) Birth of A. Rodin (d. 1917)

Some Important Events		Building and Visual Arts
	1841	Birth of A. Renoir (d. 1919) Turner—Snowstorm: Steamboat off a Harbour's Mouth
1848 Communist Manifesto		
	1848	Birth of P. Gauguin (d. 1903)
1850 Birth of G. de Maupassant	1850	Courbet—Funeral at Ornans J. Paxton—Crystal Palace
1851 Great Exhibition—London		
1852 Napoleon III Emperor		
	1853	Birth of V. Van Gogh (d. 1890)
1855 International exhibition—Paris	1855	Courbet—one-man show
1857 G. Flaubert—*Madame Bovary* C. Baudelaire—*Fleurs du Mal*		
1859 Darwin—*Origin of Species*		
	1863	Birth of E. Munch (d. 1944) Manet—Déjeuner sur l'Herbe Ingres—Turkish Bath
1865 Japan open for trade to west	1865	Manet—Olympia
1867 K. Marx—*Das Kapital*		
1869 L. Tolstoy—*War and Peace*		
1870 Franco-Prussian War		
1871 Paris Commune		
	1872	Birth of A. Beardsley (d. 1898)
	1873	Degas—First ballet pictures
	1874	First Impressionist exhibition
1877 Queen Victoria declared empress of India	1877	Rodin—Age of Bronze
1880 Dostoevsky—*The Brothers Karamazov*		
	1884– 1886	Rodin—Burghers of Calais Seurat—Island of Grand Jatte
	1886	Last Impressionist exhibition
	1888	Gauguin—Vision after the Sermon
1889 International exhibition—Paris	1889	Eiffel Tower
	1890	Van Gogh—Road with Cypresses Van Gogh's suicide
	1891	Gauguin to Tahiti
1894 *Salomé* published in England	1894	Monet—Rouen Cathedral series
	1895	Munch—The Cry (painted version)
1899 Outbreak of Boer War	1899	Signac—*From Delacroix to neo-Impressionism*

See the map on p. 146 –The Modern Movement—for a number of important late 19th-century locations.

CHAPTER FIVE

The Twentieth Century

Art in the age of Science and Technology

Perhaps the only simple statement which can be made with any validity concerning the twentieth century is to the effect that it is the most complex in the entire history of the human race.

Developments in science and technology, in scale and extent wholly unprecedented, have brought in their wake profound and often alarming changes in the patterns of human life. Amazing advances in such fields as communication, medicine and mass-production must be weighed against the horrors of modern warfare, pollution and the threat of over-population. The complexities of the century are compounded of contradictions of an almost schizoid nature!

The plethora of artistic styles and movements, which make our century unique, reflect all of this. To plot their ebb and flow adequately is a daunting task. In an attempt to clarify I have identified three major idea-streams, which for my purpose I term (1) Art and Structure, (2) Art and Emotion and (3) Art and the Subconscious.

Such classification, of necessity, is a gross over-simplification. One can only hope that historical truth has not been unduly distorted.

1. ART AND STRUCTURE

Look at the painting reproduced on this page. Does it mean anything to you? Begin with the subject matter. This is a complex of buildings of course, but painted in what could only be termed a blatantly 'unrealistic' manner. The artist has left out almost all detail; we can just about detect a variety of slanting roofs, and some windows. He appears to be unaware of the basic rules of perspective and in addition has chosen a drab colour-scheme of dull browns and dirty greys. Even the area of the picture which we may interpret as the sky is painted in the same brown colour as the buildings. It must be obvious that the artist is not trying to impress us with his subject matter, command of atmospheric effects, colour or interesting detail. What does that leave us with?

Look at the picture once more—buildings yes, but strongly reminiscent of—? A heap of wooden blocks put together by a child perhaps? Crystals? The shapes do look solid and rigid—and the clean, sharp corners which most of them have can almost be physically felt. We can say then, that 'clarity' seems to be of fundamental importance to this artist. Perhaps you would

Reservoir at Horta de Ebro, *1909, by* Pablo Picasso *(1881–1973). (Galerie Louise Leiris, Paris, © S.P.A.D.E.M., 1976). Artists that use the simplest, most complete and most logical forms have been dubbed 'Cubists'. 'The technique of the Cubists is clear and rational: it excludes school tricks, facial graces and the stylisations so much in favour nowadays. These are painters aware of the miracle that is achieved when the surface of a picture produces space...' from an article by Jean Metzinger published in Paris-Journal 16 August, 1911*

agree that the 'blocks' or 'crystals' seem to be carefully and deliberately arranged together. The central, vertical shapes appear almost to grow out of the broad curving ones at the bottom, and to form themselves into an irregular pyramid.

To 'clarity' we might add a second element—'structure'. The subject of the picture is in fact a group of buildings and a reservoir at Horta de Ebro in Spain

Seated Woman, *1917, by* Jacques Lipchitz *(b.1891).*
Lipchitz was born in Lithuania, but worked in Paris
for many years. Although he attended the Ecole des
Beaux-Arts he joined the Cubists, producing sculpture
which paralleled their pictorial experiments.

The Engineer, *1920, by* Fernand Léger *(1881–1955).*
(National Gallery of Canada, Ottawa: ©
S.P.A.D.E.M., 1976). 'If pictorial expression has
changed, it is because modern life has made this neces-
sary'—Léger, writing in 1914.

and the artist is Pablo Picasso. Picasso painted 'The
Reservoir' a few years before the outbreak of the Great
War, during a period when many other artists were
also very concerned with the same two ideas of 'clarity'
and 'structure'.

Picasso's powerful personality and his original ideas
have influenced many artists during the past fifty years
or so. Does this explain why, during those years
around 1914, large numbers of artists turned their
backs on the tradition of painting more or less what
they saw in front of them in order to make works like
these? Hardly! A number of artists working in Paris
had produced 'structural' paintings quite independent-
ly of Picasso and similar ideas sprang up almost simultaneously in several parts of the world, in Moscow,
Prague and Leyden for instance (and these were pre-
TV days!)

The suggestion that this form of art was 'right' at

that particular time seems a far more reasonable one.
In a similar fashion the perspective and anatomy based
art of the Northern Italians was 'right' in the fifteenth
century.

The period from 1890 to the Great War is marked
by a widespread optimism about the possibilities of
scientific and technological advance. The idea that a
new art, marked by precision and clarity, must be
forged in preparation for the 'brave new world' of
science anticipated by many, lurked at the back of
many artistic minds. Picasso's sheer ability, aided by
an unusually audacious temperament, had enabled
him to take the necessary steps towards the realisation
of such an art, a little ahead of everyone else.

There were other, though perhaps related, consider-
ations. The camera, for instance, was capable of producing accurate likenesses of people and places far
more quickly and cheaply than any painter. Indeed,

many painters, at the turn of the century, feared that they might go out of business because of this. Others, like Picasso, felt that painters should not bother to compete with the camera; representation of nature could safely be left in the hands of the photographers while painters found other, and more fruitful, directions to explore.

It is also worth mentioning that mechanical forms—pistons, gun barrels, aircraft screws etc.—with their economy of design, their functionalism, their polish, were beginning to impress many artists as beautiful and worthy of study.

Look at the painting by Léger again.

Now look at the object in this illustration. Obviously it is not the product of a technological society. It comes from West Africa and was made by hand. A large number of objects similar to this one found their way into the museums of Western Europe during the nineteenth century—just some of the fruits of colonial adventures. The art of 'primitive' societies was once thought to be of little value. Picasso and some of his French associates were unusual in the serious attention which they gave to such 'primitive art' and his studio boasted a number of West African carvings on its walls among his own canvases.

Can you see any connection between the paintings reproduced in this chapter and the West African carving?

Baluba Figure (detail). Wood-carving

Still Life *by* Juan Gris *(1887–1927). (National Gallery of Ireland) This picture is composed largely of stuck-on or collage elements.*

Cubism

In Paris this new 'structural' art was called Cubism. The term should not be taken too literally; there is a lot more to Cubism than pictures made from little blocks.

Briefly, the main aims of the Cubist artists—Picasso, Braque, Gris and Léger were among the most important of them—were these:

1. Art should seek to create forms based on reason rather than on retinal images (cf. Impressionism).

2. In painting, many of the traditional devices to 'trick' the eye should be discontinued. A perspective scheme gives the impression of depth. The Cubists argued that this was dishonest—paintings had flat surfaces and should not pretend otherwise.

3. The painter should not restrict himself to the single viewpoint imposed by a perspective scheme. The Cubists felt quite free to 'dismantle' their subject, whether it was still life, human figure or landscape, and to rearrange the fragments according to the dictates of harmony.

4. Elements in a picture which do not help in its structure (i.e. colour) should be given little importance.

5. Simple, everyday subjects are the most suitable for painting and sculpture.

6. Real objects—wallpaper, playing cards, letters, sand etc.—may be used, along with more traditional materials, in the making of a picture. The technique of sticking such matter onto a canvas became known as 'collage' from the French word 'coller'—to glue.

Can you think of any late nineteenth-century artists whose work might have influenced the Cubists?

A modern kitchen. (Camera Press)

De Stijl

Soon after the debut of Cubism in Paris, constructive, rational art made its appearance in many parts of the world and some groups went very much further along the road to clarity and rationalism than the Cubists.

The painting reproduced here was painted by the Dutchman, Piet Mondrian who was a member of a group of painters, designers, and architects based in Leyden. They called themselves de Stijl. Many people still find it hard to take works like this seriously as paintings. Most noticeably it has no subject matter whatsoever. It is an abstract painting. Possibly it seems too empty to you and probably not worth the effort of examination.

Composition in Grey, Red, Yellow and Blue by Piet Mondrian (1872–1944) (Tate Gallery, London, © Harry Holtzman). Mondrian began his career as a naturalistic painter of landscapes and flowers. The severe form of geometric abstraction—neo-Plasticism—which he evolved, was the result of many years' hard work.

Yet Mondrian laboured for over a quarter of a century on paintings like this. Although he restricted himself to vertical and horizontal straight lines and used only the most basic colours, every element had to be exactly right. Mondrian was both a purist and a perfectionist. His concern was to produce works which would be perfectly balanced. The suspicion that one of his lines might be a millimetre or so too thick, thus disturbing the overall harmony of the painting, would have disturbed him greatly.

All of this sounds very remote from everyday life. It is easy to imagine that the influence of an artist like Mondrian would be so restricted as hardly to be noticed. Perhaps the truth is not so simple!

Castrol House, *London. (Camera Press)*

The Futurists

We will sing the midnight fervour of arsenals and shipyards blazing with electric moons; insatiable stations swallowing the smoking serpents of their trains, factories hung from the clouds by the twisted threads of their smoke!

Marinetti, *Futurist Manifesto*, 1909.

After the cold, intellectual clarity of Mondrian the work and ideas of the Italian Futurists come as a pleasant shock. The Futurists were not simply in favour of the new technological age—they were positively ecstatic about its possibilities! Racing cars, artillery, express trains, electric light—everything that moved at speed, clanked, whistled, exploded, blasted out steam or exhaust fumes—all of these delighted them. Not surprisingly, they detested everything that was old, including Italy's magnificent artistic past, Michelangelo, Leonardo et al.

Here is a typical Futurist painting. Compare this picture, by Umberto Boccioni, with some of the Cubist pictures we have already looked at. Can you find any similarities between Boccioni's approach and that of Picasso? How do they differ? Boccioni called his painting 'Dynamism of a Cyclist'. Is the title appropriate?

Dynamism of a Cyclist, *1913, by* Umberto Boccioni *(1882-1916).*

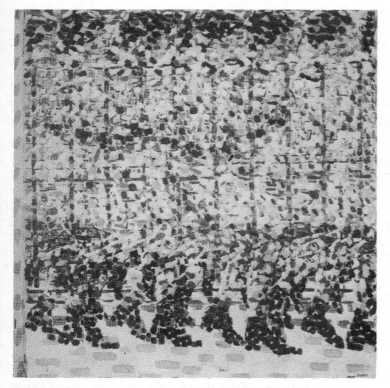

Girl Running on a Balcony, *1912, by* Giacomo Balla (1871–1958).

Giacomo Balla painted this picture, 'Girl Running on a Balcony' in 1919. What have been the two main influences on the picture?

Russia—Suprematism, Rayonism and Constructivism
We tend to regard the Soviet Union as very conservative indeed where the arts are concerned. The forceful closure of an exhibition of 'modern' art, mounted on an open-air site near Moscow, as recently as the summer of 1974, indicates that Russia is only beginning to waken up to the ideas which artists like Picasso and Mondrian were exploring over half a century ago.

This is very far from the truth however, and it can be argued that for the period of a decade or so, until 1922, Moscow was second only to Paris as a hot-bed of 'advanced' artistic activity. Many painters and sculptors in Moscow daobled with Cubism before developing their own distinctive styles. A number of rival movements emerged, the origin of whose differences owe as much to personal animosities as to genuine dispute over ideology.

Kasimir Malevich, the founder of Suprematism, developed a geometrical style even more austere than that of Mondrian. Natalia Goncharova and Michael Larionov produced a dynamic form of painting, which they called Rayonism, similar in many ways to Futurism. Naum Gabo, one of the founders of Constructivism, built geometrical structures in metal, plastic and wire. Others rapidly turned their ideas to practical use, designing stage-sets, pottery, buildings, textiles and posters.

The poster by El Lissitzky makes a very forthright political statement. Many Russian artists welcomed the October Revolution of 1917 and felt that their artistic ideas echoed those of the Bolsheviks.

Linear Construction in Space, *1949, by* Naum Gabo (b. 1890). (Gemeente Musea van Amsterdam). *The decorative constructions in coloured thread so popular today would appear to be direct descendants of Gabo's work.*

Beat the Whites with the Red Wedge, c. *1919. Street poster by* El Lissitzky (1890–1941).

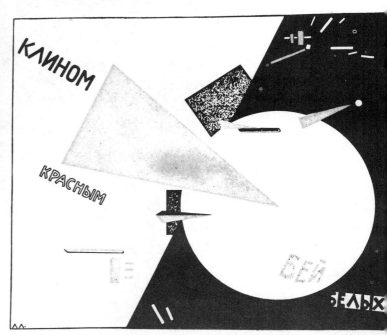

V. I. Lenin Addressing the 2nd All-Russia Congress of Soviets, *by* V. A. Serov. *(Novosti Press Agency, London)*

For a few brief years the Russian Revolution and modern art advanced together in step. Then the Soviet authorities decided that, after all, such ideas were bourgeois in origin. What the Russian people needed was a purely anecdotal art depicting peasants, workers, soldiers and politicians all striving for the good of the Soviet system—propaganda, in short!

A new academism was born.

The Great War—And After
The Great War seemed to prove to many in the western hemisphere that technology was not, in fact, leading to some paradise on earth. The new machines could destroy as effectively as they could build and lift the work-load from men's shoulders. The pessimism and bitterness generated in Europe by the war gave impetus to several artistic movements quite alien in outlook to Cubism. We shall examine some of these shortly.

Painting and sculpture based on reason and harmony survived, though no longer as a primary creative force.

Architecture—the International Style
During the twenties and thirties the field of architecture looked a great deal more hopeful. A new style of building, designed along theoretical lines laid down by movements like Cubism, de Stijl and Constructivism, found increasing favour in many European countries. The 'International Style' as it was designated, exploited materials like steel girders, pre-stressed concrete and vast amounts of glass.

Such ideas have become hackneyed and commonplace today. Our cities are increasingly overwhelmed by vast anonymous concrete and glass boxes. It is surprising therefore that we can state convincingly that the originators of modern architecture were idealists who would probably be appalled by the present state of urban development. The architects of the International Style were deeply concerned with the problems of creating an environment which would enhance the everyday existence of people generally. It would be a mistake to see them as engineers and aesthetes only.

Gerrit Thomas Rietveld, who designed both the building and the chair shown in these illustrations, was a member of de Stijl. He was therefore an associate of Mondrian's.

Do the building and the chair have any design principles in common? Refer back to the painting by Mondrian. Compare the design of the two utilitarian objects with the painting.

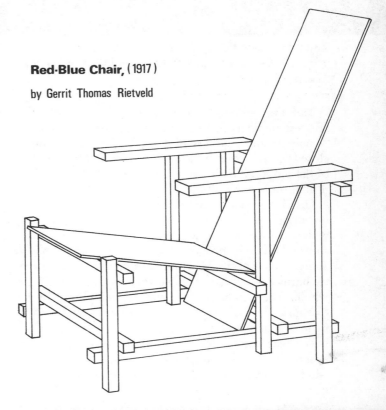

Red-Blue Chair, (1917)

by Gerrit Thomas Rietveld

Schroeder House, *1924, by* Gerrit Thomas Rietveld *(1888–1964).*

The Marseille Block, *1952, by* Le Corbusier *(1887-1965). 'The house is a machine for living in.' (Photo Lucien Hervé, Paris)*

The Franco-Swiss, Le Corbusier, is possibly the greatest single name in twentieth-century architecture. A painter and sculptor himself, Le Corbusier was a close friend of several of the Paris Cubists. He was one of the pioneers in the use of concrete and mass production of units in buildings.

His deep interest in aesthetic harmony led to the invention of the 'Modulor', a measuring principle which combines harmonious mathematical relationships with the proportions of the human body. Judicious use of the Modulor scale enables an architect to harmonise every element in a building with the whole. The Modulor scale was also employed by Le Corbusier in the design of his paintings, sculpture and furniture. If we add to all this the fact that Le Corbusier was quite a prolific writer, he begins to emerge as a modern universal genius. (His book describing the Modulor system is readily available in English translation.)

The Bauhaus

The German architect Walter Gropius was, like Le Corbusier, something of a visionary. He is remembered today, not so much for his buildings as for the foundation of a college of art and design—the Bauhaus.

The Bauhaus published the writings of artists like Mondrian and Malevich and managed to attract several leading artists as lecturers. It managed both to foster and to concentrate the ideas of many of the most creative minds in Europe. The Bauhaus courses—in architecture, painting, sculpture, typography and a variety of crafts—attempted to establish a secure and rigid basis for all design in the synthesis of the theories of the de Stijl and Constructivism.

The Bauhaus Building, *1925–28, Dessau, by* Walter Gropius *(b. 1883–). (Bundesbildstelle, Bonn). Perhaps the most celebrated building of the 1920s. Interior decoration and furnishing were undertaken by the Bauhaus workshops.*

nummer	3
jahrgang	III
bezugspreis jährlich rm.	7.20
preis dieser nummer rm.	2.00

bauhaus

juli-sept. **1929**

ihr-zeitschrift fur gestaltung. herausgeber hannes meyer. schriftleitung: ernst kállai. bauhaus dessau. verlag und anzeigen-verwaltung: dessau, zerbster strasse nr. 16

typo joost schmidt

Bauhaus typography. Cover for a quarterly magazine by Joost Schmidt. *Gropius was appointed first principal of the Bauhaus—originally at Weimar—in 1914. He intended that it should be 'a consultation centre for industry and the trades'. The Bauhaus moved to Dessau in 1925 and was closed by the Nazis in the 1930s.*

Departing in Yellow, *by* Josef Albers *(b. 1888). From the artist's Homage to the Square series. (Tate Gallery, London)*

This could possibly be summed up as *simplicity of form* and *truth to materials.* Such ideas, although no longer universally accepted, have had a profound influence on designers throughout the western hemisphere. They have been largely responsible for the 'clean lines' of so much modern design from cigarette lighters to locomotives.

Josef Albers

The painter Josef Albers is an excellent example of a Bauhaus graduate. He has served his time both as student and teacher there, only leaving when the Bauhaus was closed by the Nazis in 1933. His approach to painting is endlessly experimental yet highly disciplined and austere.

His influence as a teacher has been widespread, particularly in the U.S.A., where he has lived and worked for some twenty years.

His own long series of paintings bearing the general title 'Homage to the Square' concentrates solely on the mutual influence exerted by a small number of simple coloured shapes. Paintings composed of very simple, flat, geometrical shapes, inspired by Albers's example, are called 'Hard edge' paintings. The 'Hard edge' style has been influential during the sixties and early seventies.

Painting by Kenneth Noland *(b. 1924). (Municipal Gallery of Modern Art, Dublin)*

Op Art

'Optical'—'Op'—Art has also been influential during recent years. It too has its roots deep in Bauhaus experimentation.

Fall *by* Bridget Riley *(b. 1931). (Tate Gallery London, © Bridget Riley)*

Op paintings usually consist of arrangements of simple geometrical elements—lines, squares, dots, etc.—carefully organised in such a way that, on viewing, the retina of the viewer's eye is over-stimulated through colour or tonal contrasts. This may sound complicated but the end result is a painting which appears in some curious way to 'come alive'.

In many ways Op painting is the easiest of all forms of abstract art to appreciate. One does not have to know anything about the theory behind a work in order to enjoy the energy which appears to pulsate from its surface.

Look at this painting by the English artist Bridget Riley. Would you agree that the page of this book almost seems to buckle under the impact of those lines? Move the book slightly from side to side while still looking at the picture. What other 'optical' effects do you notice?

Because of its eye-catching effects Op Art has gained considerable popularity in recent years. Many people have become familiar with it through the numerous commercial designs—fabrics, book covers, advertisements, etc.—inspired by Op. Indeed, Bridget Riley has had to bring one manufacturer to court for illegally reproducing one of her paintings on dress fabric.

Vasarely (b. 1908)
The central figure in the movement is without doubt the Hungarian, Victor Vasarely (see front cover).

Just as long-playing records enable music to be mass-produced, so Vasarely conceives of a form of painting, constructed from simple basic units, which the artist simply designs and others put into production. A number of artists working today share

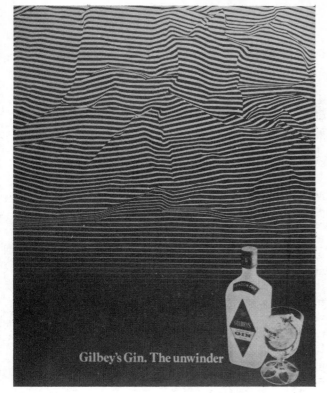

Vasarely's view.

Thus history may well have come full circle. The artist of the near future may withdraw completely from the limelight and return to the anonymity which was once his a thousand years or so ago. Do you feel that this is a possibility? The idea is worth debating in any case.

Woman with the Hat, *1905, by* Henri Matisse *(1869–1954). (© S.P.A.D.E.M., Paris, 1976)*

Surely all art stems ultimately from emotion? How could artists produce anything at all if they did not first 'feel something'? This is a valid line of argument, yet some artists go to considerable pains to cover up, to contain, their original emotion. It is not allowed to show on the surface. (This is true of most of the art dealt with in the first section of this chapter.)

There are artists of a different temper who make very clear in their work *how* they feel and *what* they feel. The late nineteenth century produced several notable examples of this type—particularly the Dutchman Van Gogh. Artists like Van Gogh, whose chief concern is to make their emotions manifest, are often referred to as 'Expressionists'.

The 'Wild Beasts'

'I put down my colours without a preconceived plan . . . I discover the quality of colours in a purely instinctive way.'

Henri Matisse, 1905

'It is not madness that stares at you from his [Matisse's] canvases but leering effrontery.'

Kenyon Cox, Art Critic

Although Expressionism has never really been 'at home' in France (Van Gogh and Munch were both northern Europeans) we begin our story once again in the city of Paris, in the year 1905 to be precise.

In that year the painting 'Woman with the Hat' by Henri Matisse was first publicly exhibited. It earned for Matisse and the small group of painters exhibiting with him a great deal of notoriety, along with the label 'Les Fauves'—'the Wild Beasts'. Matisse's painting scandalised the press and public not because of its subject, but simply because of the *manner* in which it was painted—with irregular patches of unrelieved garish colour. Even the lady's face is accented with slashes of pure green, red and yellow, while the background changes colour in a bewildering fashion from green to purple to yellow! Matisse explained that he was simply using colours according to the dictates of his emotion. He began his paintings with a patch of colour which 'suggested' a second to him and so on until the picture emerged complete.

He had not been converted to the use of pure colour overnight, but only after years of experiment and study. The majority opinion held that his pictures were like the daubings of a child or a lunatic. Some suggested that Matisse was simply a confidence trickster. The writer André Gide was almost alone in his

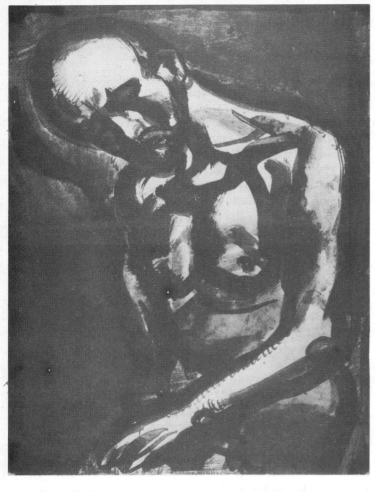

opinion that, if anything, Matisse's art was too reasonable:

'. . . the canvases that he paints today seem to be demonstrations of theorems . . . Everything can be deduced, explained . . . Without doubt, when M. Matisse paints the forehead of this woman apple colour and the trunk of this tree an outright red he can say to us, "It is because—".'

Georges Rouault's art was a different matter altogether. His colours were deep and smouldering and held together by a latticework of heavy black lines reminiscent of stained glass. And his subject matter was hardly calculated to please. There were women—obviously prostitutes—with bloated faces and bulbous decaying bodies, grossly misused creatures and objects of pity. Add to these besotted men in top hats, and clowns with sad, drawn faces. Rouault was a man of deeply religious, but no less deeply pessimistic convictions. His pessimism, his religious fervour, his deep pity for his fellow human creatures all communicate themselves to us in his paintings and prints.

This etching by Rouault—'The Tough Business of Life'—perfectly demonstrates his personal philosophy. The title confirms the impression left by the image of a man bowed down and defeated by the struggle entailed in simply remaining alive.

Le Dur Métier de Vivre, *from the Miserere series by* Rouault. © S.P.A.D.E.M., Paris, 1976.

Christ and the Soldier, *by Georges Rouault (1871–1958). (Municipal Gallery of Modern Art, Dublin, © S.P.A.D.E.M. Paris, 1976)*

The Pool of London, *by André Derain (1880–1954). (Tate Gallery, London) Derain produced some of the finest Fauve pictures. He was to renounce the use of bright colour however, and his later pictures were painted in sombre browns and greys.*

German Expressionism

. . . here there are only two possibilities: either these so-called artists really see things this way and therefore believe in what they depict; then we would have to examine their distorted eye-sight to see if it is the product of a mechanical failure or of inheritance . . . If, on the other hand, they themselves do not believe in the reality of such impressions but try to harass the nation with this humbug for other reasons, then such an attempt falls within the jurisdiction of the penal law.

Adolf Hitler

Emil Nolde's 'Prophet'—printed from a plank of wood onto paper; the white shapes, hacked with a chisel from the wood, leave an image of the human face which, although appallingly crude in its execution, is deeply moving. Look at it for yourself. What does it make you feel? The 'Prophet' is a fine example of German Expressionism.

The Prophet, *1912, by* Emil Nolde *(1867–1956). 'We live at a time when primitive man and the primitive way of life are becoming extinct . . . . I often have the feeling that they are the only real human beings alive, while we are like puppets.' From a 1914 letter by Nolde.*

Die Brücke

Nolde was one of a close-knit group of artists, centred in Dresden, calling themselves 'Die Brücke'—'The Bridge', a 'Bridge' linking the great German past to the twentieth century perhaps.

Certainly the members of Die Brücke were painfully aware of the decline which German art had suffered since the great days of Dürer and Grünewald. The fact that French art had suffered no such decline, had blossomed if anything, was a further blow to nationalistic pride. New ideas from France were received with deep interest not altogether untinged with jealousy.

On the surface, paintings by the Brücke group— Kirchner, Pechstein, Heckel, Schmidt-Rottluff and Nolde—seem very similar to those of the Fauves. The same bright unrelieved areas of pure colour are there, so too is the total disregard for academic polish and 'correctness' of drawing.

Five Women in the Street, *1913, by* Ernst Ludwig Kirchner *(1880–1938). (Wallraf-Richartz-Museum und Museum Ludwig, Cologne). 'German art is a religion in the broadest sense of the word; Latin art is reproduction, depiction, description or a paraphrasing of nature. The German paints the "what", the Frenchman the "how". That completely explains the bad technique in German art and the great dependence of the Germans on French technique.' Extract from a 1925 diary kept by Kirchner.*

The differences are fundamental, however. The German works tend to be motivated by a deep-seated disquiet, a suspicion that all is not well with the world.

Would you agree that Ernst Ludwig Kirchner's 'Five ladies' create a rather disturbing effect? There is the suggestion of menacing birds in their pinched faces and dark silhouetted bodies.

And Nolde's 'Prophet'?

This dimension of unease is missing from the work of the Fauves—with the notable exception of Rouault—as it is from most French art. How do we explain this almost medieval pathos? Many works of German Expressionism are strikingly similar, in their mood and wilful distortions, to certain medieval paintings and sculptures. Can we explain this in terms of hypersensitivity to the growing forces of destruction building up in Europe during the early 1900s and soon to engulf the continent? Or is there already something deeply melancholic and alienated in the northern European soul which the threat of war merely brought out?

Kandinsky

The Russian painter Wassily Kandinsky has related how, one evening after a landscape sketching expedition, he returned in the half-light to his studio only to be confronted by a strange, but radiantly beautiful, painting propped on his easel. The painting, composed of rhythmic shapes and rich, glowing colours, seemed to have no subject matter whatsoever! Kandinsky was overwhelmed by the shock of revelation—painting *could* be free of the restraining shackles of representation. The discovery that this painting was one of his own landscapes lying on its side made no difference. He had reached a turning point in his career which led inevitably to his first timorous attempts at painting pictures wholly without subject matter. These are among the very first 'abstract' paintings of the modern era.

Kandinsky felt that painting, once free of the necessity to represent, could move on to a higher plane of spirituality—once the unique province of the composer of music. A piece of music, after all, does not seek to reproduce sounds found in nature—a Beethoven quartet sounds only like a Beethoven quartet!

Painting had become a sort of visual music.

Der Blaue Reiter

Kandinsky had come to Munich—regarded by many as the artistic capital of Germany—before the turn of the century, to study painting. He became the central

In the Black Circle, *1923, by* Wassily Kandinsky, *(1866–1944). (Galerie Maeght, Paris). Many earlier paintings and prints by Kandinsky depict horses, but he was to write 'I love the circle to-day as I formerly loved the horse, for instance—perhaps even more, since I find more inner potentialities in the circle which is why it has taken the horses' place.'*

Jumping Ponies, *1912, by* Franz Marc *(1880–1916). Woodcut. Marc was a co-founder of Der Blaue Reiter with Kandinsky. Kandinsky has recorded how the name was derived from their shared interests: 'We both loved blue, Marc—horses, me—riders.' Marc died at Verdun, during World War I.*

Botanical Garden, *1926, by* Paul Klee *(1879–1940).*
Drawing. 'Art does not render the visible; rather it
makes visible.' Klee, 1920.

Weeping Woman, *1937, by* Pablo Picasso. *(Tate Gal-*
lery, London; © S.P.A.D.E.M., Paris 1976)

figure of Der Blaue Reiter (the Blue Rider), a group of artists domiciled in that city. The work of this group tended to be more lyrical and optimistic than that of Die Brücke, indicating that Expressionism may occasionally be more than simply the vehicle of pessimism and harshness.

Through his writing and lectures in the Bauhaus, Kandinsky sought to establish a firm theoretical basis for his 'lyrical' form of abstraction (now termed 'Abstract Expressionism').

The work of the German-Swiss Paul Klee formed a powerful buttress to Kandinsky's position. Klee's work is extremely varied—sometimes purely abstract, sometimes humorous, whimsical, gay, enigmatic or deeply pessimistic. To his many-sided abilities as a painter and draughtsman may be added the fact that he was also an extremely talented violinist, teacher and writer—one of the most richly gifted of twentieth-century artists.

Klee spent some ten years as a lecturer in the Bauhaus and his essays on painting were originally formulated for the benefit of his students. In these essays he examines the position of the twentieth-century artist and analyses the 'mechanisms' of art with great lucidity. (Essays like 'On Modern Art' are still very well worth reading and are freely available in English translation.)

Using the tree as a metaphor, Klee sees the roots as equivalent to the artist's perception (his 'sense of direction in nature and life'). The roots draw nourishment from the ground (nature) and pass this in the form of sap through the trunk of the tree (the artist). This produces the crown of the tree (the work of art). We do not expect the crown of a tree to resemble in appearance what lies beneath the ground; in a similar fashion we have no right to expect the work of a painter or sculptor to look exactly like some aspect of nature which might have inspired it.

Picasso

We have already examined a picture by Picasso in some detail. This picture 'The Weeping Woman' was painted almost thirty years later. What does it depict? The face of a woman crying—she lifts a handkerchief with her left hand to dry her tears, or to blow her nose perhaps. A blue and red bonnet rests on her head.

Does this description convey anything of the impression which the picture itself makes on you? Look at it. The harsh angularity of the shapes which Picasso has used to build up the form of the face and hat, the two eyes heavily delineated in black which appear to stare through smashed spectacles, the twisted mouth full of crooked teeth, the heavy, clumsy fingers and rope-like hair all add up to a very particular statement. One can

Guernica, *1937, by* Pablo Picasso. *(Museum of Modern Art, New York; © S.P.A.D.E.M., Paris 1976)*

hardly suggest that Picasso did all this purely for the sake of structure, as in his earlier Cubist paintings. It seems far more likely that he actually set out to create an image of provocative ugliness!

The 'Weeping Woman' was painted in 1937, a year when many signs existed to indicate that Europe was heading straight for a disaster of frightening proportions.

Disaster had already struck Picasso's native Spain in the form of a bitter civil war. Picasso made no secret of his deep concern for the fate of his country, or of his support for the Republican side in the conflict. His increasing agitation as the Spanish Republic was steadily crushed with the help of German and Italian military might is clearly seen in his pictures from that period.

The 'Weeping Woman', with her shattered face, is one example; there are many others including the celebrated 'Guernica'. This latter, indeed, was painted in a single month of feverish activity (although it measures 3·56 by 7·95 m) in response to a single incident during the Spanish Civil War. This was the destruction, by German aircraft, of the Basque market town of Guernica with the resulting loss of some two thousand human lives.

Look at the reproduction of the painting. At first it seems to be a mass of great jagged shapes; then a number of identifiable images emerge—a grief-stricken mother clutches her dead infant, a figure falls from a burning building, a screaming horse is pierced through by a lance, the dismembered fragments of a warrior lie

on the ground, his hand still grasping a broken sword. Above this scene of chaos and misery floats a form like a great eye—an electric light bulb burning at its centre. To the left of the scene is the brooding presence of a bull.

Picasso's cry of outrage, in the form of paintings and drawings, against the savagery of the Spanish Civil War and the World War which followed on its heels, continued until Fascism was finally defeated in 1945.

His use of the bull symbol (or the related bull-headed monster, the Minotaur) recurs in a number of Picasso's works from this period. It seems to constitute Picasso's personal symbol for mindless brutality. Does this interpretation make sense when applied to the 'Guernica' picture? How would you interpret the other symbols used in that picture?

After World War II—Abstract Expressionism

This painting, by the Dutch artist Karel Appel, is typical in its exuberance of the kind of painting which emerged in Europe and the United States after the Second World War. A large number of artists, on both sides of the Atlantic, seemed to rediscover ideas first

Portrait of the Sculptor Cesar, *1956, by* Karel Appel *(b. 1921). (Ulster Museum, Belfast). Appel was a member of the short-lived Cobra group of 1948–50, so called because the participant artists came from COpenhagen, BRussels and Amsterdam. The Cobra artists wished to achieve expression completely unguided by intellect.*

ainting, *1952, by* Jackson Pollock, *(1912–56). (Tate Gallery, London). Pollock was the most celebrated of the American Abstract Expressionists. His large canasses were placed unstretched on the floor of his studio and the paint was applied by vigorous dripping and splashing.*

---

pioneered by Kandinsky and Klee several decades previously.

The new revitalised Abstract Expressionism of the late forties and fifties took many forms. Often working on huge spreads of canvas, artists flung paint, dripped it and splashed it, applied it with knives, their hands and house-painters' brushes, or squirted it straight from the tube.

The Americans in particular (they called the movement 'Action Painting') fully exploited the new-found freedom. They aimed to establish a form of painting which would be distinctively American. The sheer scale and vigour of much of their work did certainly distinguish it from its European counterpart, with only a few exceptions.

Deposition—Study After Rembrandt, by Frank Auerbach *(b. 1931). (Municipal Gallery of Modern Art, Dublin). Auerbach paintings have something of the quality of relief sculpture.*

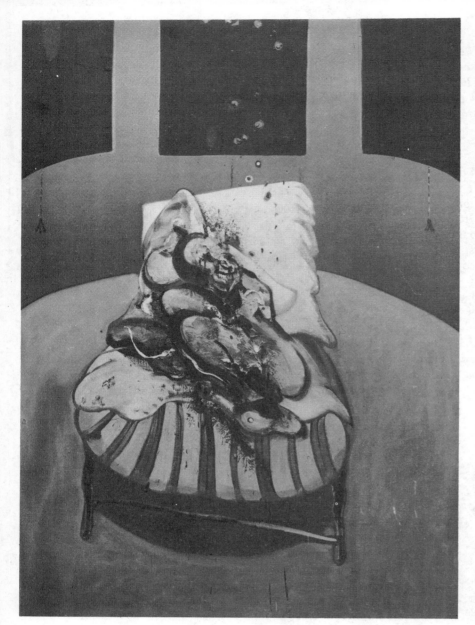

One of Three Studies for a Crucifixion, *1962, by* Francis Bacon *(b. 1910). (Solomon R. Guggenheim Museum, New York, © Francis Bacon). The centre panel of a triptych. 'When you go into a butcher's shop and see how beautiful meat can be and then you think about it, you can think of the whole horror of life—of one thing living off another.'*

Francis Bacon

A small number of important artists, whose work developed during the forties and fifties, remained aloof from the dominant current of abstraction. Among the most impressive of these is the Englishman (born in Dublin) Francis Bacon.

Bacon's paintings are not designed to reassure us. The great artists of the Renaissance—Michelangelo is the supreme example—tried to show by their art that man is a sort of God. Bacon seeks to prove the contrary. His figures—often soft, boneless, grub-like creatures—cringe, writhe in agony or scream with sheer terror or frustration. They are extremely vulnerable!

His 'Study for a Crucifixion', reproduced here, shows such a creature. In agony, this human 'thing' writhes on a bed, splashed with its own blood, as are the sheets, pillow and mattress. The bed with its tortured inhabitant seems to be situated in the centre of a featureless room or stage—everything is brightly lit and the colours are mainly reds and oranges.

This obsession with pain and injury, both physical (Bacon has made a careful study of wounds through medical publications) and emotional, might lead us to dismiss his work as that of a 'sick' mind. Perhaps—but the nagging doubt remains—how close we all are to the possibilities of experiencing pain, injury, suffering.

Is there a valid reason for expressing such feelings in a work of art? Should we, in fact, dwell on such matters at all? What do you think?

3. ART AND THE SUBCONSCIOUS

A landscape shattered by war, 1916. (Imperial War Museum, London)

During the Great War, it has been estimated, the battle of the Somme *alone* cost the lives of over a million men along with incalculable suffering. Only a tiny minority in Western Europe at the time felt that such carnage was a hideous waste, a further proof that the civilised nations had sunk to the depths of depravity and madness. The majority still spoke of patriotism, self-sacrifice, the 'war to end wars' etc.

A small number of expatriate artists and writers, from a variety of European countries, found refuge from the prevailing storm of war in neutral Zurich. During 1916 one of their number, the German poet and pacifist Hugo Ball, took the initiative and hired a small room in the old part of Zurich. Here, paintings could be displayed, music performed and poetry recited—the 'Cabaret Voltaire' was born. From a relatively harmless beginning, with Ball playing the piano and a balalika band playing Russian folk-music, the Cabaret Voltaire blossomed into something quite different and unexpected. Ball and his friends began to argue that, since the entire 'civilised' world had turned reason on its head, everyone should be made aware of that fact.

Their evenings of light entertainment were turned into a series of assaults upon the sensibility of their audiences and considerable ingenuity went into the invention of a variety of 'outrages'. Poets with stovepipes covering their heads read their poems to the accompaniment of a tin being banged and sounds like the yelping of a dog. Participants frequently hurled insults at the audiences and appeared wearing masks and dressed in ludicrous costumes fabricated from rags or painted cardboard. Poems were sometimes read simultaneously, or composed of meaningless sentences or sounds. One of Ball's 'abstract' poems began:

> gadji beri bimba glandridi laula lonni cadori
> gadjama gramma berida bimbala glandri galassassa,
> laulitalomini . . .

In short, a sort of cultural anarchy was unleashed upon the unsuspecting citizens of Zurich.

The Cabaret Voltaire was only a beginning. The group chose the word 'Dada' to describe their activities. 'Dada' in French is a child's word for 'hobby-horse'. The group felt that such a childish, almost meaningless, word was particularly suitable as a title.

Dada
'Dada is the biggest confidence trick of the century.'
'This summer elephants will be wearing moustaches. What about you?'

Dada slogans

As the movement gained momentum Dada magazines appeared. These magazines, with their unmistakable chaotic typographic style, attacked everything, including art itself.

When the war ended, and travel was no longer restricted, it became apparent that Dada was a force to be reckoned with. It rapidly took root in several great cities including Berlin, Paris and New York. Furthermore, it attracted to its banner some of the most talented artists and writers of the day. It seems ironical that while in the process of attacking every conceivable value, the Dadaists unwittingly stumbled upon a whole series of processes which helped to revitalise the arts.

Dada typography, 1918. Back and front cover for Club Dada. Only one number of this magazine was issued.

Fountain, *1915, by* Marcel Duchamp *(1887–1968). (Galleria Schwarz, Milan)*

The Law of Chance

The story is told of an important discovery made by the artist Jean Arp, one of the founders of Dada. Arp, dissatisfied with a drawing which he had just completed, tore it up and allowed the pieces to fall on the floor. He was amazed to find that the resulting pattern was a great deal closer to his original idea. The absent-minded procedure of tearing the drawing and casually allowing the pieces to drift together had produced a more vital work than all his *conscious* efforts had achieved.

His experiments with chance lead Arp to the conclusion that he had stumbled upon a real source of creative energy. He knew that this source of energy lay within himself; the secret lay in bypassing the conscious, calculating, parts of his mind and tapping the mental energy which lies much deeper, in the subconscious.

Drawings, constructions in wood, sculptures, and poems were no longer 'calculated' consciously, but allowed to 'happen' in an almost absent-minded fashion.

Arp claimed that 'Dada is *against* art, and *for* life.' By this he meant that the art of the past had been over-sophisticated and had become separated from its elementary natural roots. Dada was against such a separation of 'art' and 'life'. A return to basics was required. Throughout his long career Arp strove to make this return to basics.

Readymades

Other Dadaists echoed Arp's dictum that 'Dada is against art', but in a more direct, violent manner. The French artist Marcel Duchamp, who had begun his career as a Cubist, caused something of a scandal in the art world by exhibiting mass-produced objects purchased in a shop, as works of art. Possibly the most notorious of these was his 'Fountain', a urinal which he derisively signed 'R. Mutt'. A reproduction of Leonardo's famous 'Mona Lisa', with moustache and beard added in pencil, gave cause for further offence. Here, too, Duchamp had added insult to injury with his title 'L.H.O.O.Q'. (a pun! In French it sounds like 'Elle a chaud au cul').

What Duchamp was doing, in his own wry fashion, was to ask a few very basic questions—which still require to be asked: What is a 'work of art'? Can a mass-produced object be a work of art? Is a urinal or a shovel, or a reproduction of a painting? If not, then why not?

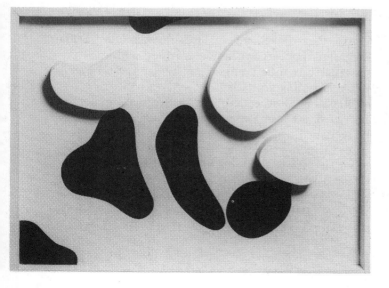

Constellation according to the Law of Chance, c. *1932, by* Jean Arp *(1887–1966). Painted wood relief. (Tate Gallery, London, © A.D.A.G.P.)*

Photomontage

The technique of cutting images from a variety of photographs and reassembling them to form a new and often highly incongruous picture is called 'photomontage'. The technique has become very familiar in recent years through exploitation by the advertising media. Nevertheless it was invented by two Dadaists, Johnnie Heartfield and George Grosz, working in Berlin.

To sum up—the Dada movement, while militating against all forms of reason and culture, helped create a climate of greater freedom which was to be of inestimable value to artists during the ensuing half century. Indeed, the rich seam of possibility, originally uncovered by Dada, is still being mined by today's artists as we shall see later.

Surrealism

Dada was amusing, thought-provoking, irritating—a breath of fresh air in any case. The fact that it consistently refused to take itself seriously, further endears it. But it was far too anarchic to last. By the early twenties its members had split into several factions and had turned to rend each other.

Then, from the ruins a new movement arose—like a phoenix from the ashes!—arguably the most powerful, influential and long lasting artistic movement of the twentieth century. It was called 'Surrealism' and was the brain-child of one man, the French poet André Breton. Breton had been quick to grasp the potential which existed in Dada and he rapidly set about gathering the pieces of that broken movement. He was also determined to rectify the one great fault which he saw in Dada—the total lack of any sense of direction. Under Breton's strong-willed leadership Surrealism coalesced into a movement which suddenly found itself with a purpose.

Breton had been deeply influenced by the ideas of the Viennese doctor Sigmund Freud. Freud, the father of psychology, had shocked the Western world by his discovery that man is dominated by powerful unconscious forces which he may be able to redirect but not control. The purpose of Surrealism was to 'tune-in' to these same unconscious forces.

Many devices, like 'automatic writing' and 'exquisite corpse', were employed by the Surrealists to further their research. Automatic writing entails relaxing completely and then writing down whatever enters the mind without any revision whatsoever. Some startling results may be obtained by anyone who employs this method *honestly*. An 'exquisite corpse' drawing is made by a number of people. The first draughtsman begins his drawing at the top of a sheet of paper and on completing his portion folds down the top and passes the sheet to the second participant. It is important that

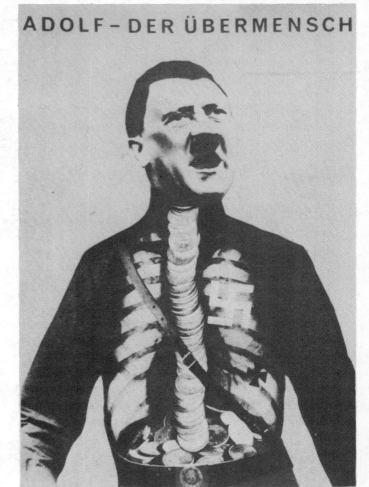

ADOLF – DER ÜBERMENSCH

SCHLUCKT GOLD UND REDET BLECH

Adolf—Der Übermensch, *by* Johnnie Heartfield (1891–1968). Photomontage. *The caption which accompanies Heartfield's derisive portrait of Hitler reads: 'Adolf the superman, eats gold and spits out rubbish.'*

the second participant should not have seen what has gone before. The drawing proceeds in this fashion until completed. Bizarre sentences may also be composed by the 'exquisite corpse' method. In fact the odd title for the process comes from one of these: 'The exquisite/corpse/shall drink/the bubbling wine.'

Max Ernst's 'Napoleon in the Wilderness' is a superb example of one aspect of Surrealist painting. There is a bland realism about the sky, the sea and the rocks covered with seaweed—but those two figures and the curious pillar which stands between them? What are we to make of them?

There is, of course, no logical explanation: in the same way many dreams have no logical explanation. Only the conscious mind is ruled by logic and reason—the subconscious has laws peculiar to itself. The Surrealist artists themselves did not seek to interpret their own works; their job was simply to dredge

Napoleon in the Wilderness, *1941, by* Max Ernst *(b. 1891). (Museum of Modern Art, New York). Ernst employed a technique called decalcomania to begin this picture. Thinned paint was pressed on to the canvas with a pane of glass; this spread the paint unevenly over the surface of the canvas and the resulting irregular areas of colour and texture then inspired the artist to interpret them as forms.*

up the imagery from the subconscious.

Max Ernst often began his pictures with random blots or drips of colour. Just as the average person may discover all manner of images in the fire or in a bank of clouds, so Ernst 'found' images in his blots. Once discovered, these images were then fully developed with the brush—the result being a painting like 'Napoleon in the wilderness'.

Artists like Jean Arp, some of whose work we have already looked at, and the Catalan Joan Miró, show us the other face of Surrealist painting.

Look at Miró's 'Person throwing a stone at a Bird'.

Person Throwing a Stone at a Bird, *1926, by* Joan Miró *(b. 1893). (Museum of Modern Art, New York)*

Here there is no attempt at photographic dream-imagery. Miró's 'person' is just about recognisable as such. A rudimentary foot, body, head and eye may all be identified, but the more immediate impression is of some amoeba-like creature which has escaped from under a biologist's microscope. Imagery in painting or sculpture which suggests a variety of basic natural forms, particularly organic, is termed 'Biomorphic'.

A further example of biomorphic imagery may be seen in this sculpture by Henry Moore (whose work may be seen in several locations around Dublin). Moore's figures in wood, stone or bronze, evoke a whole range of natural forms. There is frequently a dominant human element, with powerful suggestions of other natural forms—sea-worn stones, bones, weathered timber, and even landscapes. Although Moore was never a member of the Surrealist Movement he was deeply influenced by their ideas and exhibited with them on several occasions.

The paintings of René Magritte and Salvador Dali return us to the disturbing world of dreams and ambiguity. The shoes in the Magritte painting appear to be in the process of metamorphosing into the feet of their owner.

During the years between the two great wars, many artists, who were not actual members of the Surrealist movement, were profoundly affected by its discoveries (or developed along a parallel course by themselves). This is true of several artists whose work we have already discussed in other contexts, most notably Pablo Picasso and Paul Klee.

The late thirties saw the departure from Europe of many influential artists, a number of the Surrealists among them. Europe's loss was a gain for the United States. The influx of European talent into cities like New York had considerable effect upon the consequent development of North American art. After the

Reclining Figure *by* Henry Moore *(b. 1898). (Tate Gallery, London,* © *Henry Moore)*

Le Model Rouge *by* René Magritte *(1898–1967). (Edward James Foundation)*

Metamorphosis of Narcissus *by* Salvador Dali *(b. 1904). (Edward James Foundation). Dali was the best known member of the Surrealist group thanks to his talents as a painter but also to his many self-publicising activities. His art, although usually brilliant technically, is frequently marred by shallow showmanship. He eventually alienated himself from the movement. 'Dali insinuated himself into the Surrealist movement in 1929 . . . and since 1936 he has had no interest whatsoever for Surrealism.' André Breton*

Marilyn *by Andy Warhol (b. 1927). (Tate Gallery, London). Warhol is one of the best known of the New York Pop artists. 'I love Los Angeles. I love Hollywood. They're beautiful. Everybody's plastic—but I love plastic. I want to be plastic.' A. Warhol, 1968.*

war art in the U.S.A. appeared to blossom, first with the great wave of Abstract Expressionism already referred to, which became the dominant mode of expression in the late forties and throughout the fifties.

Neo-Dada

No situation remains static for very long in the twentieth century. Abstract Expressionism, with its frenzy and its insistence on extreme individualism was, in the main, a reaction against the restraints and the tensions generated by the Second World War. (During the same period the cinema produced some notable 'rebel' figures like James Dean, and a form of popular music —Rock and Roll—exemplified by Elvis Presley, emerged which expressed some of the same frenzy as Abstract Expressionism.)

By 1960 the Western world was beginning to emerge from a post-war situation, older, a little wiser and a lot more cynical. The process of forgiving and forgetting was well under way and, for better or for worse, a new era was dawning. The artistic heralds of the 'new era' began to show themselves during the early sixties, most noticeably in the U.S.A. and the U.K.

Many people, particularly professional art-critics, were appalled by the new art of the sixties, such was its sheer commonplace vulgarity. Paintings and sculptures, often executed with a brashness and a directness borrowed from the advertising media, took for their subjects every conceivable aspect of 'mass produced culture', from pop and film stars to Campbell's soup and Coca-Cola. The movement was first of all dubbed 'neo-Dada'. This was, at least in part, a tribute to the innovations of Marcel Duchamp whose 'readymades' seemed to find so many echoes in the 'supermarket-goods' which were appearing in the art galleries. Tongue-in-cheek references to the revered art of the past also seemed to echo Duchamp's 'L.H.O.O.Q.'

In England and America the term 'Pop-Art' eventually replaced the original 'neo-Dada' tag.

Donald Duck meets Mondrian, *1965, by* Eduardo Paolozzi *(b. 1924). (Courtesy Harry Holtzman, Lyme, Conn., U.S.A.) Silkscreen print from Moonstrip Empire News series. Paolozzi, who, despite his name, is British, is a sculptor and print maker. He was one of the originators of Pop art in England.*

Art Without Boundaries

Much has happened to the world during the past decade or so. Many old and revered values have been questioned or given a final push towards extinction. The term 'Future shock' has been coined to describe the increasing contemporary malaise produced by the feeling that nothing is static anymore; new ideas and values will be thrust upon us before we have been given time to appreciate or understand those we already have.

This state of affairs has been reflected in the arts. New movements rise and fall with appalling rapidity. Pop art is already relegated to history along with Cubism, Futurism etc. The traditional barriers between the various arts have largely been destroyed and many new 'media' have entered the arena.

One could mention 'Kinetic Art', largely derived from the experiments of the Constructivists. Kinetic works employ 'actual' movement—motor-driven parts may spin or vibrate, moving beams of light may flicker across a wall, even laser beams may be used to construct Kinetic works many miles across.

Some Kinetic works are made very much in the spirit of Dada. The machines made by the French artist Jean Tinguely tear or shake themselves to pieces!

'Environmental' and 'Earthworks' artists, although their work defies definition in any traditional sense, also owe something to Dada.

Environmental artists like Christo wrap up objects, including buildings and areas of coastline. Earthworks artists may dig trenches in the ground or build constructions from logs, bales of straw or boulders.

Untitled work by Richard Long *(b. 1945)*

Wrapped Coast, *1969, by* Christo *(b. 1935). One million square feet of Little Bay, Australia. Christo Javacheff was born in Bulgaria. He began making small-scale packages in 1958, but graduated to entire buildings during the sixties.*

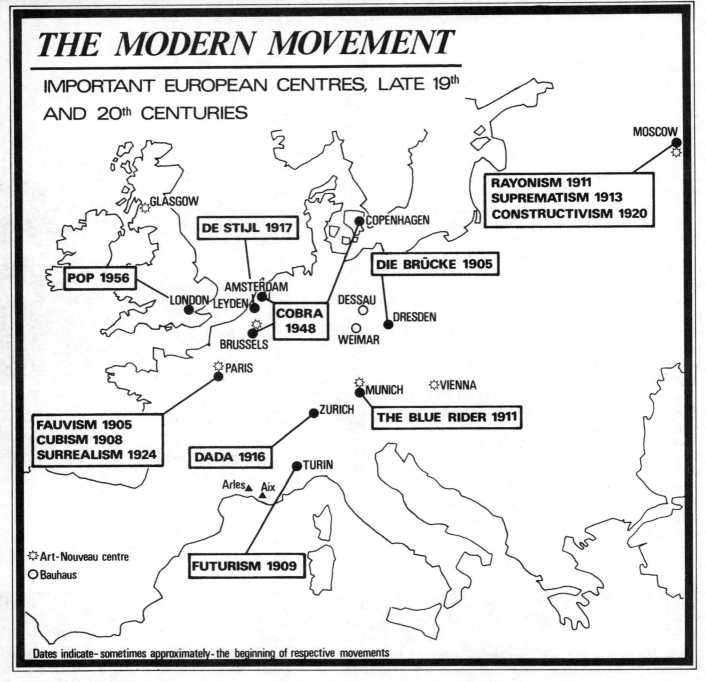

THE MODERN MOVEMENT

IMPORTANT EUROPEAN CENTRES, LATE 19th AND 20th CENTURIES

MOSCOW

RAYONISM 1911
SUPREMATISM 1913
CONSTRUCTIVISM 1920

GLASGOW

DE STIJL 1917

COPENHAGEN

DIE BRÜCKE 1905

POP 1956

AMSTERDAM
LONDON LEYDEN
COBRA 1948

DESSAU

DRESDEN

BRUSSELS
WEIMAR

PARIS

MUNICH VIENNA

ZURICH
THE BLUE RIDER 1911

FAUVISM 1905
CUBISM 1908
SURREALISM 1924

DADA 1916

TURIN

Arles▲ Aix▲

☆ Art-Nouveau centre
○ Bauhaus

FUTURISM 1909

Dates indicate - sometimes approximately - the beginning of respective movements

For further reading

General

Herbert Read, *A Concise History of Modern Painting* (Thames and Hudson)

Herbert Read, *A Concise History of Modern Sculpture* (Thames and Hudson)

A. Ozenfant, *Foundations of Modern Art* (Dover)

Larousse Encyclopaedia of Modern Art (Hamlyn)

Norbert Lynton, *The Modern World* (Hamlyn)

Edward Lucie-Smith, *Movements in Art since 1945* (Thames and Hudson)

Art and Structure

Martin Nicholson (ed.), *Circle* (Faber)

Paul Schwartz, *The Cubists* (Thames and Hudson)

Hans Jaffe, *De Stijl* (Thames and Hudson)

Umberto Apollonio (ed.), *Futurist Manifestos* (Thames and Hudson)

W. Boesiger, *Le Corbusier* (Thames and Hudson)

Le Corbusier, *Modulor* (Faber)

Frank Elgar, *Mondrian* (Thames and Hudson)

Rene Parola, *Optical Art* (Van Nost. Reinhold)

Camilla Gray, *The Russian Experiment in Art 1863–1922* (Thames and Hudson)

Jonathan Benthall, *Science and Technology in Art today* (Thames and Hudson)

John Berger, *Success and Failure of Picasso* (Penguin)

Art and Emotion
Dictionary of Expressionism (Eyre Methuen)
J. P. Hodin, *Edvard Munch* (Thames and Hudson)
Frank Whitford, *Expressionism* (Hamlyn)
Wolf-Dieter Dube, *The Expressionists* (Thames and Hudson)
Joseph-Emil Muller, *Fauvism* (Thames and Hudson)
Frank Whitford, *Kandinsky* (Hamlyn)
G. Disan Lazzaro, *Klee*, (Thames and Hudson)
Maurice Tuchman, *The New York School* (Thames and Hudson)
Paul Klee, *Paul Klee on Modern Art* (Faber)
Jean Selz, *Vlaminck* (Uffici)

Art and the Subconscious
Hans Richter, *Dada, Art and Anti-Art* (Thames and Hudson)
Dictionary of Surrealism (Eyre Methuen)
Adrian Henri, *Environments and Happenings* (Thames and Hudson)
Uwe M. Schneede, *The Essential Max Ernst* (Thames and Hudson)
Herbert Read, *Jean Arp* (Thames and Hudson)
Massimo Carra (ed.), *Metaphysical Art* (Thames and Hudson)
Michael Compton, *Pop Art* (Hamlyn)
Sarane Alexandrian, *Surrealist Art* (Thames and Hudson)
Calvin Tomkins, *The World of Marcel Duchamp* (Time-Life)

Practical Exercises

The various twentieth-century art movements provide a rich source of ideas for the practical art-class. A small number of possibilities are set out below. Many similar ideas, or variations on these, will probably suggest themselves to individual art-teachers. Topics dealt with in art appreciation classes might be followed up soon afterwards on a practical level.

1 Cubism

(*a*) Construct a picture entirely from basic geometrical solids—cylinders, spheres, cubes etc. Leave out all detail. Black and white Conté chalk, or crayons, on toned paper are possibly the most suitable materials.
(*b*) Pieces of wallpaper, newspaper, wrapping paper etc. may be stuck onto a painting, or the entire picture may be constructed as a collage.

2 Futurism

(*a*) Make an outline drawing of a figure in motion—a runner, cyclist etc., and trace this drawing a number of times onto a sheet of paper so that the drawings overlap and a line of figures runs across the paper. Develop in colour.
(*b*) Large photographs, with good contrast between figure and background may be developed to create a sense of Futurist movement. Full-page photographs from magazines are ideal for the purpose. Cut the photographs into regular vertical strips approximately 1 cm in width. Glue these carefully onto a sheet of paper so that the strip from the extreme left is stuck down on the right. All of the remainder must follow in their correct order, left always going to the right.

3 Mondrian

Make an abstract picture from strips of black paper stuck down onto white. A variety of widths and lengths may be used, the pieces being moved about until a suitable asymmetrical balance is achieved. Rectangles of coloured paper may be added, likewise strips of lettering cut from magazines or newspapers.

4 Op Art

Divide a sheet of white paper with regularly spaced parallel lines. Carefully paint the resulting strips in contrasting colours. Alternating red and green probably works best. Cut a series of concentric rings from the painting and carefully glue these onto a second sheet. Start with the centre and before sticking each circle into place rotate it slightly so that the original parallel lines are disrupted. Op Art offers many other possibilities.

5 Fauvism

Make an outline tracing from a naturalistic painting —landscape, figure, still-life—onto a sheet of white paper. Paint the drawing, ignoring naturalistic colour combinations. Aim for maximum colour-contrast (red-green, blue-orange etc.) and avoid using black, gray or brown. Try to use colours with approximately equivalent tone values.

6 Expressionism

(*a*) Try to make a picture as ugly as possible (in terms of colour, subject, distortions in drawing etc.) This is not as easy as it sounds.
(*b*) Make a large cardboard-cut. Use mainly jagged pieces of cardboard to build up the image. Ink in black or a number of colours.
(*c*) Make a self-portrait or a portrait of an acquaintance, distorting your drawing in order to stress the subject's character rather than appearance.

7 Dada, Surrealism

(a) Photomontage offers endless possibilities especially if a large quantity of illustrated magazines is available.

(b) Exquisite-corpse drawings (see text).

(c) Biomorphic abstractions may be tackled in a number of ways: as free-flowing pencil 'scribbles' developed in colour, as cardboard or hardboard reliefs built up rather like contour maps, or as carvings made in soap, plaster, or wood (particularly driftwood).

8 Pop-Art

This movement also suggests a vast number of possibilities:

(a) A single frame from a comic may be projected by means of an overhead projector onto a large sheet of paper. Use a broad black felt marker for the lines, and paint in flat, bright colours.

(b) Make a large soft sculpture in cloth, or a papier-mâché sculpture, based on some common commodity—a toothpaste tube, vegetables, slice of cake etc.

9 Kinetic Art

Mobiles may be constructed from a variety of materials. A small electric motor could easily be geared to power a mobile, or mobile relief, of modest dimensions. A cluster of small mirrors (tin plate or aluminium pieces with bright surfaces) allowed to hang in a darkened room and illuminated by spotlamp can produce spectacular results.

	Some Important Events		Building and Visual Arts
		1866	Birth of W. Kandinsky (d. 1944)
		1867	Birth of E. Nolde (d. 1956)
		1869	Birth of H. Matisse (d. 1954)
		1871	Birth of G. Rouault (d. 1958)
		1872	Birth of P. Mondrian (d. 1944)
		1879	Birth of P. Klee (d. 1940)
		1881	Birth of P. Picasso (d. 1973) Birth of F. Léger (d. 1955)
		1883	Birth of W. Gropius
		1887	Birth of Le Corbusier (d. 1965) Birth of J. Gris (d. 1927) Birth of J. Arp (d. 1966) Birth of M. Duchamp (d. 1968)
		1890	Birth of N. Gabo
		1891	Birth of M. Ernst
		1893	Birth of J. Miró
		1898	Birth of H. Moore
1900	Freud—*Interpretation of Dreams*	1900	Impressionist and post-Impressionist art shown at Paris World Exhibition
1901	Marconi—demonstration of radio		
1903	Wright brothers—powered flight		
		1904	Birth of S. Dali
1905	Einstein—special theory of relativity	1905	The Fauves at Autumn Salon Formation of Die Brücke—Dresden
		1907	Picasso—Les Demoiselles d'Avignon
1908	H. Ford—First model T cars	1908–9	First Cubist pictures

	Some Important Events		Building and Visual Arts
1909	Blériot—flight across Channel	1909–10	Kandinsky—first experiments in abstract painting
		1909	First Futurist Manifesto
		1910	Birth of F. Bacon
		1911	Blue Rider formed in Munich
1912	Suffragette riot in Whitehall	1912	Birth of J. Pollock (d. 1956)
1913	Cinema—D. W. Griffith's Birth of a Nation Stravinsky—Rite of Spring	1913–14	Extensive use of collage by Cubists
		1913	Armory show—New York's first extensive view of modern European art
1914	Outbreak of First World War	1914	W. Gropius appointed first director of Weimar Bauhaus
1915	Freud—The Unconscious		
1916	Battle of the Somme Einstein—general theory of relativity	1916	Cabaret Voltaire, Zürich—Dada
		1916–27	Rouault—Miserere series
1917	Eric Satie—Parade, a 'Cubist' ballet Bolshevik revolution in Russia	1917	G. T. Rietveld—Red, blue chair
1919	First trans-Atlantic flight Rutherford—nucleus of atom split		
		1920	International Dada Fair, Berlin Klee invited to join Bauhaus
1922	James Joyce—Ulysses	1922	Kandinsky invited to join Bauhaus
		1924	First Surrealist Manifesto
		1925	Bauhaus moved to Dessau
		c. 1925	Picasso—beginning of Surreal phase
1926	General Strike in Britain		
		1927	Birth of A. Warhol
		1929	H. Moore—first reclining figure
1933	Hitler Chancellor of Germany	1933	Many artists leave Germany
1936	Beginning of Spanish Civil War	1936	S. Dali—Premonition of a Civil War
1937	Guernica destroyed by German bombs	1937	Picasso's mural Guernica Exhibition of 'Degenerate Art' organised by Nazis in Munich
1939	Outbreak of Second World War		
1944	D-Day landings in Normandy		
1945	Atomic bombs used on Japan		
1948	Beginning of Cold War	1948	Drip technique evolved by Pollock Picasso—ceramics
		1948–50	The Cobra Group
1949	G. Orwell—Nineteen Eighty-four		

	Some Important Events		Building and Visual Arts
1950	Korean War	1950	Le Corbusier—Ronchamp chapel Matisse—large pictures in cut paper.
		1952	Le Corbusier—Marseille block
1953	Watson and Crick—Model of DNA Beckett—*Waiting for Godot*		
		1955	Professorship for Albers—Yale
1957	Sputnik 1 launched Cinema—Bergman's Seventh Seal		
		1958	Christo—first packages
1960	Berlin Wall erected	1960s	Hard Edge, Pop Art and OP Art
1961	First man in space		
		1962	Bacon—three studies for a Crucifixion
1963	Assassination of J. F. Kennedy		
		1964	A. Warhol—Brillo boxes
1969	Armstrong and Aldrin on the moon	1969	Christo—wrapped coast, Little Bay, Australia
		1971	Christo—Curtain hung across valley in Colorado
1974	Revolution in Portugal		
1975	Viet Cong victory		

PART II

General Remarks

When we look at a representational painting we tend to respond to far more than just the subject matter. Whether we are aware of it or not the various elements of the work—colours, tones, textures, lines, forms etc.—will affect us in some way. There are, for instance, 'sad' colours and 'happy' ones, shapes which seem to be intrinsically violent and those which exude calm. It is often the case that the *treatment* of subjects in a work is far more important than the actual subjects themselves.

Where abstract art is concerned we are forced to confront only the raw materials—the elements like colour, tone etc. They must convey the artist's 'message' without the aid of subject matter (cf. music).

And with sculpture and architecture the same or similar principles apply; how the artist organises his materials is all important.

In this part of the book we shall look briefly at some of the 'raw materials' of the visual arts, and at some of the ways artists work with them.

CHAPTER SIX

Colour

The Spectrum

When sunlight passes through a piece of glass triangular in section—a prism—it breaks up, or decomposes into a number of clearly distinguishable colours. Something similar occurs when, after a shower of rain, sunlight filtering through the atmosphere becomes decomposed by the minute droplets of water in its path. A rainbow is formed. And in the rainbow we find the same basic colours, six in number, and always occurring in the same order. From these, the colours of the spectrum—red, orange, yellow, green, blue and violet—all other colours (at least in theory) may be mixed. They are therefore of considerable interest to the artist. The colours used by the Impressionists and Pointillists, for instance, were drawn almost exclusively from this range.

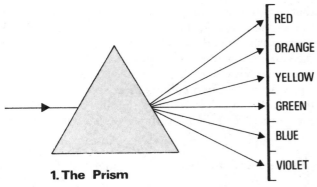

1. The Prism

One word of caution: colour in the form of light (i.e. stage lighting, colour television, coloured light used in the physics lab etc.) does not behave in exactly the same fashion as colour in the form of pigment—artist's paint. It is only with the latter that we are concerned in the ensuing discussion.

Colour Mixing

Our basic six colours may best be appreciated if we arrange them in the segments of a circle. We can now examine their properties more closely. Perhaps the most obvious point worth noting is that of the six, only three cannot be mixed: red, yellow and blue. These

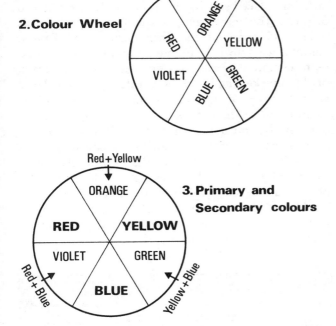

2. Colour Wheel

3. Primary and Secondary colours

Red+Yellow

Red+Blue

Yellow+Blue

three are the *primary colours,* and by mixing them in pairs we may obtain, in turn, the three *secondaries:* orange, green and violet. When we mix a primary with a secondary colour the result is a tertiary—blue and green yield turquoise, for instance. This process of mixing may continue, again in theory at least, ad infinitum.

Warm and Cool Colours

Now we must say a little about the psychology of colours: how they affect us emotionally. Most people would agree that the six basic colours mentioned above readily form two distinct families. Red, orange and yellow seem to belong naturally together; they suggest cheerfulness, liveliness and warmth. Green, blue and violet, on the other hand, suggest rather different characteristics; these are restful, cool and sometimes depressing (people once spoke of feeling 'blue', and 'the Blues', a modern form of North American Negro folk music, essentially sad and soulful, derives its title from this concept).

The two families of colours are referred to as 'warm' and 'cool' respectively.

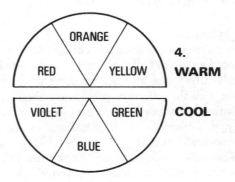

4. WARM COOL

Most colour schemes devised by designers and painters contain representatives from both temperature families; warm colours are used to balance, or complement, cool ones. Occasionally however, the designer or painter wishes to create a particular effect, and deliberately chooses *only* from one or other of the two families.

The designer advertising a well-known brand of cigarette, 'cool as a mountain stream' (*sic*), chooses only blues and greens for his visual, and thus hopes to lend greater emphasis to his message.

During the early years of the present century Pablo Picasso painted a number of pictures concerned largely with depressing themes like poverty and starvation. These, the paintings of his Blue Period, were composed almost exclusively in deep sombre blues and greens. Even flesh was given an unpleasant greenish hue. The colours chosen by Picasso, while they were not at all naturalistic, seem perfectly appropriate to the images which he created. The cold and depressing blues and greens somehow make the plight of his blind beggars and other unfortunates seem all the more desperate.

If blues and greens can be positively employed to express concepts ranging from pleasant coolness to depressing coldness it follows that reds, yellows and oranges may, in their turn, be used for similar ends. Once again we might quote an example from cigarette advertising. This time the product is marketed in a golden packet; the selling point here is richness, mellowness and pleasant warmth. The golden packet is therefore presented against a background of exclusively warm tones—polished mahogany or autumnal trees.

Many painters have used warm colours to great effect. Vincent Van Gogh, soon after his arrival in Arles, painted several pictures to celebrate his immense enthusiasm for the Mediterranean sun, and the great sense of optimism which he felt at that time. These were his 'Sunflowers', composed in yellows and rich golden hues.

Renoir too has used exclusively warm colour combinations to emphasise his feeling of *joie de vivre*, particularly in his late pictures of nude bathers, voluptuously basking in the summer sun.

Colour Harmony

As every painter soon discovers colours have a 'life' or 'force' of their own. Colours when placed side by side invariably affect one another to some degree; sometimes they clash violently, sometimes they 'destroy' one another and sometimes they appear to work together, to *harmonise*. Colour harmonies are arrived at in a number of ways:

(*a*) When all the colours are derived from the same temperature family, as described above, or are very close neighbours on the colour wheel.

(*b*) When all the colours are diluted by mixing each with the same colour. This might be black or gray or any one of the spectrum colours.

(*c*) The neutral colours, or browns, also tend to harmonise.

But harmony is only one way to use colours; it is certainly not the only 'right' way, and is quite possibly not the most exciting or creative way. According to the influential teacher of visual design Maurice de Sausmarez, the above concepts of harmony are 'of interest only to fifth-rate interior decorators and pseudo-sophisticated amateurs'. Strong words, but useful in that they remind us that the most obvious and safest paths don't necessarily lead to areas of richest discovery.

Colour Contrast: Complementaries

Try the following experiment. Take a piece of paper coloured bright red, and two smaller pieces coloured orange and bright green respectively. First place the red piece on a flat surface and then lay the orange piece in the centre. Note the effect which one colour has on the other. Now remove the orange piece and replace it with the green.

You will probably find the difference in effect very marked indeed.

Orange and red are so closely related to one another that when they are placed together nothing really interesting happens; they blend or harmonise. Red and green clash violently however. They seem to bring out the best in each other, when placed side by side; the red becomes even redder' and the green 'greener', and the edges where the two colours meet seem to vibrate as though the two colours were literally trying to repel each other. This is an example of *'colour contrast'*.

7. Complementaries

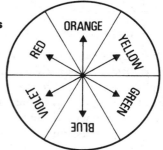

Now look at the colour wheel once more. Notice how the green and red segments occur diametrically opposite to each other. So also do the other sets of complementaries: orange—blue, and yellow—violet. Each colour has its complementary; a colour wheel with twelve segments, which included all the tertiary colours, would yield six pairs.

The vibrant effect created when the two complementaries are placed side by side is naturally of interest to painters. The Impressionists and Post-Impressionists were well aware of the phenomenon, and Fauvist painting was virtually founded upon it. Find a good reproduction of a Fauve painting—by Matisse, Derain, or Vlaminck—and note how often blue is placed against strong orange, red against green and yellow against violet. The Fauves believed that by using colours in this most violent fashion they would best express the true vibrancy of nature. Expressionist artists—Van Gogh, Die Brücke and the Blue Rider—have also made great use of colour contrast, often in a way very similar to the Fauves. This is also true of the later work of the Irish painter Jack Yeats, and of the work of many of the Op artists, particularly Victor Vasarely (see front cover).

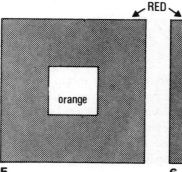

5.

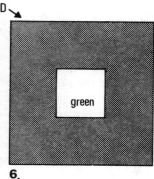

6.

When a pair of complementaries are mixed together they 'destroy' one another, and a neutral colour or brown is formed. Some painters prefer to use only neutrals: the Cubists for instance.

Practical Exercises

1 Analyse a number of paintings purely from the point of view of colour. Use good reproductions, or go to see the real thing if possible. Choose a number of painters who approach the use of colour in widely differing ways: Rembrandt, Monet and Vasarely, for instance. Note what range of colours each employs and whether each works towards harmony or contrast.

2 Make three versions of the same picture, (*a*) in naturalistic colours, (*b*) in either warm or cool colours, or in a range of browns, (*c*) in clashing pairs of complementaries, (i.e. a Fauve painting).

CHAPTER SEVEN

Tone

Tone means simply how light or how dark something is by comparison with one or other of the two extremes black and white. It follows that every colour has a tone value; pure blue for instance, is obviously a much deeper tone than pure yellow, although both have exactly the same amount of colour value or *'chroma'*.

The ability to distinguish degrees of light and dark is fundamental to seeing. Many animals rely on this alone, being unable to distinguish colours. Those of us with full colour vision are still able to make sense of pictorial matter—moving or still—presented only in tonal form. Witness the reproductions of paintings in this book. And most people were perfectly happy with black and white—or purely tonal—pictures on their TV screens before the advertising industry made it clear that colour reception was really so much better!

Between the two extremes of black and white there exists the possibility of an infinite number of grays. Whereas this may seem an intriguing concept to the mathematician it is hardly helpful to the painter. How does one go about manipulating an infinite number of tones? One doesn't even try, of course, and many painters solve this problem in practice by reducing the number of tones to something manageable; say four or even less. Some Rembrandt paintings may be resolved into just two areas of tone—a distinctly light and a distinctly dark area. This ignores a number of small transitional passages where light fuses with dark, but it is, in essence, a true statement.

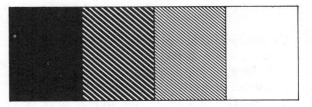

8. Four Tone Scale

Daumier's superb 'Blanchisseuse', already discussed in Part I, readily breaks down to three distinct tones. Compare the tonal analysis (diagram 9) with the reproduction. Here the artist is not merely making life simpler for himself by reducing his tones to an easily manageable few. He uses his blatant contrasts to intensify his chief image—to make it both more forceful and more memorable. It is the stooped head of the washerwoman, along with her shoulders and powerful right arm which are emphasised with greatest clarity.

9. Tonal Analysis: Daumier

While a simplified tonal structure may be used to lend dramatic effect to a single image, it may also be used as a means of simplifying a composition containing a large number of elements. Both Rembrandt and Rubens were masters in this field. If we make a tracing

AH—6

from a reproduction of a painting like Rubens's 'Horrors of War', ignoring the individual figures and instead pencilling around the areas of light and dark, a purely abstract concept emerges as may be seen in diagram 10. The outlines of the figures have been indicated here so that the diagram may more readily be related to the reproduction in Part I.

Practical Exercises

1 Analyse the tonal schemes of a number of paintings. Remember that an analysis is essentially an oversimplification so when making tracings ignore the subtleties and concentrate only on broad areas.
2 Make a tone scale like that shown in diagram 8. Use the four tones to make a simple painting of say, a landscape. Make sure a tonal pattern clearly emerges as in the Daumier or the Rubens. Trace the outlines of your painting onto a new sheet of paper. Use the same tone scale for the second picture but this time reverse the values, i.e. make the lightest areas the darkest etc. How do the two pictures differ in effect?

10. Tonal Analysis: Rubens

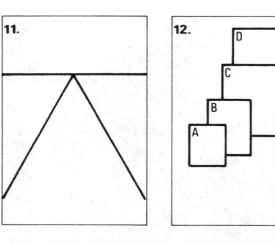

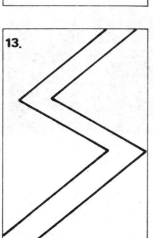

CHAPTER EIGHT

Space

Look at these three diagrams. All are very simple yet each clearly suggests the idea of space—that the lines in diagrams 11 and 13 and some of the shapes in diagram 12 are some distance 'behind' the surface of the paper. In the first diagram the two diagonals are automatically read as representing the sides of a road stretching off into the distance; the horizontal automatically becomes the horizon. Yet there are merely three straight lines drawn here.

In the second diagram shape D seems to be located furthest away from us, behind all the others, while shape A appears to be in front. This illusion persists although the shapes grow larger as they appear to recede.

It follows that creating the illusion of space is basically a very simple matter indeed: controlling it and using it creatively is something else however.

The following diagrams indicate in simple terms how painters at different periods have tackled the problem.

The painters of the Middle Ages created space in a very similar fashion to that indicated in diagram 12. The figures are flattened and stacked like playing cards on top of one another. This creates a feeling of very shallow space. Oblique or diagonal lines were often employed, however, to increase the pictorial depth.

The painters of the Renaissance (and sculptors like Donatello) created deep tracts of space in their paintings by the use of mathematical perspective. Their perspective schemes often involved very complex geometrical drawing. The subject of perspective itself is really far too complex for thorough analysis here, but a simple perspective scheme is set out at the end of this section (diagram 20).

The painters of the Baroque period were well acquainted with the various concepts of perspective and frequently made use of them to create deep space in their pictures (cf. Baroque ceilings). Painters like Rubens frequently created a feeling of depth by means of a series of diagonal bands of tone which lead the eye ever deeper into the pictorial space.

The Japanese artists of the eighteenth century did not use perspective in the Renaissance sense; they were very conscious of space however and used a system of diagonals similar to diagram 13.

Towards the end of the nineteenth century a number of European artists were influenced by the Japanese. In some of the pictures of Degas and Toulouse Lautrec, for instance, a space-making system very similar to the Japanese is employed.

With Cubism, particularly in the late, or synthetic phase, we have a return to the 'playing card' system of the medieval artists. The various components of many Cubist paintings look as though they were painted onto separate pieces of paper and stuck down one on top of the other. And indeed certain Cubist paintings —the collages—were made in almost this way.

Aerial Perspective

We have all noticed how distant objects—a range of mountains for instance—become vague or softened in outline, and bluish in colour. These effects are caused mainly by vapour in the atmosphere, and are of particular interest to landscape painters. The Impressionists were among those who have made a close study of what has been termed 'aerial perspective'.

Practical Exercises

1 Analyse a number of paintings from different periods. Use good reproductions if possible; trace the main outlines of figures, buildings etc., and try to determine in each case exactly what space-making concept the artist is using.

2 Find some reproductions of abstract paintings by artists like Mondrian, Pollock and Vasarely. Is there a feeling of space in the work of any of these artists? Are abstract paintings always flat?

3 Invent a simple picture of a landscape, with buildings, people, trees, roads etc. Make at least three different versions of it, using a different space-making concept for each one.

14. Medieval

15. Renaissance

16. Baroque

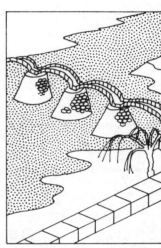

17. Japanese

18. Late 19th c.

19. 20th c. Cubism

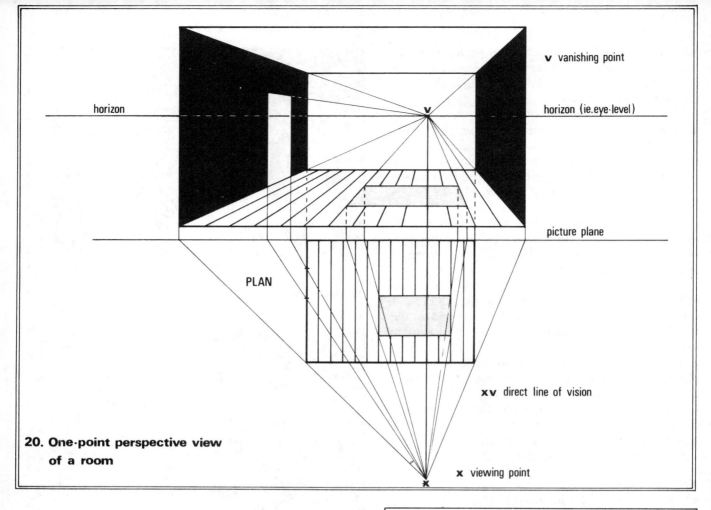

v vanishing point

horizon

horizon (ie. eye-level)

picture plane

PLAN

x v direct line of vision

20. One-point perspective view of a room

x viewing point

CHAPTER NINE

Movement

We have already noted, in the discussion on space, how we tend to attribute a feeling of depth to certain combinations of straight lines. This is really a cultural phenomenon, part of the way most of us have learned to 'see'. Now look at diagram 21.

Although a sense of illusory depth is not created here, the lines do seem to add up to something more than just lines. Most people will tend to follow the direction indicated by each line, and automatically jump from the end of one line onto the next, thus keeping the 'movement' going. These lines appear to flow or move about a vaguely defined centre.

And how much greater this effect is when the lines are suitably broadened and tapered, and arrow heads are added. The designers of directional signs and technical diagrams know all about this apparent property of lines and arrows to convey a strong sense of *direction*. So too do painters.

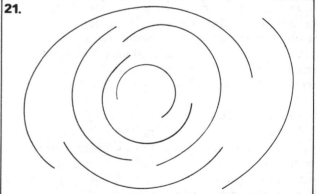

21.

22.

Now look back to the reproduction of Turner's 'Snow-storm—Steamboat off a Harbour's Mouth' in Part I. Turner's painting was concerned with violent natural movement—the turbulence of sea and airborne sleet. How does diagram 22 help to clarify the compositional machinery of this picture?

The very striking composition of Tintoretto's 'Origins of the Milky Way' has also been discussed in Part I. There are many beautiful subsidiary currents of movement in this painting, but only the major ones have been isolated in the analytical diagram (23).

The 'story' which Turner's painting tells is a simple one and might be summed up as 'the power and violence of nature rendering the works of man utterly insignificant'. The dynamics of his composition powerfully drives this message home. Tintoretto's 'story' is rather more complex, however, but exactly the same general principle applies: the dynamics of the composition are all directed towards making the story more dramatic. You may remember that the infant Heracles, who has been put to the breast of Hera, is central to the story. Notice how his figure is also central to the composition; the major lines of movement all seem to converge upon him. Thus even if we did not know the original legend upon which the painting was based, its composition alone would still act as some kind of guide.

Diagram 24 analyses the movement in Poussin's composition 'Bacchanalian Revel before a Term of Pan' reproduced in Part I. How does this composition compare with the other two discussed in this section?

23. Dynamic Composition: Tintoretto

Practical Exercises

1 Analyse the dynamic composition (or movement) of a number of paintings from different periods. Trace the main lines of each composition and arrow—preferably in red—what you consider to be the most important lines of movement. Suggested painters: Uccello, Michelangelo, El Greco, Delacroix, Van Gogh, The Futurists, Kandinsky, Pollock.

2 Try to make use of dynamic composition in your own painting, both figurative and abstract. For figurative paintings choose violent subjects: 'a storm', 'fight', etc.

24. Poussin

Sculpture and Architecture—Art in Real Space

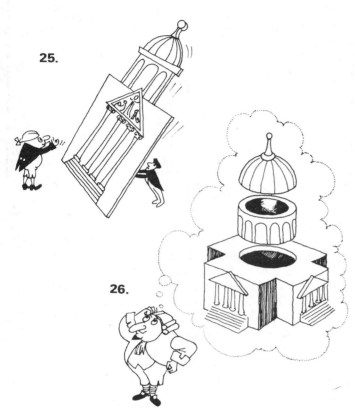

25.

26.

When a painter creates the feeling of space or weight in his picture he creates an illusion; in fact his painting remains just as flat as before. One stands in front of a painting in order to view it, and there are a limited number of angles from which it may be seen properly; step too far to the left or the right and the images become distorted. All of which is very obvious, and only stated so baldly in order to emphasise some of the main differences between painting and the two other major visual art forms: sculpture and architecture.

Both the sculptor and the architect work with real solid forms, real weight and real depth. Because their work exists 'in the round' one must walk around it (and, in the case of buildings, also through it) in order to appreciate it fully. And, of course photographs in books, no matter how excellent, are of far less value than photographs of paintings because of this.

The work of the sculptor and the architect exists 'in the round', so it follows that both these artists tend to think 'in the round'. The architects responsible for building Europe's great churches for instance—Gothic, Renaissance or Baroque—did not simply design the façades and the sides as though they were a series of flat stage sets. They must have been conscious at all times that essentially they were working with solids—blocks, cylinders and hemispheres etc.

Consider this work by the English sculptor Henry Moore (q.v.). The subject is quite obviously that of a reclining woman though Moore is hardly trying to tell

27. *(National Gallery of Canada, Ottawa/Henry Moore)*

us 'a woman looks like this'. He has taken far too many liberties with her form for this to be the case. The figure does have head, arms, breasts, legs, etc. but these merely tell us that the female form was the artist's starting point. What he has to tell us about his material is probably of more importance: this figure is made of stone, hard, heavy and unwieldy; she was cut from a block and so remains block-like. The sculptor is concerned to remain 'true to his material'. And this is by no means a modern concern. Compare Moore's figure with other works in stone from different periods: from Egypt and Greece, for instance, as well as figures by Michelangelo, Maillol and Brancusi.

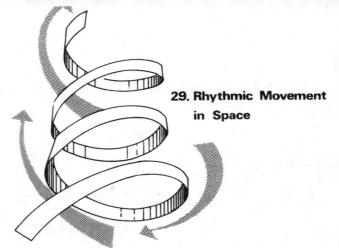

29. Rhythmic Movement in Space

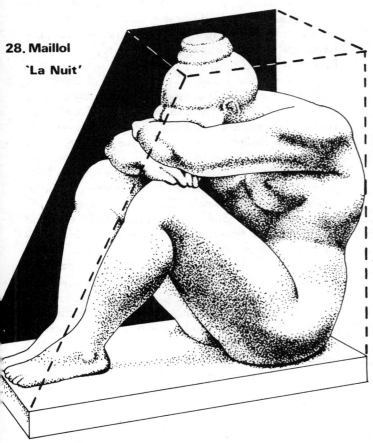

28. Maillol 'La Nuit'

Figure related to the block

30. Jean de Bologne

Sculptors from many periods have been concerned to stress the solid, block-like quality of their work; others have gone to the other extreme. In Part I we have seen how Baroque art was essentially an art of movement, and above we have discussed some of the mechanics of movement when applied to painting. Baroque sculptors working in stone often went to some lengths to escape from the heaviness of their material and the simple form of the block (cf. Bernini). Their work was often based on the form of the coiled spring (diagram 29), a three dimensional form which

seems to twist rhythmically back and forth in space. Compare diagram 30, based on a sculpture by Jean de Bologne, with the previous drawing of a coiled spring and this point should become clearer. Now turn back to the chapter on Baroque art and look at the photographs of work by Bernini and Pierre Puget.

Can you think of any works of architecture which seem to contradict the heavy quality of the stone from which they are built?

CHAPTER ELEVEN

Some Notes on Cézanne's Composition

31. Decorative Arabesques: Cézanne

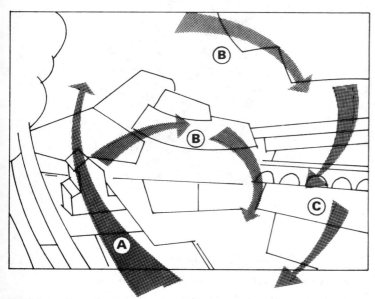

32. Composition with Space: Cézanne

A Movement into space
B Movement A deflected
C Movement back to picture plane

The paintings of the great Post-Impressionist Paul Cézanne have already been discussed in some detail in Part I. We have seen how the elements of his pictures were conceived on several simultaneous levels: colour is both harmony and structural agent; forms (i.e. lines and shapes) are both flat and decorative, but also help to describe deep three-dimensional space.

Let us look again at the view of Mont-Sainte-Victoire. The flat decorative quality of this painting is easy to appreciate. Diagram 31 stresses only the curves and makes clearer the decorative relationship between the three main elements: the mountain/landscape, the tree-trunk and the rhythmic arabesques of the branches.

This painting also conveys a great sense of depth and Cézanne, like all great artists, was not merely content to create an effect; it had to be completely under his control. The various pieces of the landscape—buildings, trees, hedges, bridges etc.—are conceived as a series of coherent steps to guide the observer into the picture space, and, very subtly, back out again. Diagram 32 demonstrates, albeit rather crudely, the basic mechanism of Cézanne's 'Composition with space'. Find some good (and large) reproductions of some landscapes and still-life paintings by Cézanne and attempt to analyse them from this point of view.

Diagram 33 is an analysis of the still-life painting reproduced in Part I. This demonstrates, perhaps more clearly than the landscape, Cézanne's space-making and composing mechanisms (because its forms are larger and simpler). An obvious point to be noted is how the form of the table has been 'broken' in two, and 'bent' so that part of it is tilted forward in the direction of the picture plane. Basically what Cézanne has done has been to take the twisting rhythms suggested by the little Baroque Cupid (by Puget q.v.) and apply them to all of the other forms in the picture. Thus various elements—those indicated at XX, AA and BB for instance—are distorted to conform with the central motif in the composition, and a harmony is achieved.

Finally diagram 34 demonstrates a favourite device of Cézanne's for binding together many of his large, and purely invented, compositions of bathers. This is the triangular composition. When placed on its base, a triangle (particularly an isosceles triangle) gives the appearance of great stability. Its effect might be described as almost the opposite to that generated by curved lines. Artists have known about this property of the triangle for a very long time. Many Renaissance compositions, for instance, make use of its stabilising influence. Look through the reproductions in this book and try to discover a number of such compositions.

The various types of analysis suggested in this section are useful aids for understanding paintings and sculptures. They must never be regarded as the be-all and end-all, and by no means provide a full and comprehensive understanding of a work. However, a person who has analysed a painting in terms of tone, colour and the various aspects of composition, and has also given due consideration to its subject matter, must at least have given it more than a casual glance.

For further reading

Johannes Itten: *Design and Form: The Basic Course at the Bauhaus* (Thames and Hudson)

Kurt Rowland, Looking and Seeing—*4 volumes (Ginn and Company)*

Maurice de Sausmarez, Basic Design; the Dynamics of Visual Form *(Studio Vista)*

Peter Cook, Architecture: Action and Plan *(Studio Vista)*

Guy Brett, Kinetic Art: the Language of Movement *(Studio Vista)*

Patricia Sloane, Colour: Basic Principles and New Directions *(Studio Vista)*

[161]

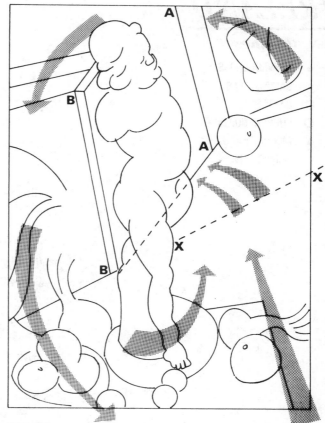

33: Cézanne

X X `Normal´ line of table

A A, B B Lines tilted out of the vertical to create tension or movement from right to left

34. Cézanne

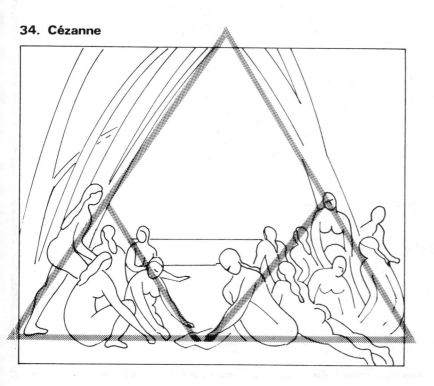

35. ?

IRELAND

KEY TO MAP

+ CARVED CROSS
s CARVED SLAB
□ CASTLE
○ CHURCH BUILDING
▲ MEGALITHIC SITE
t ROUND TOWER

Tory Island

Carndonagh
Clonca
Carrowmore

Fahan
Rathmullan

Connor

Donegal

Donaghmore

Clogher

Downpatrick

Drumcliffe
Corracloona
Armagh

Creevelea

Killala

Clones
Donaghmore

Drumlane

Fenagh

Dromiskin

Meelick
Strade

Boyle

Castlekeeran
Kilary
Monasterboice
Termonfeckin

Ballintubber

Kells

Cong

Roscommon
Inchcleraun

Newgrange
Duleek
Athcarne

Tuam
Knockmoy

Castle-
strange

Abbeyshrule

Killucan

Lusk
Swords
Howth

Claregalway

Bealin

Maynooth
Taghadoe
Finglas
Clondalkin
Kilgobbin
Tully

St Macdara's Island

Clonmac-
noise

Durrow
Tihilly

Kildare

Fassaroe

Clonfert

Old Kilcullen

Corcomroe

Lorrha

Moone
Baltinglass
Glendalough

Kilfenora

Kinnitty

Castledermot

Dysert O'Dea
Ennis

Roscrea
Timahoe
Clonmore
Killeshin

Quin
Bunratty

Holy Cross

Kilkenny

Ferns

Limerick

Ullard

Mungret

Craiguenamanagh
St Mullins

Lough Gur

Cashel
Killamery
Ahenny
Jerpoint
Enniscorthy

Dingle ○ s
Peninsula □ +

Tonaknock
Ardfert

Toureen
Kilkeeran

Gallerus oratory

Kanturk

Labbacallee

Waterford

Drumlohan s
Slade

Killarney

Blarney
Cloyne
Ardmore

Kilcrea

Kinneigh

Bantry

General Remarks

Here we shall consider the art, not of a period but of a geographical entity—Ireland. As our story begins in the prehistoric past and ends in our own period, a vast span of time must be covered within a very short space. It is impossible therefore to give a comprehensive picture; instead we shall attempt a broad sketch, highlighting certain significant works and artists. Naturally, the periods of greatest artistic richness will tend to receive most attention, while others will have to be dismissed with a few lines.

CHAPTER TWELVE

The Neolithic Period 3000 B.C.–2000 B.C.

In Part I of this book we covered a period of less than one thousand years. During that relatively brief time the artist's role in society altered radically; art has a vastly different significance for us today than that which it had for people of the Renaissance period or of the Middle Ages. Indeed the typical artist of the early Middle Ages is scarcely recognisable as such to the modern man, so greatly has our way of thinking altered since then. These points must indicate certain of the difficulties which arise when we come to assess the art of the distant past, and we should never make the mistake of applying our own preconceptions too rigidly to the various works of our ancestors. What may, for instance, seem like trivial decoration to us, may very well have possessed the deepest magical or religious significance for its creator.

We must look to a period during the third millennium B.C. if we wish to discover the earliest surviving works of Irish art. These are the passage-graves located in several parts of the country—and also in several other parts of Europe—but most especially in the Valley of the Boyne in County Meath. A passage grave is basically a corridor formed of two rows of vertical, and massive, stone slabs called 'orthostats', with other slabs resting on top to form a roof; this opens on to a chamber also constructed of stone. Such structures are buried beneath an artificial hill of stones and earth called variously a 'tumulus', 'barrow' or 'cairn'. Many of the huge stones of which the passage graves were constructed have patterns carved on them. Such patterns are almost always apparently quite abstract, but we have only to consider the sheer labour involved in carving hard stone without the aid of modern power tools or even steel chisels, to understand that they must have had a great deal of significance for the people who carved them. In any case their original meaning still quite eludes us.

Nor do we know very much about the people who built the passage graves, who they were, what language they spoke, or what they worshipped. We are fairly certain that they came to Ireland from the Iberian peninsula, some as early as 3000 B.C. They knew how to work with copper and they must have been skilful sailors. We are not certain why they should have come to Ireland and can only guess that it was to search for metal deposits.

Newgrange

The passage grave at Newgrange is undoubtedly the finest in Ireland, and, like Stonehenge in England, it ranks as one of the showpieces of what has been termed 'Megalithic' (great stone) culture. It has been estimated by the latest methods of radio-carbon dating that the Newgrange passage grave was constructed around 2500 B.C. and of course it may have been worked on over a period of many generations. Considering its great age it is still in a remarkable state of preservation. The tumulus measures over eighty metres across and it may once have been covered with white stones and surmounted by a large vertical slab of stone, or 'megalith'. The chamber, which is reached by a passage almost nineteen metres in length, has a central portion and three recessed cells, cruciform in layout. It is roofed with a number of horizontal slabs forming what is known as a 'corbel vault'.

The carvings at Newgrange, on many of the horizontal kerb stones which define the edge of the tumulus, as well as in a number of the slabs comprising the tomb itself, form spirals, zigzags, lozenges, circles and other less easily defined shapes. These patterns were picked out on the surface of the slabs with sharp pointed instruments, probably of flint or quartz. Chisels made of metal seem also to have been used occasionally. Sometimes a picked-out line was rubbed smooth, presumably with a pebble.

Some of the finest carvings of the Newgrange site are

Entrance Stone, *Newgrange, Co. Meath, c. 2500 B.C.*
(Commissioners of Public Works in Ireland)

to be found on the surface of the great kerb stone
which lies before the entrance to the tomb. The bands
which form the rhythmic curves, spirals and lozenges
are about four centimetres wide, so too are the channels between them. These channels were rubbed
smooth to produce an even surface and the entire
worked face of the stone was picked all over with a
fine point to remove the original weathered surface.
The artist who carved this kerb stone seems to have
been something of a perfectionist; not all of the stone
carvings on the area are as well finished. And there is a
great wealth of megalithic carving to be found at
Newgrange and at nearby sites within that region
between Drogheda and Slane which S. P. O'Ríordáin
has aptly called the 'bend of the Boyne'. The two great
tumuli of Knowth and Dowth, for instance, lie virtually within sight of Newgrange.

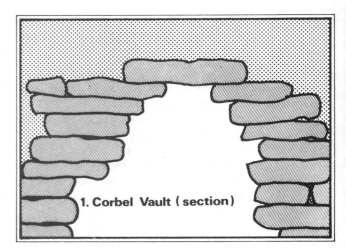

1. Corbel Vault (section)

CHAPTER THIRTEEN

The Bronze Age
2000 B.C.–500 B.C.

The Bronze Age in Ireland saw the production of large
numbers of ornaments in metal, often gold, as well as
weapons, trumpets, shields and tools. By the middle of
the second millennium B.C. Irish bronze and goldwork
was being exported overseas. The late Bronze Age
seems to have been a period of comparative peace and
prosperity to judge by the sheer number of gold ornaments which have survived from that time. These
include neck ornaments of twisted gold called torques,
and others made of sheet gold called gorgets. Gold
dress fasteners, similar to the northern European fibula
used for fastening cloaks, have also been found. Many
bronze objects have proved impossible to date and we

2. Gold Dress - fastener (fibula)

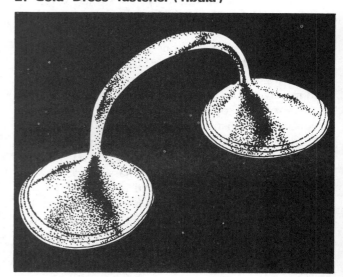

know about as little of those who made them as we do
of the makers of the megalithic passage graves.

The Iron Age 500 B.C.—A.D. 500

Castlestrange Stone, *Co. Roscommon. La Tène period. (Commissioners of Public Works in Ireland)*

With the arrival of Celtic-speaking people in Ireland the picture becomes a little clearer. The Celts, a loosely knit group of peoples of different origins, shared a language and other cultural traits in common. They knew how to use iron and began to establish themselves in Europe some time around 600 B.C. Their arrival in Ireland was a gradual process over a number of centuries, but they had firmly established themselves here by about 150 B.C. The Celtic culture of the late Iron Age has been called 'La Tène', after a site located in Switzerland. The last wave of Celts to arrive in Ireland, during the second century B.C., who were possibly fleeing from the advancing legions of Rome, brought La Tène culture to this country. In Ireland it took firm root, and because the country remained free of invasion for the better part of a thousand years, it was left free to develop to an extent unknown in the rest of Europe.

Celtic Art

A variety of objects in several materials has survived from the Celtic La Tène period: stone carvings, weapons, vessels and ornaments. The Castlestrange stone from County Roscommon, approximately a metre across, curiously suggests the spiral forms of Newgrange in its surface patterning. Again we are at a loss to know just what function this carved dome-shaped stone served, but presumably it, and others rather like it such as the Turoe stone from County

Galway, fulfilled some religious purpose. We can still admire the skill with which the carver has brought the domed surface to life, and although he has limited his repertoire of forms very severely to spirals and ellipses, he has managed to ring an amazing number of subtle variations from them. The result is a well balanced but apparently free and spontaneous design.

The spiral and elliptical decorations on the surface of the Castlestrange stone are typical of La Tène design and they recur in a number of materials. Notice how similar are the curvilinear decorations on the surface of the gold neck ornament to those we have seen on the stone. This neck ornament dates from the first century A.D. and is called the Broighter Collar. The decorations on both objects seem to have a geometric basis yet they

The Broighter Collar. *First century A.D. (National Museum of Ireland)*

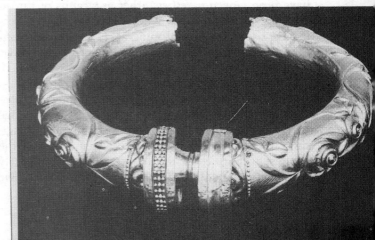

always appear to retain an element of irregularity or spontaneity about them. This is an important aspect of Celtic design continually encountered; the designers were happy to use a certain amount of geometry to start them off, as it were, but it was never allowed to dominate their work totally. This curious stone figure, a warrior apparently, with horned helmet and wide open mouth, shows us another side of Celtic art. Judged purely as representation the figure is not very impressive; the forms are rather clumsily articulated and perhaps oversimplified to the point of naïvety. Something similar might be said regarding the egg-shaped head with its three faces, from the National Museum. Yet this apparently clumsy and inept approach was typical of the Celtic artist once he left the field of abstract decoration for that of representation. Must we conclude then that the Celts were merely clever decorators but out of their depth once they turned to the visible world for their forms? Perhaps the truth is rather more complex.

3. Stone Figure from Armagh

4. Three-faced Stone Head

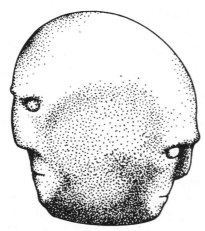

The Nature of Celtic Art

Irish Celtic art grew in complexity, developing highly intricate designs in metal, stone, and (later) in paint, based largely on the spiral and on the interwoven 'strapwork'. This latter decorative form conveys the idea that a number of straps, or ribbons or threads, have been woven together rather as strands of thread are woven to form cloth. Whereas the spirals frequently gave rise to leaf-like protuberances, suggesting plant life, the strapwork often ended in the heads and claws of fantastic animals or birds (and sometimes humans).

Such decorative surfaces had, for the Celtic Irish, a meaning far more significant than that of merely pleasing the eye. In a similar way to the art of Newgrange they possessed a symbolic, or more probably, a magical value. Françoise Henry who remains one of the greatest authorities on the art of prehistoric and early Christian Ireland, has speculated that these decorative

5. Strapwork (from the Book of Mac Regol, late 8th C.)

surfaces were believed to possess protective powers. And again it must be added that we have lost the secret of interpreting the symbolism and the exact significance of the decorations. But they may very well have their origins in some fertility cult from the very far distant past.

With regard to the problem of representation already mentioned, it might be argued that a people who, for countless centuries had been trained to 'see in a pattern the visible sign of an idea, as decorative words of a mystical language' (Françoise Henry), would, when they turned to figurative work, use the very same instincts and view their representations of nature primarily as symbols. This helps, at least partially, to explain why the early Irish made little or no attempt to develop a truly naturalistic art; their basic attitude rather than any lack of skill was the determining factor.

Their art seems very carefully to pursue a path which avoids the two extremes; total geometric abstraction on the one hand and naturalistic appearance on the other. Françoise Henry mentions these two extremes in terms of pitfalls which the Celtic mind actually seemed to fear. Creative vitality—the power to endow the surface of stone or metal with a magical potency—could only be retained so long as the artist retained some independence of those two worlds of 'absolute' forms.

CHAPTER FIFTEEN

The Early Christian Period
A.D 500–800

The history of St Patrick's mission to Ireland during the mid fifth century, and the consequent conversion of the country to the Christian faith, are familiar but some points are well worth mentioning here.

Ireland was converted to the Christian faith during that period when the Roman Empire was crumbling in ruins before the advancing Germanic peoples. So, far from making Ireland a part of the Roman world at last, Christianity served rather to isolate her to an even greater degree than before. The frequent raids into Roman Britain by various Irish chieftains ceased, for instance.

And the Irish seem to have suffered no deep traumas in their acceptance of the Christian faith; there was no bloodshed and no sudden and radical social upheaval. Ireland remained a land of tiny squabbling kingdoms, or *tuatha*, devoid of cities or roads. The ancient and elaborate laws of the Brehons remained in force; the law schools continued to flourish alongside those established by the Christian clergy. And the artists, poets and musicians retained their high social status, some-

where between that of the traditional aristocracy and that of the common man. Eventually even the Brehons —the traditional custodians of Celtic law—were converted to the new faith. For their part, the Christian clergy attained a position in Irish society comparable in status to that of the aristocracy.

Although the Christian faith brought new concepts, symbols and forms, these in no way alienated the native Celtic artistic tradition. On the contrary, they were readily accepted and the new was simply added to the old. Those artifacts closely associated with the Christian faith brought from Roman Britain by St Patrick and others—chalices, books, patens, bells, croziers etc.—were readily adapted to the Celtic language of forms.

The Beginnings of Christian Art in Ireland

The sixth century saw the rapid spread of monastic communities throughout the country. These communities were housed in collections of huts grouped about a church and usually set within a stockade. Sometimes the disused rath of some petty king was taken over by the monks. Many of the early monastic buildings, often constructed of wood or wattles and clay, have now perished. Those that have survived tend to be situated on the west coast, in Clare, Kerry and Mayo. Here timber was very scarce and the huts of the monks were built of stone, as were the oratories or chapels.

The oratory of Gallerus, on the Dingle Peninsula, County Kerry, is still remarkably well preserved. It looks a little like an upturned boat and, like many of the surviving oratories and huts, is built of carefully dressed stone, held together without the aid of mortar by a system of corbelling similar to that used in Newgrange, but very much more refined.

The building is seven metres long and five metres high approximately. Like all the other oratories it is orientated with a doorway in the west wall and a window in the east.

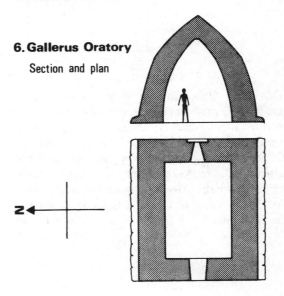

6. Gallerus Oratory

Section and plan

The Development of Stone Carving

Slabs of stone, incised with a symbol of the cross, were often placed beside these buildings and in all probability marked the tomb of some venerable person, the founder of the monastery for instance. A number of such stones, ranging from engraved boulders which retain their original natural form intact, to rough hewn pillars anything up to two metres in height, have been discovered on the sites of nearly all the early monasteries.

This stone pillar, from Aglish in County Kerry and now in the National Museum, has the form of a Greek Cross, inscribed in a circle, cut into its surface, along with an inscription written in ogham. Some slabs bear Latin inscriptions, and later, inscriptions in early Irish. Decorations, often the familiar Celtic spirals, made their appearance on the surface of stone slabs. And eventually the stones themselves were more carefully shaped and made more regular.

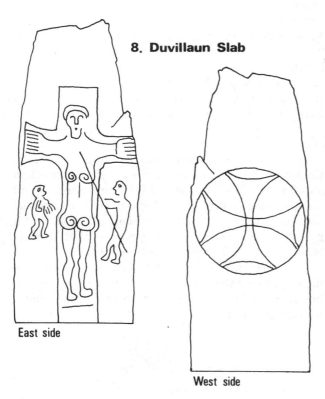

8. Duvillaun Slab

East side

West side

7. Aglish Pillar

The Duvillaun Slab, County Mayo, has a design carved on its two main faces. On one side is a Greek cross inscribed in a circle, very similar to the one from Aglish; on the other is a rather primitive representation of the Crucifixion. Again we must keep in mind the Celtic attitude to representation. This very simple drawing was probably deemed quite sufficient as a symbol of the sacrifice of Christ. Notice too how the artist has introduced the form of the spiral into his design.

The Fahan Mura slab, County Donegal, might be regarded as a further development; the surface area of the slab which surrounds the form of the cross has been cut back, allowing the cross to stand out in relief. The form of a Greek cross, this time with a stem, has been carved in a powerfully decorative manner on both sides. The decoration of both crosses takes the form of vigorously interwoven strapwork. On both faces also the border of the slab itself has been clearly marked and one of the crosses is accompanied by two

9. Fahan Mura Slab (west face)

we have already seen in the Fahan Mura slab; indeed Françoise Henry has suggested that both originated from the same workshop. The shapes of six birds, two groups of three, have been blended with the strapwork decoration. This whimsical mixture of the figurative and the purely abstract is one of those constants which we shall meet continually in Celtic design.

We have now seen how the form of the free-standing high cross gradually evolved from the carved slab. It is as well to keep in mind that, in reality, the process was undoubtedly much more complex than indicated here, and the emergence of the free-standing crosses does not mean that slabs were no longer produced.

Manuscripts—The Cathach

It seems likely that St Patrick and his followers brought books with them to Ireland, and that these served as the original models for the first Irish books. Very little written matter indeed was produced in pre-Christian Ireland; the law schools of the Brehons, for instance, transmitted learning via the spoken word, and human memory rather than writing on page or slab, served to record the wisdom of the past.

Carndonagh Cross, Co. Donegal. Possibly late sixth century A.D. (Commissioners of Public Works in Ireland)

very simple figures who stand on either side of the main stem. Notice too how the carver has left a 'bump' on both sides of the slab which seems to continue the horizontal arms beyond the frame.

By the end of the sixth century the cross form had been freed from the surrounding slab. The process had been a long one; it seems that the early Christian Irish artists retained a reluctance to interfere unduly with the natural form of the stone on which they worked, a phenomenon which may be traced back to Megalithic times. The Carndonagh Cross, County Donegal, is one of the earliest examples. It has a primitive, vigorous outline. Strapwork decoration is used here also. This decoration covers one side of the cross while the other is an interesting mixture of decoration and figures. This latter side, shown in the photograph, is dominated by one large figure, presumably a representation of Christ in Majesty. He is surrounded by four small figures who are packed tightly into the spaces beneath the upraised arms and on either side of the head. Beneath is a small rectangular panel with three more figures, this time seen in profile. The strapwork itself forms a Greek cross above the figurative section. The Carndonagh Cross has something of the vigour which

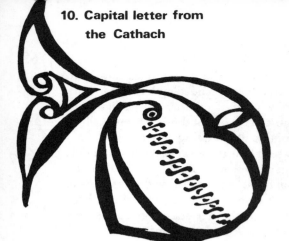

10. Capital letter from the Cathach

11. Ardakillin Brooch

The first Irish books—those produced during the fifth and early sixth centuries—have all been lost, but one important manuscript, dating from the second half of the sixth century has, at least partially, survived the ravages of time. This is the 'Cathach', a copy of the Psalms, now in the keeping of the Royal Irish Academy. Tradition maintains that the Cathach was the work of St Columba, the very copy which he made without permission from a book owned by his master, Finnian, and which led to bloodshed and Columba's self-imposed exile on Iona. Irrespective of whether this tradition regarding the Cathach is true or not, the book was certainly associated with the shedding of blood. Its name means 'battler', and it was carried into battle by the O'Donnells—the clan to which St Columba had belonged—who believed that its presence made their armies invincible.

The Cathach is rather sparsely decorated. The beginning of the book is missing and we can only presume that the first page was more elaborate than the remainder. The capital letters, which begin each Psalm, have a rude strength about them, reminiscent of the decoration of some of the early stone slabs. These letters form strong black scrolls, sometimes giving rise to simplified leaf forms, crosses or animal heads. A limited amount of colour was used; many of the capital letters were surrounded by a field of red dots, and occasionally some yellow was used for the patterns inside the letters.

Metalwork

Where work in stone or manuscript is concerned, there is usually little doubt as to whether it pre-dates the conversion of Ireland to Christianity or not. Stone carving took on a distinctly Christian orientation and manuscripts did not exist in the pre-Christian era. Work in metal often poses a very different problem however; the form and decoration of purely secular objects—brooches, bowls, buckles etc—were scarcely affected by the advent of the Christian religion. There are a number of such metal objects which may be

12. Bronze Disc

dated with some accuracy only because of the location in which they were found.

A number of large bronze discs with high relief decoration have been discovered. Their exact function is not known. The various curves of the decoration were probably hammered out from the back, a technique called 'repoussé'. A very obvious stylistic similarity exists between the decorations on this object and those on the other two illustrated here. All three recall the curvilinear motifs of La Tène design.

The object shown in the photograph, the so-called Petrie Crown, may have been used as a tomb decoration. Its various components seem to have been rearranged, and originally it may have formed part of some horse trappings. The delicately wrought decorations on the surfaces of the crown afford us yet another example of a design which has been 'rescued' before it

The Petrie Crown, *detail. (National Museum of Ireland)*

could become too rigidly geometrical. Notice how the ends of the various spirals blossom into a variety of animal or bird heads.

To objects like those mentioned above we might add numbers of penannular—or ring-like—brooches and disc-like fasteners or latchets. The penannular brooch, particularly in its later and more complex form, has come to be regarded as a distinctly Celtic, or early Irish invention. In fact its form was borrowed from the Romanised world.

13. Penannular Brooch

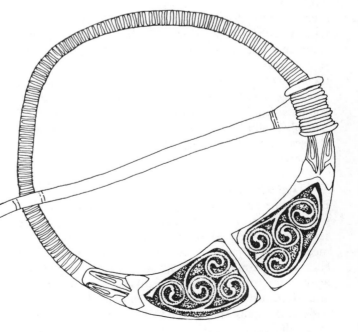

CHAPTER SIXTEEN

[172]

The High Period of Christian Irish Culture—
Seventh and Eighth Centuries

The Christian civilisation in Ireland seems to have reached its full flowering during the seventh and eighth centuries. That period saw the final fusion of the Irish and Latin traditions; the poets and Brehons learned to read and write so that they might at last record their wisdom and culture in permanent form. And they applied their new knowledge to the Irish language. The Church too was flourishing; Irish missionaries had for some time been carrying their message to Britain and the continent, founding many monasteries in the process. In Ireland the monastic centres had risen to positions of power and wealth; they had become the true cultural centres of the country, attracting like a magnet many types of people other than the purely religious, among them scholars, poets and craftsmen. At the same time the power of the petty kings was in decline. Writing in or around the year 800, Óengus, of the Céilí-Dé, relates how the great fortresses of the old kings had crumbled into ruins, and contrasts their wasted state with the flourishing condition of such ecclesiastical centres as Armagh, Clonmacnoise and Glendalough: 'Tara's mighty citadel has perished with the passing of her princes, with a multitude of champions of wisdom great Armagh abides.' And again, 'Emain's citadel has vanished . . . Rome of the Western world is multitudinous Glendalough.' So we must imagine these monastic centres as small cities, teeming with activity. From their workshops and scriptoria emerged large quantities of beautifully wrought objects: metalwork — chalices, bells, croziers, brooches, their surfaces enriched with fine gold filigree and gleaming enamel; manuscripts with decorated pages as complex, colourful and rich as the work of the gold and silver smiths; and finally great carved stone high crosses, with surfaces enlivened by figurative panels and intricate interlacing patterns.

The High Crosses

High stone crosses were erected both inside and outside of the monastery enclosures. They seem to have served several functions: they formed focal points for meetings and prayer, and were placed outside the enclosure presumably to act as a protective barrier against the forces of evil. In terms of size, proportion and decorative or figurative content they differed widely. Basically they tended to take the form shown in the diagram. The distinctive 'wheel' connecting the four arms of the cross occurs on most, but not quite all, of the crosses.

The crosses at Ahenny, County Tipperary, are, for the most part, remarkably well preserved examples dating from the eighth century. Compare the photograph, which gives a view of the South Cross, with the earlier Carndonagh Cross. Here the form is both regular and very firmly stated, and a narrow wheel connects the four arms. We may imagine that the sculptor who made the Carndonagh Cross felt rather reluctant to break with the form of the block of stone; the two horizontal arms still seem to hug the broad central column. This is certainly not the case with the cross at Ahenny; the sculptor confidently allowed the horizontal arms to spring clear of the vertical column. Notice too how clearly he has emphasised the overall cross-form by raising a thick, rope-like border, which catches the light, around the perimeter of it. The decoration on the surface of this cross is mainly ab-

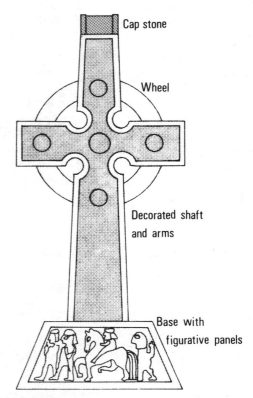

14. High Cross

Cap stone

Wheel

Decorated shaft and arms

Base with figurative panels

South Cross, *Ahenny, Co. Tipperary. View of the west face. Possibly eighth century A.D. (Commissioners of Public Works in Ireland)*

large heads. Yet it must be stressed immediately that there is absolutely nothing 'crude' about these carvings; the sculptor has worked with a repertoire of forms which are both consistent and perfectly under his control. Their intrinsic simplicity is also perfectly appropriate to the nature of the material out of which they are carved — granite, a singularly unwieldy stone.

Look at the photograph showing one of the large panels from the base of the cross. Three rows of little men occupy this panel; at a glance they look very like those little figures which young children are allowed to make out of scraps of dough by indulgent mothers. Individually they can hardly be described as sophisticated yet the composition itself has considerable visual impact; the three rows of little men add up to a blatant but memorable piece of design. Nor are they as

The Cross of Moone, *Co. Kildare. West face. Possibly eighth century. (Commissioners of Public Works in Ireland)*

stract: spirals and interlacing. The panels on the surface of the base, a truncated pyramid, are in fact figurative, but these are so badly weathered as to be almost indistinguishable.

The Cross of Moone

The cross of Moone, located in the south of County Kildare, is one of the finest of the eighth-century crosses (it may date from the early ninth century). The first striking feature about it must surely be its proportions; compared to the Ahenny Cross with its heavy base, the one at Moone seems amazingly tall and slender. It is in fact quite high, over five metres, and this is emphasised by the smallness of the wheel-head and the slender pyramid-shaped base which merges with the shaft far more gracefully than does that of the Ahenny Cross. The panels on the surfaces of this cross are also markedly different; these are almost entirely figurative, depicting biblical stories, scenes from the life of St Anthony the Hermit, and a variety of animals.

Most of the important panels are carved on the base, as was common practice during the period. Close inspection reveals their remarkable style; the human figures, for instance, frequently have square or rectangular bodies devoid of details — even arms — and very

The Twelve Apostles, *from the Cross of Moone.*
(Commissioners of Public Works in Ireland)

15. The Three Hebrews

uniform as might appear at first glance; subtle differences may be detected from one face to the next, and the proportion of the bodies changes from nearly square to decidedly oblong, from the bottom to the top row. These are small matters but they help to lend the necessary tension to a design which otherwise might run the risk of being too blatantly mechanical and therefore boring. As there are twelve of the little men it is easy to guess that the subject is 'The Twelve Apostles'.

Françoise Henry suggests that the various panels on the base of the Moone Cross are best read in sequence, starting on the east side and moving around the monument in a clockwise direction.

On the east side are some scenes from the Old Testament: Adam and Eve standing on either side of the tree around whose trunk writhes the Serpent, Abraham about to sacrifice his son Isaac on the altar, and finally Daniel surrounded by the seven lions.

Moving to the south side, we discover representations of 'The Three Hebrews in the Furnace' (often referred to as the 'Three Children in the Furnace'. The story, which relates how Shedrach, Meshach and Abednego were miraculously delivered from the wrath of King Nebuchadnezzar, is taken from the Book of Daniel), 'The Flight into Egypt' and a curiously 'abstract' and symbolic rendition of the 'Miracle of the Five Loaves and Two Fishes'.

On the west side is the panel representing the Twelve Apostles, and above that is a small 'Crucifixion'. Finally, on the remaining side of the cross we encounter some scenes from the life of St Anthony, the archetypal holy hermit who lived in the Egyptian desert: in the topmost panel St Anthony and St Paul sit facing one another on high-backed chairs and break bread; immediately below, St Anthony is tempted by two demons — one with a goat's head and the other with a bird's. The bottom panel depicts a frightful, many-headed monster, or dragon, presumably an evocation of the 'wilderness'.

The underlying theme of these stories — from the Old and New Testaments and from the early history of the Church — might be described as the help and protection given by God to the faithful throughout the ages. The figure of Christ in Majesty, placed high up on the east side of the cross where the arms join, may also be seen as part of this thematic scheme. Thus the cross of Moone, as well as being a symbol of *the* 'Cross' and a beautiful visual object, is also a sort of pictorial sermon, a charactaristic shared with most of the high crosses of the period and later.

Before leaving the Moone Cross it might be as well to mention briefly the small panels on the shaft depicting various animals. These animals are more obviously decorative than the human figures, and are far more

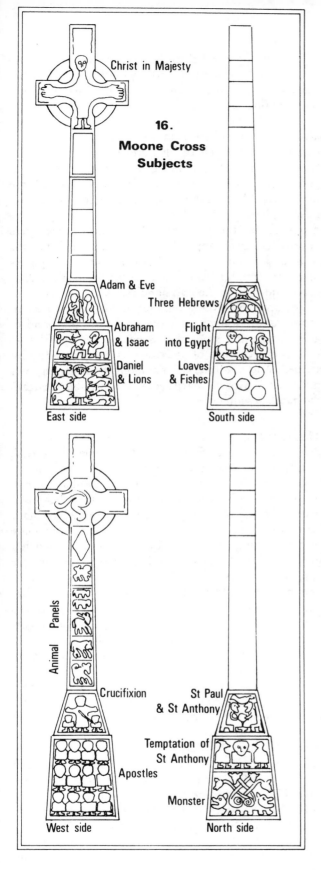

Christ in Majesty

16.
Moone Cross
Subjects

Adam & Eve

Three Hebrews

Abraham & Isaac

Flight into Egypt

Daniel & Lions

Loaves & Fishes

East side

South side

Animal Panels

Crucifixion

St Paul & St Anthony

Temptation of St Anthony

Apostles

Monster

West side

North side

supple in outline. They give the impression that the artist made them purely for his own enjoyment.

The Ardagh Chalice. *Eighth century A.D. (National Museum of Ireland)*

Metalwork

Many of the high crosses from this, the great period of Irish civilisation, remain more or less intact. The same cannot, unfortunately, be said for the great abundance of metal objects — chalices, croziers, shrines, brooches etc., wrought in silver and gold — made during the period. They proved far too tempting to the raiders who came from the northern lands in later centuries. We are lucky that a few superb specimens remain intact, as an indication of the riches that have been lost forever.

The Ardagh Chalice

The Ardagh chalice, one of the treasures of the National Museum, was discovered in the 1860s by a boy who was digging for potatoes. It is basically very simple in form: a hemispherical cup of beaten silver joined to a base, also roughly hemispherical, by a thick stem of gilded bronze. This shape is further modified by two handles, and greatly enriched by inlaid panels of very fine gold filigree, and some large studs of metal and coloured glass. The overall impression is one of great refinement; the broad undecorated surfaces of the silver act as the perfect foil for the richly worked gold panels and the red and blue studs.

The chalice, like all the best examples of Irish metalwork, requires close scrutiny if the full richness of the various decorated surfaces, and indeed, the sheer ingenuity of craftsmanship, are to be fully appreciated. It is worth keeping in mind while studying the panels of gold filigree, for instance, that all those fine lines which writhe and twist into a variety of patterns are in fact gold wires, each one of which had to be soldered into place. These panels of gold filigree are to be found on the two handles, in the band which runs around the

The Ardagh Chalice. *Detail showing a section of the band of gold filigree and studs which runs parallel to the rim. Also visible is some of the inscribed lettering.* (National Museum of Ireland)

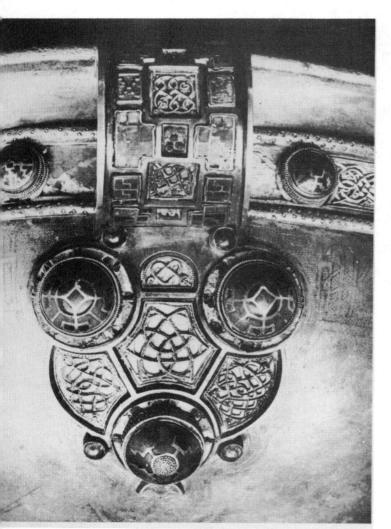

The Ardagh Chalice. *Detail showing a handle of the chalice.* (National Museum of Ireland)

top of the cup parallel to the rim, in two large round panels on the side, and also on the base. The gilded surface of the bronze stem blends, in terms of colour, with the filigree work.

The various glass studs are also worthy of attention. These are hemispherical in form and give the impression that tiny panels of blue and red glass have been fitted into a metal framework. The metal frame or grille was probably prepared first, placed in a close fitting mould and the red areas of enamel then carefully applied. A molten blob of blue glass could then be deposited into the framework, filling those areas where no red had been applied, and of course making the stud solid at the same time. There are also some panels of more straightforward enamel work, in blue, dark green and red, on the two handles.

The areas of silver should not be described as completely undecorated; immediately below the band of gold panels and studs the names of the Apostles — with the exception of Judas — have been lightly inscribed. And two interlaced animals, their gaping jaws filled with rows of sharp teeth, are inscribed beneath the handle escutcheons.

The Tara Brooch

Before we consider that supreme example of the Irish metalworker's skill and ingenuity, the Tara brooch, a word of caution: this object looks so familiar to Irish people mainly because of the innumerable cheap and insensitive mass-produced versions of it which have been available over the years. Our ability to appreciate the 'real thing' may therefore have been somewhat impaired due to exposure to these. The same principle applies, of course, to many other examples of Celtic design; our ability to appreciate the high crosses has not been enhanced by exposure to the mass-produced versions which adorn our cemeteries, and the vulgarised versions of Celtic strapwork which have been applied to every conceivable article, from copy books to calendars, don't help us much either.

But the real Tara Brooch is truly a marvel; indeed the National Museum is worth visiting to examine this piece of jewellery alone. Its title is purely fanciful; in fact it has no known connection with Tara. It is believed to have been discovered not too far from Tara however, near the mouth of the Boyne, in a wooden box along with several other objects. These, no doubt, were the fruits of some raid on a monastery.

The brooch itself is of the familiar penannular variety, which evolved from models originally Roman. It consists basically of a closed ring with a long straight pin. The fact that a length of fine silver mesh chain emanates from one side of the ring suggests that it was once one of a pair.

The brooch ring is of cast silver, both sides of which

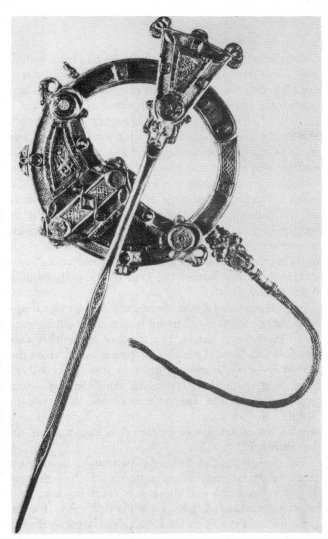

The Tara Brooch. *Eighth century A.D. (National Museum of Ireland)*

The back, which could not be seen when the brooch was worn, is worked in a slightly broader technique than the front. Here are a number of coiled serpents, near relatives of those whose heads punctuate the outer rim of the brooch, and a border of plump birds whose beaks are firmly fastened on the legs of those immediately preceding.

The design of both front and back is further enhanced by glass studs and raised areas of amber. Some of the glass studs on the front of the brooch have been crowned with gold filigree and granules, while several on the back are again reminiscent of those which we have seen on the Ardagh chalice.

A number of metal objects — penannular brooches, buckles, reliquaries etc. — from approximately the same period may also be seen in the National Museum, but the two we have looked at in some detail are undoubtedly the most splendid. Before leaving the subject of metal work we shall consider one more piece, rather different in style from the brooch and the chalice.

The Tara Brooch. *Detail of the front showing gold filigree and studs. (National Museum of Ireland)*

have been decorated by a variety of delicately worked gold panels and glass studs. The gold filigree panels on the front of the brooch are strongly reminiscent of those from the Ardagh chalice, and the quality of workmanship is at least as fine. The possibility exists therefore, that both these objects originated from the same workshop, or were even the work of the same craftsman. This, of course, is mere speculation.

The wonder which we may very well feel before the craftsmanship of the chalice is augmented when we encounter the brooch, for this is a relatively tiny object; the ring is less than nine centimetres in diameter. Yet packed into this small area is an entire world of ornament: strands of fine beaded and twisted gold wire evoke the forms of fantastic beasts and birds, as well as innumerable interlacings, loops and spirals. A number of the filigree panels are missing from the front of the brooch, but enough remain for us to imagine the complete object without difficulty.

The Athlone Crucifixion Plaque. *Possibly late seventh century A.D. (National Museum of Ireland)*

The Athlone Crucifixion Plaque

The Athlone Crucifixion plaque, which probably dates from the late seventh century, is one of the earliest representations of that sacred subject in Irish art. This open-work plaque may have graced the cover of some manuscript; again its origins are fairly vague. The composition, which comprises five figures in all, is dominated by the impassive figure of the crucified Christ. He wears a long robe which reaches to the ankles, a curious feature to be found in several Irish, as well as continental, versions of the subject.

Much of the surface of the plaque is covered with decorative motifs; particularly noticeable is the series of large spirals which occupy roughly the area of the torso of the Christ figure. Again we are reminded of the probable sacred or magical significance of this motif. The angels too are covered in patterning, spirals again and also a herring-bone pattern not often encountered in Irish art.

Manuscripts

With the sixth-century manuscript which we have examined briefly, the Cathach, a tendency to turn certain letters to decorative purpose has been noted. This decorative predilection of the scribes became very greatly enhanced during the next century, as skills and confidence grew. Decoration became as important a feature of the manuscripts made during the seventh and eighth centuries as it was with work in metal and stone. Curiously, even in this field the difficulty of dating, attribution and place of origin often remains. Colophons (i.e. inscriptions made on the last page of a book indicating authorship etc.) when they do occur are frequently found to have been altered, added to or simply forged, for a variety of reasons. We must remember that our near obsession with accuracy is a fairly recent cultural phenomenon (or aberration?) and certainly did not bother the men of the early Middle Ages unduly.

Several types of book were produced in the scriptoria. Large numbers of hymn books and psalters were in all probability made, but none of these have survived. We do have a number of gospel books from the period however; some are more or less intact, others have been reduced to fragments consisting of a few pages. Several very fine examples are preserved in Dublin, in the Library of Trinity College, while a number of others are to be found in England and on the continent.

The gospel books fall into two main categories: small, relatively undecorated editions which might easily have been carried about for everyday use, and larger sumptuous editions, carefully decorated, for use at the altar. We shall concern ourselves largely with the second type.

With regard to their schemes of decoration, these tended to have a number of points in common: the first page of each gospel was elaborately decorated; this decoration usually took the form of a huge initial letter followed by a few lines of ornamental text. Such pages were usually placed on the right hand so that the left-hand facing page could be given over entirely to elaborate ornament. Some of the more complex pages of this type are referred to as 'carpet' pages. Often in addition to this—occasionally instead of—a page was given over to a representation of the symbol of the relevent Evangelist. These symbols, which frequently recur in medieval art, were derived from the first chapter of the Book of Ezekiel: a man for St Matthew, a lion for St Mark, an ox for St Luke and an eagle for St John. 'Portraits' of the Evangelists also sometimes occur.

The Book of Durrow

The Book of Durrow, now in Trinity College, is a fine example of the seventh-century gospel book for use at the altar. It was once in the possession of the Columban monastery of Durrow, near Tullamore in County

Offaly. Before it passed to Trinity College in the seventeenth century, it was owned by a farmer who was in the habit of 'curing' his sick cattle by dipping the book in their drinking water. Nevertheless it has survived with most of its colours fresh and bright.

The book opens with two decorative pages: a double cross shown against a background of interlacing on one, and the symbols of the four Evangelists on the other. The four gospels, which follow, are each decorated in a systematic fashion. Each begins with a page bearing the symbol of an Evangelist. The text of each gospel begins on a right-hand page dominated by a large decorated capital letter. The photograph shows the beginning of St Mark's gospel, with its superb long-stemmed capital N.

The left-hand pages which face the beginnings of the gospels are elaborately decorated. The page which precedes St John's gospel is particularly intriguing. As may be seen from the photograph it consists largely of

---

The Book of Durrow. *Carpet page from the beginning of St John's Gospel. (Trinity College Dublin; The Green Studios Ltd.)*

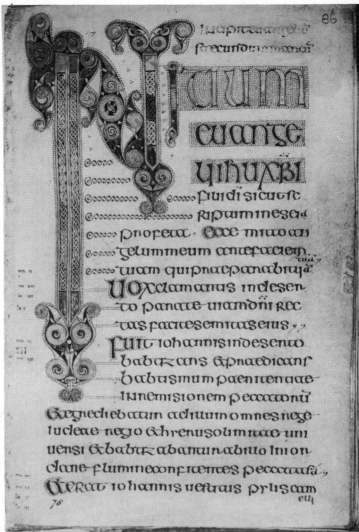

Page from The Book of Durrow. *Seventh century A.D. The opening words of St Mark's Gospel. (Trinity College Dublin; The Green Studios Ltd.)*

---

panels occupied by fantastic intertwined beasts. Those in the upper and lower panels are reminiscent of serpents, those on the sides bear some resemblance to greyhounds. The equivalent carpet pages from the other three gospels are decorated with intertwined ribbons and spirals.

Four main colours have been used on the decorations: a rich green (copper acetate), a strong golden yellow (orpiment or arsenic trisulphide), red (lead oxide) and finally a dark rich brown which may once have been black. These colours are employed with considerable sensitivity on the various pages and contrast beautifully with the subtle creamy colour of the vellum itself.

The page with St Mark's symbol, the lion, demonstrates the use of colour very well. We see the lion in profile, mouth open to reveal a row of sharp teeth and a lolling tongue, tail swishing fiercely into a tight S-shape. His body and legs are decorated with a

The Book of Durrow. *The symbol of St Mark. In this book the symbol of St Mark is unaccountably placed at the beginning of St John's Gospel. (Trinity College Dublin; The Green Studios Ltd.)*

uncoloured apart from a single line of red dots. The patterns which they form are set against a variable background of dark brown, yellow and green.

The missionary activities of the Irish monks caused many Irish books to be carried to Britain and the continent. Irish monks working abroad continued to labour at their manuscripts and inevitably their styles became influenced by the indigenous art of the regions in which they had settled. Native disciples were also taught to work in the Irish manner. These factors led to a diversification of styles, and, in the case of a number of books it is impossible to ascertain for certain either their place of origin or that of their authors.

Some such uncertainty exists regarding the origin of the Book of St Chad, also known as the Lichfield Gospel, which is now kept in Lichfield Cathedral, Staffordshire, England. It seems probable that this book was made in Ireland however. It was roughly handled during the course of its existence; the whole of St John's Gospel and part of St Luke's are missing, and the edges of the pages have been clipped, thus reducing the size of the book. Some of the preliminary pages are likewise missing, others are worn and areas of colour have been damaged or washed away altogether.

A larger and more subtle range of colours than those in the Book of Durrow have been used here. The ornament too is sometimes far more complex; the carpet page before the gospel of St Luke, for instance, contains a truly bewildering number of phrenetically entwined beasts and birds, as well as the form of a large cross. This book also contains pages with 'portraits' of the Evangelists accompanied by their symbols.

St Mark is shown, book in hand, before a large and elaborate chair which incorporates the forms of two curious beasts. Above his head sails the lion, also clutching a book.

A number of other manuscripts, made during the late seventh and eighth centuries, are worth mentioning. These include the Lindisfarne Gospels, written and illuminated by Eadfrith, Bishop of Lindisfarne, the Book of MacRegol, the Book of Mulling and the Book of Dimma. This latter, also in Trinity College, is a good example of the small portable form of gospel book. It was made during the eighth century at the monastery of Roscrea in County Tipperary. The style is simpler and less sophisticated than that of many of the larger altar gospels, but vigorous nevertheless.

diamond pattern, harlequin style, in red and green. The red is used again on his paws and on his head where it has been muted by application in the form of a careful stipple. This stippling, or dotting, is employed to great effect on various pages of the book, sometimes to decorate part of a figure, sometimes to emphasise a particular letter or word. The yellow has been used for the strongest accents, on the eye, tail and paws as well as the two decorative forms which underscore the belly and neck.

The border which surrounds the lion consists of four panels of strapwork interlacing. The horizontal panels at top and bottom are particularly forceful, presumably to echo the essentially horizontal form of the lion. Here all three colours are set against a background of deep brown, emphasising their luminosity. The straps or ribbons which form the two vertical decorations are

The Lichfield Gospel, *also called the Book of St Chad. Portrait of St Mark. Possibly eighth century A.D.*

CHAPTER SEVENTEEN

The Period of Viking Invasions–
–Ninth and Tenth Centuries

Bitter is the wind to-night
It tosses the ocean's white hair
To-night I fear not the fierce warriors of Norway
Coursing the Irish Sea.
from a poem written in the margin of the St-Gall Priscian c. 850.

The Anglo-Saxon Chronicle tells us that on 8 June 793, 'The Ravages of the heathen men miserably destroyed God's church on Lindisfarne, with plunder and slaughter.' In the early years of the ninth century these same 'heathen men' plundered the monastic settlement on Iona, causing great loss of life and the eventual abandonment of the island by the monks; they settled again in Kells, County Meath. The raiders were, of course, the Vikings, who travelled across the northern seas in their beautifully constructed long ships, from

their homes in the west coast of Norway. They soon learned that Ireland was a land rich in silver and gold, and their arrival here brought to an end the many centuries of comparative peace which had allowed Irish civilisation to flourish to such a degree.

The Viking invasions, during the course of the ninth and tenth centuries, affected Irish civilisation in a number of ways. A great deal was destroyed; monasteries, mostly built of wood, were burned, monks were slaughtered or forced to flee for their lives. Many objects of silver and gold were taken, often to be broken up and divided, or even melted down to make coins. Gilded objects too, were taken home to Norway, where they frequently made fine gifts for the ladies. A reliquary, for instance, its sacred contents flung away, might end up as a jewel box for some Viking lady. The relics of the saints were of no interest to these warriors, nor were books, since they were illiterate. So books were burned, or thrown into the sea, once they had been wrenched free of their gold and silver covers. Ireland endured further loss in that many monks and scholars simply fled the country and sought refuge on the continent. Here they were made welcome by Charlemagne and his successors. And these exiles frequently carried with them such easily portable treasures as illuminated manuscripts, to Ireland's further loss.

Not all the consequences of the Viking invasions were negative however. The Vikings established the first real cities in Ireland. These were originally fortified camps built near the mouths of navigable rivers and established as bases for raiding parties plundering the central parts of the country on horseback. Gradually they evolved into more permanent trading centres; towns like Wexford, Waterford, Limerick and Dublin. And the Irish themselves seem to have learned a great deal about building during this period; churches built of cut stone and mortar began to appear, and so too did the tall and graceful round towers

The Round Towers
The round towers, which were built very close to the churches, served several functions. Primarily they were bell towers, and from the lofty elevation of their upper stories the monastic hours were sounded for the benefit of those monks working in nearby fields. Irish bells were small affairs, most could easily be rung by hand. And the great height of these buildings—something between thirty and forty metres—made them ideal as watch towers, perhaps their most useful function. They were also relatively safe places of refuge, for both human beings and treasure. Having walls over a metre in thickness, often of very well cut stone, and an entry door several metres above the level of the ground, they could not easily be breached. In the event

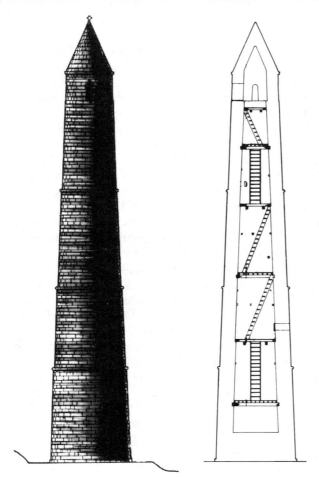

The round tower *at* Ardmore, *Co. Waterford together with a cross section. Possibly twelfth century. (Commissioners of Public Works in Ireland)*

of an impending Viking raid there might just be time for the monks to bundle themselves into this sanctuary, draw up the entry ladder and bolt the door securely. The most valuable of the monastic treasures were probably already kept within the tower.

The interior was quite spacious, towers were built with diameters of over five metres, and there were up to seven floors of wood, each accessible by ladder. Fire was the only real hazard. If the entry door could be breached and the interior flooring set alight nothing could save those within; round towers, by their very shape, made very efficient chimneys.

Quite apart from architecture, the other arts and crafts not only managed to survive but, for a time during the ninth century, actually saw a marked development. Stone carving in particular entered a new creative phase; the high crosses became even taller and their surfaces were enlivened with an almost purely figurative art. And at the very beginning of the period of Viking invasions during the last few years of the eighth century and the first of the ninth century, perhaps the greatest, and certainly the most celebrated

of the Irish illuminated manuscripts was made. This was the Book of Kells.

The Book of Kells

The Book of Kells was conceived and begun in the scriptorium of the Columban monastery of Iona. Work on the manuscript was interrupted by the Viking raids on the island, and it was brought to Kells in 806 where, presumably, work was recommenced on it. It is a large book, both in terms of the number of pages—originally there were about three hundred and fifty—and in terms of page size; each at present measures 330 mm by 250 mm although originally they were larger, having been trimmed during the last century. Along with some pages of lists of Hebrew names, tables of cross-references, prefaces and summaries of the gospels, the text consists of the four gospels themselves in Latin.

The scheme governing the decoration of the book is basically the same as books from earlier years like the Book of Durrow, but there are certain important additions in the form of full-page illustrations in colour which help to account for the extra length, as does the profusion of other illustrations which occur on the other pages.

Each of the gospels begins with a page of huge initial letters, heavily decorated, which leave scarcely any room for words of text. These initial pages fall on the right, as with earlier books, but only in one case is an accompanying carpet page included. This is the carpet page which faces the beautiful Chi-Rho, the Greek monogram of Christ used traditionally in chapter one of St Matthew's gospel. The initial pages of the other three gospels are faced in each case by a page bearing the symbols of the four Evangelists, but each page is framed differently.

The Illustrators of the Book of Kells

Such an extremely sumptuous book was obviously not designed for everyday use; it was in all probability intended only for use by the celebrant in the public worship of the most important religious feasts. Nor was it the work of one man, but rather of an entire scriptorium. Françoise Henry has detected the presence of the work of four major artists, who were naturally entrusted with the most important sections of the book and also the work of a number of lesser artists who carried out various lesser tasks. The Book of Kells is therefore somewhat variable in quality, but we shall concern ourselves with the work of the four master illustrators only.

The first illustrator was the master decorator of the Book. He was probably responsible for the carpet page (the so-called page of the eight circles), the initial pages of three of the gospels (the exception is St Luke's) and the Chi-Rho page mentioned above, which is illus-

Book of Kells. *The Chi-Rho page from St Matthew's Gospel. End of the eighth century A.D. (Trinity College, Dublin; The Green Studios Ltd.)*

large 'portraits' of St John and St Matthew, the Teaching Christ who stands between two peacocks and holds a red book, and possibly the symbols of the Evangelists. Although his repertoire of ornament is similar to that employed by the 'Goldsmith'—strapwork, interwoven bodies etc.—the effect which he creates is very different. Compare the two photographs showing the Chi-Rho and the figure of St John respectively, and the differences of approach should immediately become apparent. The first is the work of an artist most at home in the realms of abstract design, the second is the work of an artist primarily concerned with the human figure: there are certainly decorative elements—the writhing curves of cloth and hair, the interlacings in the border and in the huge halo—but these take second place to the figure of the Evangelist himself. Notice too how the artist has insisted on the symmetry of his design, resulting in a less exciting composition than the Chi-Rho perhaps, but ultimately stressing the monumental character of the figure. The colours employed by this artist also tend to be muted and harmonious.

Book of Kells. *Portrait of St John. (Trinity College, Dublin; The Green Studios Ltd.)*

trated in the photograph. Françoise Henry calls him the 'Goldsmith', and it is easy to see why. His skill speaks for itself, and certainly we must be reminded of the work of the finest Irish metalworkers, those who made the Ardagh Chalice and the Tara Brooch. The modern reader may also be reminded of the wheels and springs of some extremely delicate watch movement. But amid this bewildering profusion of decorative detail—the spirals and strapwork, the plaited bodies of beasts and humans—there is amazing clarity. Notice how powerfully the forms of the two Greek letters—Chi and Rho—are stated on the page. And how firm and supple (and subtle!) are the curves which form these letters. His colours too are extremely subtle, and have been conceived in terms of delicate harmonies: silver-blue, muted green, golden yellow, purple and red.

The second illustrator might be termed the official portrait painter of the Book; from his hand come the

Book of Kells. *The Temptation of Christ, a rarely treated subject in early Christian art. (Trinity College, Dublin; The Green Studios Ltd.)*

Next we meet the illustrator whose talents lay in the direction of dramatic story telling. Among his contributions are 'The Arrest of Christ', 'The Temptation of Christ' and the 'Virgin and Child'. His concern for decoration was minimal, his frames are merely settings for his powerful figure groups, and are of little interest in themselves. His colour is usually more adventurous than that of the first two artists; his searing greens and blues, his strong purples and reds actually call to mind certain modern painters like Henri Matisse.

St Luke recounts how Satan brought Christ to Jerusalem and set him upon the pinnacle of the Temple, 'and said unto him, If thou be the Son of God, cast thyself down from hence: For it is written, He shall give his angels charge over thee, to keep thee . . . And Jesus answering said . . . Thou shalt not tempt the Lord thy God.'

It is this story which we find depicted in the complex picture shown in the photograph: a very large figure of Christ stands upon the sloping roof of the Temple (based on the form of the small Irish churches of the period). His gesture towards the black and shrivelled form of Satan is one of dismissal. Immediately above Christ's head float two rather anxious looking angels, ready to fulfil the prophecy if called upon to do so. Around the Temple we see crowds of people, all of them shown in profile.

Although none of the pages of primary importance

Book of Kells. *Detail, animals from the Chi-Rho page. (Trinity College, Dublin; The Green Studios Ltd.)*

Conjectural reconstruction of the monastery *at* Kells, *Co. Meath as it might have been* c. 1100. (© Brian O'Halloran)

appear to have been entrusted to the fourth important illustrator, he makes his presence felt in many parts of the book. His work is to be seen on many of the small capitals and in a number of the borders. He seems to have been a keen observer of everyday things, particularly animals, and his delightfully drawn creations —cats, mice, cocks and hens, dogs and warriors—add a refreshing down-to-earth note to the otherwise rather austere pages of the manuscript. Even the majestic Chi-Rho has been invaded by some of his animals; near the base of the stem of the letter Chi two rather plump cats have seized two unwary mice, or possibly rats, by their tails. In an adjoining space beneath the letter Rho a black cat devours a large fish—pilfered from the monastery kitchens?

The Book of Kells, although largely Celtic in its inspiration, demonstrates a distinct widening of the horizons of Irish art. Over the centuries Irish artists had continually absorbed certain influences from abroad—from Britain and Europe for instance —without disturbing their own tradition unduly. By the end of the eighth century the old Celtic repertoire of forms seems no longer to have been adequate to express everything that was felt necessary. As we have seen, certain of the illustrations in the Book have moved away from the realms of the purely symbolic, and towards the dramatic and the representational.

Scholars have speculated on the existence of other great gospel books comparable to the Book of Kells.

Some such may have existed, but books on so lavish a scale, the work of many artists over a long period, could never have been common and could only have been produced by the largest and wealthiest of the monasteries. A variety of lesser books have survived from the ninth and tenth centuries. These include gospel books like the Book of Mac Durnan, and the Book of Armagh, several psalters and grammar books.

The Book of Armagh is yet another of the treasures of the library of Trinity College. It was the work of a scribe called Ferdomnagh and would appear to have been written around the year 808. This book contains a number of interesting texts: documentation, including a biography, relating to St Patrick which seeks to uphold the claim of Armagh to its primacy over the other Irish monasteries, the only complete New Testament which has survived from early Christian Ireland, and finally, a life of St Martin of Tours, held by tradition to have been St Patrick's uncle.

Stone Carving

The carving of stone crosses continued during the ninth century and into the tenth at a number of monastic centres including Armagh, Kells, Clonmacnois, Durrow, Monasterboice and Castledermot. The basic form of the stone cross established in previous centuries—heavy pyramid-shaped base and wheel head—continued, but often with modifications. Figurative panels were no longer confined to the base but were extended over the entire east and west faces. As a consequence decoration became far less important and tended to retreat to the sides of the shaft and

The North Cross, *Castledermot, Co. Kildare. View of the east side. Ninth century A.D. (Commissioners of Public Works in Ireland)*

onto the wheel. The figure compositions themselves became increasingly complex and sophisticated, and owed a great deal to continental models, particularly to carved ivory panels and paintings from Carolingian Europe which found their way to Ireland during the period.

We have already seen, in the case of the cross of Moone, how various panels formed a coherent sequence in terms of subject matter. The panels on a high cross were, in effect, a pictorial sermon. This remained very much the case with the great figured crosses of the ninth and tenth centuries. The sequence of subjects was of primary importance, and was worked out before the sculptor considered his compositions in purely visual terms. A number of such themes may be discerned: the 'help of God' theme, which we have seen on the Moone Cross, and sequences which demonstrate a widespread belief of the early Church that events in the New Testament are often prefigured or paralleled by events in the Old (i.e. the 'Sacrifice of Isaac' was regarded as an event prefiguring the Crucifixion; Isaac was sometimes depicted carrying the wood for his own sacrificial altar). The theme of Redemption was yet another.

The north and south crosses at Castledermot, in County Kildare, relate in several ways to the Moone Cross which is located a short distance away. The Castledermot crosses are also of granite and the subjects depicted are similar to those on the earlier cross. Compare the photograph which shows the north cross with the photograph of the Moone Cross. Certain distinct dissimilarities should be immediately apparent: the proportions are quite different, and in the case of the Castledermot cross the most important subjects now appear on the shaft and arms. On the west side of the cross, we find Adam and Eve in a large eight-sided panel; surrounding that are panels depicting 'Daniel in the Lions' Den', 'David playing the Harp', the 'Massacre of the Innocents', and the 'Sacrifice of Isaac'. On the east side is a large depiction of the 'Crucifixion', surrounded by panels representing the Apostles. Other panels on the shaft seem to refer to St Anthony, the Hermit and possibly to the 'Three Hebrews in the Furnace'. A large panel on the side of the base presents us with a version of the 'Miracle of the Five Loaves and Two Fishes', somewhat more explicit than the Moone version.

The Cross of Muiredach

The most celebrated high cross of the Viking period is undoubtedly Muiredach's Cross in Monasterboice, County Louth. An inscription at the bottom of the west side of the shaft reads, 'OR DO MUIREDACH LAS NDERNAD I CHROSSA' (Pray for Muiredach who has caused this cross to be erected). This same Muiredach has been identified with an abbot of Monasterboice, who died in the year 923, thus helping us to date the cross itself.

Both the east and west faces are almost entirely covered with figure compositions, carved in high relief. A new and vigorous style has been introduced into Irish sculpture by the artist who carved this cross. The thematic structure of the panel sequence is also new and rather complex.

On the west face we find five subjects: starting at the bottom, 'The Arrest of Christ', 'Doubting Thomas', 'Christ giving the keys to Peter and the Book of the New Law to Paul', the 'Crucifixion' (which spreads across the arms) and finally a subject from the Old Testament, Moses, with arms raised, between Aaron and Hur.

Carved on the east face there are six panels in all, but these are far more crowded than the first set, some panels bearing two subjects. The panel at the bottom of the shaft, for instance, depicts both 'Adam and Eve' and also 'Cain slaying Abel'. Above this is a panel with 'David and Goliath' and also 'Saul and Jonathan'. Then come two panels with only one subject in each: 'Moses striking the Rock', and the 'Adoration of the Magi'. An elaborate 'Last Judgment' occupies the large panel formed by the crossing arms. Christ the Judge

divides the Blessed from the Damned, while below his feet the souls are weighed.

The revolutionary style of carving and the themes depicted on this cross, seem to have had considerable influence, and among those crosses with certain similarities might be mentioned the tall west cross at Monasterboice, the 'Cross of the Scriptures' at Clonmacnois, the high cross at Durrow and the Market cross in Kells.

This profusion of figured crosses appears to have occurred during the early decades of the tenth century. The years between 875 and 915—the so-called 'forty-years recess'—had seen a great lull in Viking raids upon Ireland, and the Irish used this period of comparative peace to regroup their forces. Monasteries were rebuilt, stone architecture, including the round towers, was developed and the new generation of stone carvers came to maturity. The crosses which they carved seem almost to have been a gesture of defiance towards the Invader, who continued to occupy a number of Irish towns. Then, towards the middle of the tenth century the carving of the crosses ceased and when it was revived again, a century or so later, styles and concepts had changed radically.

Of the metalwork produced during the Viking period our knowledge is very scanty. Among the few surviving examples are a number of croziers, heavy cast-bronze bells, brooches and plaques. Standards of craftsmanship suffered; decorative work became broader and coarser, and enamel work became rare.

Muiredach's Cross, *Monasterboice, Co. Louth. View of the west side. Early tenth century A.D. (Bord Fáilte Photo)*

CHAPTER EIGHTEEN

The Romanesque Period—Eleventh and Twelfth Centuries

The power of the Vikings was effectively curtailed, at least so far as Ireland was concerned, by the great pitched battle fought at Clontarf in 1014. The country returned to the comparative peace which it had known before the coming of the invaders. There was much to be done: ruined buildings to be rebuilt, many treasures to be repaired or replaced, stability, both political and religious, to be regained. Even before Clontarf this process had been set in motion. Brian Boru had done much for the political stability of Ireland by establishing his authority with great firmness; indeed he had been declared 'Emperor of the Irish' in Armagh. He was also conscious of what Ireland had lost culturally, and we learn from one of the annals, *Cogad Gaedel re Gallaib,* that the Ard Rí sent messengers abroad to buy books and bring them back to Ireland.

The process of repair lasted right into the middle of the eleventh century, and it appears that very little original work was actually undertaken. By mid century many of the monasteries had been restored to something resembling their old position, and the workshops and scriptoria were again turning out precious objects, high crosses and manuscripts. As we have already seen in the very first chapter of this book, a similar process of rebuilding was under way on the continent at the same time. We have seen too how in various European countries the architects and artists sought continually to modify and improve their creations, and how this adventurous spirit led to one of the greatest upsurges of artistic activity that Europe has ever known. Compared to this Ireland remained rather conservative, perhaps the consciousness that a 'golden age' was separated from the present by only two centuries was too great, and the Irish longed to restore the glories of the past rather than rush headlong into some new cultural adventure.

Irish people travelling on the continent—on pilgrimages to Compostella and Rome, for instance—certainly noticed that something new was happening in the realms of architecture, sculpture and painting. Inevitably certain aspects of the Romanesque style began to exert an influence here. Little or no attempt was made to emulate the grand scale of continental (and after the Norman Conquest in 1066, English) church building. Irish churches remained modest in scale and essentially rectangular in plan; foreign ideas like transepts, or apses curved or hexagonal in plan, simply did not appeal. Distinctly Romanesque features did begin to appear on Irish buildings however; carved doorways, windows, arches and pillars, usually combined with traditional Celtic motifs and therefore given a local flavour. Perhaps too the idea of combining the form of a round tower with that of a church—as we find in St Kevin's Church, Glendalough, or in Temple Finghin, Clonmacnois, County Offaly—was continental in inspiration. Irish buildings with distinctly Romanesque features are to be found at Roscrea and Cashel in County Tipperary, Dysert O'Dea and Inis Cealtra in County Clare, Tuam and Clonfert in County Galway, Clonmacnois in County Offaly, Killeshin, County Leix and Mellifont, County Louth. This list is, of course, by no means a complete one. And many of the buildings are now in a ruined state.

Clonfert Cathedral—Romanesque Portal

Clonfert Cathedral, in County Galway, is situated approximately three kilometres to the south of the junction between the rivers Shannon and Suck. The main structure probably dates from the ninth or tenth century, and occupies the site of a monastic church originally founded by St Brendan the Navigator. Its

The portal of Clonfert Cathedral, Co. Galway. *Possibly mid twelfth century A.D. (Commissioners of Public Works in Ireland)*

proximity to a major river has facilitated those intent upon plundering the building—the Vikings, and later the O'Kellys and the O'Rourkes. It has been modified several times during the Middle Ages, and it seems likely that the remarkable Romanesque portal was added about the middle of the twelfth century.

The deeply recessed doorway is flanked by two sets of columns, each covered with traceries of decorative carving. Above, the voussoirs of the arches are deeply cut with a variety of patterns: bosses, rings and a row of animal heads—possibly dogs—carved in high relief, each of which bites a section of moulding.

The most striking feature of the entire portal is probably the gable which rises steeply above the arches. Here we discover a number of relief carvings: an arcade composed of six columns with connecting arches, below each arch is a carved human head. This feature recurs in the triangular section which appears to rest on top of the arches and which is divided into smaller panels carved alternately with human heads and a marigold pattern.

Several other Irish portals display rows of heads. The portal at Dysert O'Dea in County Clare, for instance, has a row of heads carved on the voussoirs. Each of these has been carefully individualised however; some are beasts and some human. Other interesting Irish doorways from the period may be seen at Killeshin, County Leix, Clonmacnois (Nuns' Church), Roscrea, County Tipperary and Clonkeen, County Limerick.

Cormac's Chapel, Cashel

Cormac MacCarthy, King-Bishop of Cashel from 1122 to 1138, was responsible for the erection of the fine Romanesque chapel which stands, still intact, on the Rock. It was consecrated in 1134 with full pomp and ceremony, and occupies one of the most impressive architectural sites in Ireland along with a tenth-century tower, the ruins of a thirteenth-century cathedral and several later additions. So the site is a crowded one, and it may have been so for a considerable period before the chapel was built; the Rock of Cashel has probably been the seat of kings since the fourth century. For a period the site on the great limestone outcrop was jointly occupied by a lay court and the clergy; then, in 1101 the King, Muirceartach Ua Briain, handed it over entirely to the Church.

The chapel itself consists basically of a barrel-vaulted nave flanked by two square towers, and with a groin-vaulted chancel at the east end. The two towers occupy the position where we would normally expect to find the transepts in a French or English church.

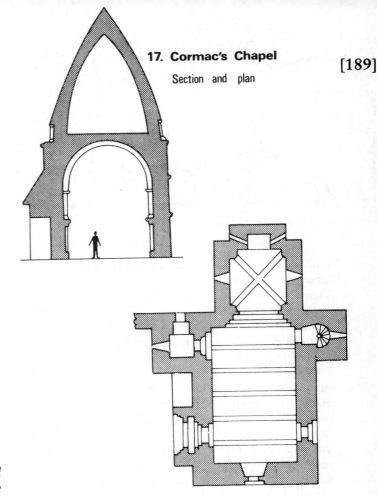

17. Cormac's Chapel [189]

Section and plan

Cormac's Chapel, *Cashel, Co. Tipperary. Consecrated in 1134 A.D. View from the south-east. (Bord Fáilte Photo)*

Above the vaulting are two apartments reached by a stairway in the southern tower. The high pitched stone roof is built on the corbel principle which we have encountered several times before in Irish architecture. Several features of the chapel's design suggest a certain German influence, particularly the two towers, and it is worth noting that there were a number of Irish monastic foundations in the Rhineland and central Germany during the period. Records show that direct contacts existed between Germany and Cashel, so the Germanic features are not altogether surprising.

The south tower, which is approximately three metres square, served as a belfry as well as housing the stairway. The north tower, which has no windows in its upper stories, served some other function, possibly that of treasury. It is entered by an elaborate doorway off the nave, and originally had another door opening to the east.

The massive barrel-vault which spans the nave is strengthened by a series of unmoulded arch ribs. These spring from a set of short, half columns which stand upon a broad stone shelf above an arcaded lower wall.

The interior is now lit very badly though originally there were three windows in the west wall which must have admitted ample light. Two of these were entirely

Cormac's Chapel – Tympanum carving

built up when the later cathedral was constructed. The larger building now encroaches upon the chapel in such a way that the north portal—the chapel's most impressive exterior feature—looks onto a narrow, triangular courtyard. The great depth of this portal was achieved by simply increasing the thickness of the wall several-fold.

Over the door is a very attractive tympanum sculpture of a curious helmeted centaur who shoots an arrow at a great leonine creature. Above the entire portal rises a wide and steep gable, similar in proportion to the one we have seen at Clonfert, but quite dissimilar in terms of decoration. Here the decoration suggests the beams of a timbered gable, of a kind found in Germany, in fact. The stone 'beams' are carved with a simple chevron design, and a number of the intervening spaces have large carved rosettes.

A high cross from the Romanesque period is also to be seen on the Cashel site. This is now in a ruined condition, however, due to weathering. A much better preserved example exists at Dysert O'Dea.

High Cross, Dysert O'Dea

The contrast between the cross at Dysert O'Dea, which dates from the mid twelfth century and those we have seen from earlier periods is very striking. The wheel-head is gone and the two figures, carved in very high relief, dominate the surface. The upper figure is that of the 'Crucified Christ', while the figure immediately below is that of a Church dignitary with mitre and crozier. The right arm of this figure is now missing, but in all probability it was raised in a gesture of benediction. The squarish hole where the arm once was indicates that the missing arm was carved originally from a separate piece of stone and inserted into the main piece. This appears to have been fairly common practice during the period. In a similar fashion two decorative pieces once protruded from each of the horizontal arms. The head of the Christ figure is also cut from a separate piece, and is now held firmly in place with cement.

The cross was repaired on several occasions, and placed on a new plinth. An inscription is carved on the original base below the bishop figure and reads: 'This cross was newly repaired by Michael O'Dea son of Connor Crone O'Dea in the Yeare 1683'.

The Cross of Dysert O'Dea, *Co. Clare. Mid twelfth century. (Commissioners of Public Works in Ireland)*

By way of contrast to the figures in high relief the remaining surfaces of the cross have been lightly carved with a variety of decorative and figurative motifs. The decorations on the back and sides of the cross include marigold patterns and intricate animal interlacings. On the original base is a pattern of interwoven snakes and some figurative scenes. These latter include 'Daniel in the Lions' Den' and 'Adam and Eve', both treated in a highly schematic fashion. The figure of Daniel, for instance, is flanked by two grotesque seated lions whose bodies are enmeshed by interwoven snakes.

Metalwork

A wealth of metalwork has survived from the Romanesque period; croziers, reliquaries and book boxes. We shall examine two examples briefly which indicate the high level of craftsmanship attained, although we shall encounter nothing quite like the sheer finesse of work from the greatest centuries of Irish craftsmanship.

St Patrick's Bell Shrine and the Cross of Cong

The shrine of St Patrick's Bell and the Cross of Cong, although differing widely in form, have this much in common: they were both constructed to house sacred relics. As its name implies the former was made to house a bell, made of iron, supposed by tradition to have belonged to St Patrick. The shrine was made in Armagh on the orders of the Ard Rí Domnall Ó Lochlainn around the year 1100. Basically it is a box measuring approximately 26 cm high and 14 cm by 10 cm at the base. It is made of heavy sheet bronze. Decoration consists of very finely cast gilt silver panels of openwork interlacings, and large bosses of crystal and coloured glass. The back bears a panel of silver-plated bronze pierced by a very repetitive cruciform pattern and inscribed with details of the shrine's manufacture.

The Cross of Cong was made on the orders of another Ard Rí, Turlough O'Conor, during the mid 1120s. Its purpose was to enshrine a splinter of the True Cross, which the King had begged of the Pope, Calixtus II. This sacred splinter was mounted beneath the large hemisphere of rock crystal which dominates the centre of the cross.

The Cross of Cong is basically a structure of oak, approximately three quarters of a metre in height, encased in panels of gilt bronze and further embellished by some glass studs. The metal casting is of a very high quality indeed. The panels, both front and

Shrine of St Patrick's Bell. *Made for the Árd Rí, Domnall Ó Lochlainn, c. 1100 A.D. (National Museum of Ireland)*

The Cross of Cong. *Made for the Ard Rí, Turlough O'Conor, c. 1123. Originally kept in Tuam and later transferred to the Abbey of Cong, Co. Mayo. (National Museum of Ireland)*

back, are decorated with animal interlacings. The same animal, vaguely reminiscent of a rather thin sea-horse with long snout, recurs again and again. On the back the design is fairly broad and repetitive but on the front the artist has managed to ring an amazing number of changes on his basic motif. One of the most intriguing aspects of this otherwise rather austere cross is to be found at the base. Here, quite unexpectedly, the two-sided head of a rather replusive little beast, covered with scales, bites savagely into the bottom of the shaft.

Manuscripts

Some twenty manuscripts in all have survived from the period: gospel books, psalters, books of poetry, epics, histories and others. These tend to be rather sparsely decorated when compared with the great early books. In style too they are often much broader. They include the Laber Hymnorum and the Book of Leinster, both in Trinity College.

The Cistercians

The period of Viking invasions had sadly disrupted the Irish way of life, but several events of the second half of the twelfth century effected deeper changes than anything since the beginnings of Christianity itself in the fifth century. The powerful current of the emerging continental civilisation became increasingly irresistible, and Ireland was soon to be swept along with the flood, and to lose much of her former identity.

The arrival of the Cistercians in Ireland effectively marked the end of the purely Irish monastic tradition. St Malachy of Armagh, while on a visit to Rome during the early 1140s had paid a visit to St Bernard of Clairvaux (q.v.) and was sufficiently impressed by the Cistercians to request that French monks be sent to Ireland to help found a branch of the order. The first Cistercian foundation was at Mellifont, in County Louth, and many others followed in the course of the next century or so. The austerity and dicipline of the French order had considerable appeal for Irish monks who began to forsake their traditional and far less organised way of life in large numbers. Among those monks dispatched by St Bernard were some with architectural training, and these helped to establish the very distinctive form of Cistercian building here.

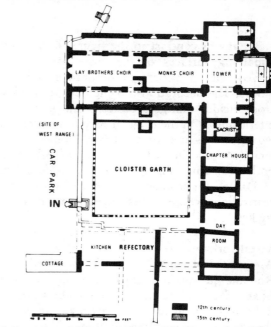

Plan of Jerpoint Abbey. *(Commissioners of Public Works in Ireland)*

The Cistercian System of Building

Cistercian buildings were organised according to a definite plan which echoed the austere discipline of the order. They were grouped around an open square or quadrangle. The church, with nave and transepts, was usually located on the north side, while more mundane buildings like refectories (dining-halls) and kitchens were placed on the opposite side. The sacristy and chapter (meeting-hall) were on the east, and store rooms etc. were on the west. The monks had their sleeping accommodation in first-floor dormitories above the rooms on the east and west. The result of all of this was a tightly knit and functional unit, quite unlike the old Irish monasteries with their casual scattering of huts.

By the late thirteenth century there were some thirty-eight Cistercian monasteries in Ireland. Among the

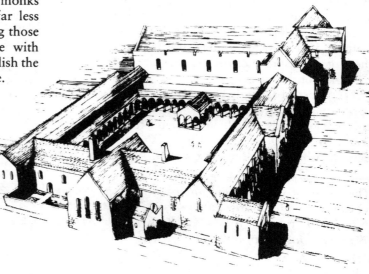

Conjectural reconstruction of Jerpoint Abbey, *Co. Kilkenny as it might have been in the thirteenth century.*
(© Brian O'Halloran)

best known of these, apart from the parent foundation at Mellifont, are Jerpoint and Graiguenamanagh in County Kilkenny, Boyle in County Roscommon, Holycross and Kilcooly in County Tipperary and Corcomroe in County Clare.

The 'invasion' of Ireland by the Cistercians, (and other orders like the Dominicans and Franciscans) was, of course, essentially peaceful, and enriched Irish monastic life. The invasion of the Anglo-Normans in 1169 and 1170 was altogether different in character.

CHAPTER NINETEEN

The Anglo-Norman Period, and After

Conjectural reconstruction of Trim Castle, Co. Meath, *as it might have been* c. 1250. (© D. Newman Johnson)

We shall not attempt to deal in any great detail with those centuries of struggle for control of this island, the net result of which was almost total domination from Britain, and the resulting eclipse of any culture recognisably Irish, particularly where the visual arts were concerned. It might be as well to note, however, that even before the coming of the Normans, the course of Irish culture was already beginning to falter and would possibly have deferred to pressures from the continent and Britain in any case.

In chapter one we saw how the Normans brought their concept of building to Britain after 1066. In Ireland too they began an extensive programme of building, erecting many castles and churches and replacing traditional concepts of work in metal, stone and wood with those of their own.

Churches

The first half of the thirteenth century was a prolific period for the building of churches and cathedrals. The two Dublin cathedrals, Christ Church and St Patrick's date from this time.

Christ Church, which was begun around 1173, occupies a site within the boundaries of the old Viking city. Of the Gothic buildings erected in Ireland by the Anglo-Normans it is probably the most important.

Double capital from Christ Church Cathedral *Dublin,*
c. 1200 A.D. (Roger Stalley)

Originally the building was almost purely English in
concept. Masons and sculptors were imported from
Somersetshire to undertake a major part of the project
and even some of the stone for its construction—
oolite, a granular limestone—came from the same
region. The present building is the product of a
number of extensions and reconstructions made over
the centuries. The only parts of the original twelfth-
century construction which survive are the north and
south transepts. The nave was probably begun around
1212, and other sections were added later in the
thirteenth century and in the fourteenth. In 1562 the
nave vaulting and the south wall suffered collapse, and
were rather crudely repaired. These were restored to
something resembling their original condition late in
the nineteenth century.

Other important church buildings from the period
include St Mary's Church, New Ross; Kildare cathedral; the Cathedral of SS. Peter and Paul, Newtown,
Trim, County Meath and Killaloe cathedral, County
Clare.

Church building entered a period of decline after the
mid thirteenth century. The Black Death, which, as we
have seen, had a profound effect on Europe, struck
Ireland during the middle of the following century,
bringing building activity virtually to a standstill for
some time. It was not until the beginning of the
fifteenth century that the country had recovered sufficient strength to enter another creative phase. From
that century came a whole series of important Francis-
can establishments: Muckross, County Kerry;
Timoleague, County Cork; Creevelea, County Leitrim;
Claregalway, Kilconnell, and Ross Errilly in County
Galway. A very widespread campaign of alteration
and rebuilding also took place; new doors were inserted, as were new broad traceried windows which let
in a great deal more light than those they replaced.
This period is also rich in metalwork, wood and stone
carving.

Many of the finest of the stone carvings are found on
the sides of box tombs. These remained fairly common
until the seventeenth century and consisted of a large
stone box, usually bearing a carving of the deceased in
high relief on top, with carvings of religious subjects
around the sides. The photograph shows a panel from
the MacMahon tomb which is in Ennis Friary. The
subject here is 'Christ being laid in the Tomb'. There
are many other subjects depicted on the sides of the
box, among them 'The Arrest of Christ', 'The Scourg-
ing at the Pillar' and 'The Crucifixion'.

After about 1200 free standing metal crucifixes,
used to adorn altars, were introduced to Ireland. The
Ballylongford Cross, now in the National Museum, is
a good example from the late fifteenth century. Its
distinctly unIrish character may readily be appreciated

Christ Laid in the Tomb, *from the MacMahon*
tomb, Ennis Friary, Co. Clare. c. 1475.
(Commissioners of Public Works in Ireland)

Ballylongford Cross. *Late fifteenth century. (National Museum of Ireland)*

Christ on Calvary, *from Fethard, Co. Tipperary. Early sixteenth century. (National Museum of Ireland)*

by comparing it with an earlier Irish example like the Cross of Cong. With the fifteenth-century cross, much of the emphasis is laid on the gaunt, rather expressionistic figure of Christ. Decoration is largely confined to the floral sprays which project from the shaft and arms. As was common with this type of altar cross, the symbols of the Evangelists were included as openwork designs inserted into small panels on the arms and shaft.

The remarkable figure of 'Christ on Calvary' from Fethard, County Tipperary, probably dates from the beginning of the sixteenth century. It is of painted wood and seems to indicate a strongly Spanish influence. Compare it with some of the Spanish works illustrated in Part I. Here the depiction is unmistakably expressionistic: the drapery upon which the gaunt figure of Christ sits is blood red; his only companion is a skull. Great emphasis is laid on the elements of suffering and apparent helplessness—the binding of Christ's wrists with rope and the large coarse thorns which adorn the head.

The carving of stone high crosses was revived for a period during the sixteenth and seventeenth centuries in County Meath. Several stone crosses were erected by Dame Jennet Dowdall in or around 1600 as memorials to her husband William Bathe who died in 1599. These are at Duleek and Athcarne. The Duleek cross bears an inscription recording William Bathe's death, and asking a prayer for the repose of his soul. There are also a number of carved figures, including those of an angel with a coat of arms, and a number of saints.

In 1541 Henry VIII assumed the title 'King of Ire-land'. During the course of his reign the abbeys were dissolved and large amounts of Church property were confiscated. The Church's role as chief patron of the arts in Ireland was effectively brought to an end after a period of over a thousand years virtually without interruption.

Cross *erected by* Dame Jennet Dowdall *at Duleek, Co. Meath in 1601. (© Ruth Brandt)*

CHAPTER TWENTY

The Georgian Period

The proliferation of fine buildings in any country is usually a sign of two things; affluence and confidence. During the eighteenth century, particularly during the latter half, many superb buildings were constructed in Ireland; indeed many of the very finest ever to be erected in this island. While the quality of these buildings is not in question, they still pose one or two problems. Should buildings, very often designed by foreign architects, and at the very least overwhelmingly influenced by styles from abroad, be regarded as Irish at all? Often the answer to such a question, when it can be answered, must be in the negative. They find a place in this chapter simply because they are an important part of the heritage of the country, rather than because of any specific 'Irishness'. And while the great eighteenth-century Irish buildings were certainly indicative of affluence and confidence, these attributes applied only to a very small minority of Irish citizens. The majority of Irishmen living during that period were both poor and politically impotent.

The eighteenth-century buildings were of several distinct types. There were, first of all, the houses of the landed gentry, often extremely lavish both in scale and in decoration. These are to be found in many parts of the country. Then there were the buildings which so utterly transformed the city of Dublin, and signified the new-found status of that city as a true metropolis, with its own (almost) independent parliament. We have that period of pride and affluence, late in the eighteenth century, to thank for Dublin's great wide thoroughfares like O'Connell Street and Baggot Street, her beautiful civic buildings like the Bank of Ireland, the Custom House and the Four Courts, and the various squares surrounded by elegantly proportioned red brick terraces.

Sir William Chambers (1726–96)

The English architect William Chambers designed a number of important buildings in Dublin, both for Trinity College, and for his patron Lord Charlemont. The two buildings which face one another across the front square in Trinity College—the Chapel and the Public Theatre (usually called the Examination Hall) were both designed by him. The Public Theatre was completed in 1791. The stucco (plaster) work on the ceiling was by Michael Stapleton, and gives us some idea of the quality of Dublin craftsmanship from the period.

The Casino at Marino, shown in the photograph, which Chambers designed for Lord Charlemont, has been described as the most perfect building in the country. This elegant and small-scale pavilion, Palladian in inspiration, was completed in 1771. The parent house for which it was built has long since disappeared. Not wishing to spoil the external perfection of his building with such mundane details as chimneys and drainpipes, Chambers very cleverly concealed both; the decorative urns on top of the building serve as chimneys while the columns have been hollowed, enabling rainwater to drain from the roof. Look at the photograph and try to assess the style of the building for yourself, and compare it with other eighteenth-century buildings discussed in an earlier chapter. The Municipal Gallery of Modern Art, originally Charlemont House, was also the work of Chambers.

James Gandon (1743–1824)

James Gandon was born in London, the son of a French father and a Welsh mother. A pupil of William Chambers, he spent much of his working life in Ireland. Gandon had already made a name for himself in London when, in 1781, he accepted an invitation to come to Dublin to build the new Custom House. He seems to have encountered opposition almost from the start; there were those who believed that their vested interests would not be served by the position of the new building, as it was some distance down river from the previous one and thus would tend to shift the existing centre of commerce. The bold way in which he tackled the problem of building the foundations on

The Casino, Marino, north-east Dublin, by Sir William Chambers, 1771. Built for James Caulfield, 1st Earl of Charlemont. It cost £60,000, a great deal of money in the 1770s. (Bord Fáilte Photo)

The Custom House, *1781, by James Gandon. View from across the Liffey. (Commissioners of Public Works in Ireland)*

what was then rather soft reclaimed slob-land also drew some criticism. He decided to use a base of timber, with brick and granite, instead of piling alone. His judgement would seem to have stood the test of time. So indeed has his design.

The building must surely still rank as one of the most pleasing buildings in Dublin; this is particularly apparent when it can be viewed from the opposite side of the Liffey. Its long horizontals blend so perfectly with the greater horizontal form of the river. It might be added that the close proximity of several recent structures, the railway bridge and more particularly, the new Liberty Hall, do a great deal to disturb the sense of scale which Gandon achieved in his building. Viewed against the rather brutal vertical form of Liberty Hall the Custom House tends to take on the aspect of a toy. There are, of course, many other examples both in Dublin and other cities, where insensitive modern development, while not actually destroying works from the past, has a rather detrimental effect upon them.

The Four Courts is another, and slightly later, work by Gandon. This building, another architectural tour de force, also occupies a site on the banks of the Liffey. Fortunately there are no high-rise structures nearby to detract from its appearance. Again it might be useful to compare these buildings with others from England and the continent which we have already discussed.

Gandon was to remain in Ireland for the rest of his life; he died in his house in Lucan, aged eighty. Among his other Irish buildings are the King's Inns in Henrietta Street and that best known of Dublin structures, O'Connell Bridge.

Edward Smyth (1749–1812)
An edition of the Dublin *Evening Post* published in 1784 enthusiastically described some of the stone carvings used to decorate the exterior of Gandon's Custom House: 'Colossal heads, emblematic of the principal rivers of this island, with singular descriptive ornaments, in a style of sculpture admirably executed.'

The River Boyne, *carving by* Edward Smyth. *From the Custom House. (Commissioners of Public Works in Ireland)*

These were the work of an Irish sculptor, Edward Smyth, whose carvings were much appreciated by Gandon—so much so that Smyth's work is featured on all of the other buildings in Dublin by that architect.

The appeal of Smyth's carvings may readily be appreciated. Their surfaces are richly animated with a variety of textures. Their forms are weighty and full, and well modelled. Yet they have, after all, a light-hearted quality about them.

The subjects symbolically depicted on the Custom House have been open to some speculation, but it is usually agreed that if one starts from the O'Connell Bridge end they are: the Foyle, Lough Erne, the Liffey, the Boyne, the Nore, the Blackwater, the Atlantic Ocean, the Bann, the Shannon, the Lee, the Lagan, the Suir, the Barrow and the Slaney.

Thomas Ivory (c. 1732–86)

Accounts of Thomas Ivory's origins are vague; it has been suggested that he may have been born in Cork, and there served his apprenticeship as a carpenter. Be this as it may, we do know that he was appointed Master of the Dublin Society School of Architectural Drawing some time around 1760.

Ivory's relatively brief career, although attended by a small share of success, was beset with frustrations. He was forced to contend with the contemporary preference for English architects, with the spectacle of the greater success of his rival and inferior Cooley, with the frustration of being unable to finish several of his most important projects as he would have wished and finally with the disappointment of total eclipse by the formidable Gandon.

His best-known building is the Blue Coat School (King's Hospital) in Blackhall Place. A competition, sponsored by the school governors, was held in 1772, to attract designs for the new school. Ivory had the double gratification of being awarded the sum of fifty pounds and seeing his rival Cooley disgraced. He did not win the commission at this juncture however; all the entries were ultimately rejected and some hopes were expressed that William Chambers might be tempted to accept. A second competition held during the following year resulted in the job being given to Ivory.

The Blue Coat School is now owned by the Incorporated Law Society of Ireland. The building is somewhat Baroque in conception. A massive central block (which was originally to have been surmounted by an elaborate tower) is flanked by two lesser edifices linked to it by curving wings. The central tower was one of several features uncompleted, and its place has been taken by a rather unimpressive copper dome. Ivory's own drawings of the building convey a feeling of considerable elegance, as does the view, reproduced here, (by a contemporary, the topographical artist James Malton). The actual building has a certain oppressive heaviness about it, however, which is not compensated for by the finely conceived details of the façade.

Dublin is still rich in buildings from what is usually termed the Georgian period, although many have either sadly decayed or have been destroyed altogether. Areas like Merrion Square, Fitzwilliam Square and College Green still retain much of their original splendour. So too do many of the superbly executed Rococo and Adam style stucco ceilings of the period, in buildings as various as Newman House and the David

The Blue Coat School, c. *1790. Drawing by* James Malton. (National Gallery of Ireland)

Hendrick's Gallery (both on Stephen's Green), the Chapel of the Rotunda Hospital and the Dominican orphanage in Lower Dominick Street.

It is hardly surprising that such a period of prosperity should have encouraged the art of painting, particularly portraiture, although very little of the painting seems to have approached in excellence the best architecture. Several members of the Hone family stand out, particularly Nathaniel (1718–84), whose work may be seen in the National Gallery, and his son Horace. We shall encounter members of this artistic family again, in both the nineteenth and the twentieth centuries.

Unrest leading to rebellion, the threat of invasion from France, these were but two of the factors which led to the Act of Union in 1801 which effectively took away so much of Dublin's status. London had once again become the magnetic centre, politically and culturally, inevitably drawing talent away from this country.

CHAPTER TWENTY-ONE

The Modern Period: Nineteenth and Twentieth Centuries

So the modern period begins on quite a low note; through much of the nineteenth century Ireland lost many of her most gifted painters, sculptors and writers. Several carved out very successful careers in London, others were attracted to France.

The mid nineteenth century was deeply marked by the potato famine, with the resultant death toll and emigration on a large scale. But this was also the period which saw a revival of national pride, the age of O'Connell, Thomas Davis and Young Ireland, and later of Parnell.

The early years of the twentieth century brought together those forces which were once again to make of Ireland a nation, as opposed to a colony. Perhaps it is significant that this period also produced one of the greatest of all Irish painters, Jack Yeats, as well as a number of literary figures of immense stature, including the painter's brother, the poet, William Butler Yeats.

John Henry Foley (1818–74)

John Henry Foley was born in Dublin, and at the age of sixteen he emigrated to London to study sculpture. A certain amount of success came very early in his career; his neo-classical works like the 'Death of Abel' and 'Ino and Bacchus' were exhibited at the Royal Academy. He had increasing successes with his portraits also, and by the early 1850s he had established himself as the leading portrait sculptor in England. And he was soon to be accepted as a full member of the Royal Academy.

The Memorial to Prince Albert, constructed in Hyde Park, was one of the most grandiose monuments conceived in Victorian England. Foley was one of the eight sculptors chosen to work on the project (two others were also Irish) and such was his artistic standing that he was asked to execute the portrait figure of the late Prince as well as one of the large allegorical groups to be placed at each of the corners of the monument. But Foley was also to undertake some important civic sculpture for the city of his birth.

His equestrian statue of Field Marshal Gough was cast from fifteen tons of gun metal from the cannon captured by that stalwart soldier during his various campaigns. The figure was placed in Phoenix Park but was rather unceremoniously removed some years ago. Two other figures by Foley are unlikely to meet a similar fate however; Edmund Burke and Oliver Goldsmith still stand on either side of the main entrance to Trinity College. The best known of all of his Dublin monuments has not been so lucky; the O'Connell Monument recently lost one of the large figures from its pedestal in a manner rather similar to that used to remove the Field Marshal. Happily this figure has since been restored, thanks largely to the efforts of another Dublin sculptor, John Behan.

The O'Connell Monument

The O'Connell Monument is one of those works of art which has probably suffered through being too well placed. Many thousands of people pass it daily, but probably almost no one actually looks at it! Yet, from several points of view, it is well worth the effort.

First of all the entire monument is conceived as a coherent and satisfying architectural unit; the dominant form is that of the central vertical drum which culminates in the massive figure of the Liberator himself. The smaller figures grouped around the centre of the drum, far from destroying its integrity as a simple form, add articulation to its surface and emphasise its vertical quality. The four great winged figures who sit at the corners of the pedestal serve, from the purely aesthetic point of view, to create an easy transition from the vertical of the drum to the horizontal of the pedestal and ultimately the street below. Notice how their wings reach out to embrace the form of the drum

The O'Connell Monument, *Dublin, by* John Henry Foley. *(Bord Fáilte Photo)*

figure pointing dramatically upwards towards O'Connell is Erin; she clutches a traditional Irish harp, while the chains of bygone servitude lie broken at her feet. The various figures are those of a bishop, poet, historian, artist, musician, soldier and sailor. Others represent farming, trade, law, and science. Below these figures, on the drum, are the four heraldic coats of arms of the provinces. And above all this stands Daniel O'Connell; the Liberator receives homage from a grateful people.

Daniel Maclise (1806–70)

Although a number of parallels may be found between the careers of John Henry Foley and the painter Daniel Maclise, time has not been quite so kind to the latter. Yet in his own day Maclise enjoyed both fame and financial success; to his friend Charles Dickens he was 'the gentlest and most modest of men' and possessed 'prodigious fertility of mind and wonderful wealth of intellect'. He was even offered the presidency of the Royal Academy and a knighthood.

Like Foley he was Irish born (in Cork probably in 1806) and like the sculptor he emigrated to London to further his artistic career. Already in Cork he had begun to make a name for himself, while still in his teens he had set up a small sudio in Patrick Street and there turned his hand to producing small skilful portraits in pencil and watercolour. From the proceeds he was able to go to London to study at the Royal Academy schools.

He continued to produce portraits, including several of Dickens and his family. But he was soon to develop a taste for that genre so beloved of the Victorians, the large composition based upon historical or literary subject matter. Among such pieces submitted to the Royal Academy exhibitions we find 'Henry the Eighth's first interview with Anne Boleyn', 'Alfred the Saxon King, disguised as a minstrel' and 'Malvolio in Olivia's Garden'.

During the 1860s Maclise was one of a number of artists selected to paint a series of mural decorations for the Houses of Parliament. His enthusiasm for this task was soon to wane however; he encountered great difficulties in trying to master the fresco technique, and he felt that the payment was insufficient. Nevertheless he completed 'The Meeting of Wellington and Blucher' and 'The Death of Nelson'.

His 'Wedding of Strongbow and Aoife', originally intended as part of the mural scheme, now exists as a large oil painting on canvas, and hangs in the National Gallery. This painting will probably be familiar to many Irish people through frequent reproduction in school text-books, and on account of this may seem rather hackneyed. Consider it afresh. It is a forceful picture, both in terms of composition and symbolism.

and how the subtle rhythm of the feathers seems to merge and blend with the folds of the drapery. Foley has articulated his large architectural mass very successfully, but he has also paid considerable attention to detail—each of the figures is beautifully made, and each plays a particular role in the elaborate symbolic scheme.

The four large winged female figures represent 'Patriotism', 'Courage', 'Fidelity' and 'Eloquence' (the attributes of O'Connell) respectively. It is relatively easy to tell which is which, Patriotism clutches a sword and shield indicative of readiness to defend her country, for instance, while Courage strangles a serpent. The bronze figures which encircle the centre of the drum symbolise the people of Ireland. The large female

The Wedding of Strongbow and Aoife, c. *1860 by* Daniel Maclise. *(National Gallery of Ireland)*

Make an assessment of it for yourself from both of these angles.

Nathaniel Hone (1831–1917)
With the work of Nathaniel Hone we enter an artistic world distinctly different from that of academic history painting and portraiture. Hone was essentially a painter of landscapes, and his particular vision was nurtured in France, more particularly by the French Realist movement.

He was born in Dublin, a descendant of Berkeley Hone (brother of the original Nathaniel, the seventeenth-century painter). He studied engineering in Trinity College, and worked for some time as an engineer before resolving to take up painting. In Paris during the 1850s he spent his time drawing and painting the human figure (Part I gives details of nineteenth-century French artistic training), and also diligently copying the pictures of the Old Masters in the Louvre.

A move to the village of Barbizon brought him into

Off Lowestoft *by* Nathaniel Hone. *(National Gallery of Ireland)*

contact with artists like Jean François Millet (q.v.) and here he seems to have discovered his true path. His work was painstaking and keenly observed, but ultimately rather conservative. Contact with Manet and others of the Impressionist movement left no appreciable mark upon his painting, for instance.

Returning to Ireland he settled in Malahide, County Dublin, where he lived for the remainder of his long life. As he was a man of independent means he very rarely sold or exhibited his work. Although he was a prolific water-colourist—his studies made in this medium tended to be much broader and spontaneous than his oils—even his close friends were not allowed to see what he modestly dismissed as 'blots'. He died virtually unknown, and left most of his large output to the National Gallery.

Hone's colours often seem unduly heavy and subdued; his taste tended towards browns and grays, soft greens and blues. His sensitivity to atmosphere however, is very well demonstrated by a picture like the seascape, 'Off Lowestoft'. Here there is a strong evocation of the elements: the sea is a cold gray, the heavy 'wetness' of it well expressed in the forms of those ponderously rolling waves. Upon this turgid surface the sailing boats appear to ride free as birds, while the great cloud, buff-coloured with just a hint of pink, evokes a feeling of lightness as well as light.

Roderick O'Conor (1861–1940)

Roderick O'Conor's landscape, painted in 1894, would seem to indicate an awareness of many of the exciting new discoveries being made by French painters of the period. His paint is applied in broad strokes, reminiscent of the Impressionists, and his colours—bright pinks, reds and purples contrasting with blues and greens—suggest the paintings of someone like Van Gogh or even the Fauves (q.v.)

O'Conor spent much of his life in France. He was a friend of Paul Gauguin (q.v.) and was, in fact, one of those painters who worked with the great French artist at Pont Aven. Gauguin is alleged to have invited O'Conor to accompany him to Tahiti; accounts vary, however, as to why the Irishman refused.

A number of O'Conor's paintings may be seen in the Municipal Gallery of Modern Art, including an intense, brooding self-portrait. These vary very considerably in conception. The 'Breton Girl', which he presented to the gallery in 1906 is curiously conservative; the colours are subdued and the composition very rigid and formal (compare it with any of Gauguin's depictions of similar subjects). Several figure studies are painted in a far more fluid manner, in subdued blues and purples, while a small seascape, 'Rocks', is almost pure Fauvism.

Lézaver, Finistère, *1894, by* Roderick O'Conor. *(Municipal Gallery of Modern Art, Dublin)*

Jack Yeats (1871–1957)

During the 1950s Oskar Kokoschka, the Austrian Expressionist painter, was fond of addressing letters to 'Jack B. Yeats, The Last of the Great Masters in the World, Dublin, Ireland'. A slightly exaggerated tribute perhaps. Nevertheless, it is probably no exaggeration to call him the greatest Irish visual artist of modern times.

He was born in London, the son of John Butler Yeats, an accomplished painter in his own right. Many of his formative years were spent in the West of Ireland, however. 'Sligo was my school, and the sky above it', he was later to declare. And although it was not until 1900 that he settled permanently in this country, it is basically true that from the start Ireland, her people and traditions, served as the raw material for his art. His art was to undergo great changes as he grew in maturity, and it continued to do so, and to divide him from all of those artists whose work we have just examined.

Yeats's early pictures—mostly drawings and watercolours—have often been likened to some of the literary creations of his friend John Synge. Works from the late nineteenth and early twentieth century are filled with figures just that little bit larger than life, and sometimes verging on caricature (cf. Synge's 'Playboy of the Western World'). There are tinkers, jockeys and Aran fishermen, fairs, circuses, pubs and race-meetings. Some of his characters—jockeys or fishermen—with fierce dark eyes and bristling moustaches, gaze with haughty disdain upon the world. They are aware of their own worth and vitality, and intent upon living their own lives to the full. Not all of Yeats's characters are proud; some are humorous, others pathetic, while others are slightly sinister.

With all of them we can feel the artist's involvement on a human level. The people whom he painted were not merely the raw material for aesthetic experiment, as was so often the case with painters like Degas or Seurat, for instance. When he poked fun it was all done with good humour; Yeats lacked the malicious cutting edge of Lautrec or Rouault.

The Rogue, his hat perched at a rakish angle above his shock of red curls, sits on a public house bench. Beside him is a pint of Guinness. Outside the sun is shining; are we to assume that he doesn't bother with anything as mundane as work? But he is not really as casual as he would like us to believe; the apparent carelessness of his dress and posture are not quite confirmed by the distinctly alert and shifty cast of his eyes. Is he on the look-out for some unwary stranger who might be naïve enough to swallow a hard-luck story, or perhaps even engage in a 'harmless' game of cards?

Yeats's technique in oil paint developed very gradu-

The Rogue, *by* Jack B. Yeats. *An early watercolour. (Municipal Gallery of Modern Art, Dublin)*

ally. His early works in that medium are painted in broad flat areas of fairly subdued colour, and rely for their dramatic effect on simple and powerful tonal contrasts. During the mid twenties he was beginning to apply his paint more thickly, allowing the actual texture of the pigment to play an important role in the structure of his pictures. His drawing and composition became increasingly simple, sometimes almost rudimentary—the vertical columns of figures are opposed to broad horizontal areas of land, sea or sky. And colour was becoming increasingly important.

The work of Yeats's mature years is quite extraordinary: figures, horses, landscapes and buildings remain, but swimming in a veritable torrent of colour—brilliant yellows, powerful reds, biting acidic greens and ice-cold blues. Paint is applied in the most unrestrained manner—plastered on like soft butter.

Men of Destiny by Jack B. Yeats. *(National Gallery of Ireland)*

Here Yeats has reduced his drawing and composition to a remarkably simple state; the light, and above all the colour, are all important. Against the deep cold blue of sea and cloud-heavy sky the thickly plastered colours of figures and foreground—orange, scarlet, yellow—seem to burn like embers. The peculiar sense of excitement generated by this picture, that something important is about to happen, is almost entirely conveyed by means of colour.

There are really no other Irish figures with whom one may compare or relate Jack Yeats, at least not in the visual arts. We may discover a number of parallels between his work and that of the German Expressionists however. In terms of technique his later work is often reminiscent of artists like Schmidt-Rottluff and Emil Nolde (q.v.). The same pure, searing colours are there and so too is the broad, extravagant technique. But these are ultimately exterior characteristics: Yeats's particular brand of Romantic exuberance, and his optimistic outlook seem somehow out of sympathy with the Germans. He comes closest, in terms both of technique and vision, to his friend Oskar Kokoschka, several of whose paintings may be seen in the Municipal Gallery.

Evie Hone (1894–1955) and Mainie Jellett (1896–1943)

Evie Hone and Mainie Jellet seemed to know what they were looking for when, in 1920, they journeyed to Paris to study painting. Mainie Jellett called it the 'inner principle and not the outer appearance', and they both felt that the way to this 'inner principle' lay in the study of Cubism (q.v.). For a time they became pupils of André Lhote, a thoughtful, rather scholarly painter, whose approach to art was in essence academic, but with a Cubist veneer. Moving on from Lhote, the two Irish painters persuaded Albert Gleizes to accept them as pupils. Gleizes was also, in a sense, a Cubist, but he had rejected subject matter and had reduced his paintings to flat, rhythmic areas of colour and texture. For a period of ten years Evie Hone and Mainie Jellett worked under his guidance. At the same time they were living and working in Dublin, making frequent visits to Paris.

Not surprisingly the style which both artists evolved owed much to that of Gleizes himself. Mainie Jellett's 'Deposition', now in the Municipal Gallery, is a good example. Whereas many of her paintings from this period were totally abstract (this is also true of Evie Hone), she also attempted to explore the possibilities of figurative work without in any way compromising the integrity of rhythm and compositional balance. This painting works like a well-oiled machine; every element has its logical place. The composition, which is largely composed of fluid curving forms, is lent some 'backbone' by the introduction of a number of well placed straight lines. The central vertical, which approximates to the shaft of the cross, is the most important of these. The curving forms of the figures rise on either side of this axis and culminate in the large circular form at the top which tends to absorb the upward thrust and deflect it back into the picture space. Notice too how the artist has placed a decorative form of straight lines and curves in each of the top corners.

exhibition of the Royal Hibernian Academy was something less than 'living'.

Both artists were to develop a style more obviously their own. This is particularly true of Evie Hone who eventually channelled her energies into stained glass rather than painting. Several fine examples of her work may be seen in various parts of the country: Collins' Barracks Chapel in Cork, Tara Church of Ireland church and the Catholic churches at Cloughjordan, County Tipperary and on the Ennis road in Limerick. In Dublin her most accessible piece is undoubtedly the large symbolic 'My Four Green Fields', in the C.I.E. offices in O'Connell Street. This may quite easily be viewed from the pavement. Other examples in Dublin include the superb 'Resurrection' in the chapel of Ivory's Blue Coat School, and the two small panels in the Municipal Gallery.

Resurrection *by* Evie Hone. *Stained glass window of the Blue Coat School. (Courtesy of Mr Ronald Anderson)*

Can you judge their function in the composition? This picture, because of the clarity of its structure, is an ideal subject for analysis. Make a tracing of the main curved and straight lines, and notice how carefully they have been related to each other and to the shape of the panel. Make an analysis of the tonal structure also.

In 1943 Mainie Jellet, in collaboration with a number of other Irish artists (including Evie Hone and Louis le Brocquy) was instrumental in founding the annual 'Irish Exhibition of Living Art'. This was to provide a regular venue for artists whose work was beginning to reflect the new concepts of the twentieth century. The title chosen also implied that the annual

Louis le Brocquy (1916–   )

It is no easy task to write meaningfully about a painting like Louis le Brocquy's 'Isolated Being'; in fact one may far more readily say what his picture *is not* rather than what it is. The image is too tentative to be regarded seriously as representational or expressionistic, far too blandly stated—it is basically a simple vertical form, virtually colourless, placed in the centre of the canvas—to be seen as an exploration of some purely aesthetic principles, composition, colour etc.

What then is it all about? Merely by asking this question we are perhaps beginning to approach the artist's intention. In common with many recent works of art, in a variety of media, le Brocquy's painting poses far more questions than it answers. Traditionally, the arts had content; they told stories, acted the part of religious or philosophical symbol, had coherent structure. In a sense they 'answered questions'; one could say what they were 'about'.

'Isolated Being' is a painting of a human figure, yet it tells us remarkably little, in positive terms, about the nature of its subject. What it does is to pose one or two questions which have troubled thoughtful people for some decades at least: do we ever really see or understand other people; is it ever possible to communicate meaningfully with another, and are we, each one of us, 'islands' effectively cut off from each other at the deepest levels? A disturbing theme, but one which has occupied the energies of a number of painters and writers in recent years (cf. Beckett, Sartre, F. Bacon etc.)

But le Brocquy is by no means always disturbing. Although he is best known for paintings similar to the one we have discussed (from his 'White Period', which began in the late fifties) he has also been responsible for some remarkable tapestries and book illustrations. His tapestries, most of which were executed during the early fifties, demonstrate the artist's strong sympathies with the modern French school. The influence of Picasso (q.v.) is particularly evident in designs like 'Allegory' and 'Adam and Eve in the Garden'. A more recent tapestry may be seen in the modern offices of P. J. Carroll and Company which are on Grand Parade in Dublin. This is the large work depicting the legendary sixth-century voyage to America of St Brendan the Navigator.

His vivid illustrations in black ink for Thomas Kinsella's translation of the Táin demonstrate yet another side to this artist.

Colin Middleton (1910–   )

The work of the Belfast painter Colin Middleton has passed through a number of phases reflecting several of the great artistic movements basic to the twentieth century. Cubism, Surrealism and Expressionism have

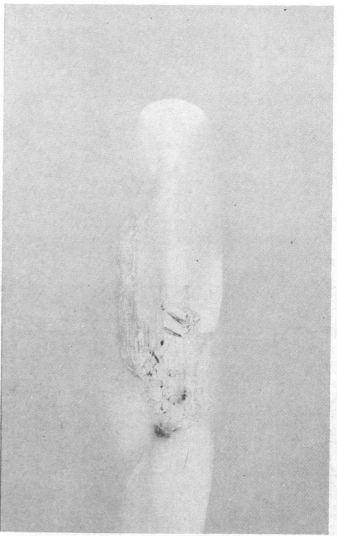

Isolated Being, c. *1958, by* Louis le Brocquy. *(Municipal Gallery of Modern Art, Dublin)*

Figure with Owls, *1970, by* Colin Middleton. *(Gordon Lambert Collection; © Colin Middleton)*

Urban Landscape, *1972, by* Jonathan Wade. *(Neptune Gallery, Dublin)*

all, at various times, left their mark.

Middleton can be austere and coldly formal, banishing colour almost entirely and working with clear-cut geometrical shapes and finely incised lines. But he can also be humorous, exploiting playful imagery with a surreal flavour, and using bright colours. He is a sensitive painter of landscapes as well, a talent which he shares with a number of fellow Ulstermen, like Arthur Armstrong or T. P. Flanagan.

There is, however, a 'real' Colin Middleton behind all this eclecticism. In a picture like his 'Figure with Owls' his own strong personality predominates over borrowed concepts and mannerisms. It is, first of all, a pleasing piece of abstract design; the forms are clearly defined and simple, yet have just the right degree of irregularity to avoid the pitfall of boring over-simplification. Middleton's sensitive use of textures, the bland flatness of paint contrasting with surfaces of plaster and wood, and the superb craftsmanship which

he invariably displays, are also apparent in this picture. The rather whimsical nature of the subject matter helps to soften the feeling of austerity generated by the forms. That bulky, rather matronly figure with the owl perched upon her shoulders is surely a distant relative of one of Miro's amoeba-like people.

Jonathan Wade (1941–73)

Of Jonathan Wade one can say several things with some certainty: he was an artist with a very clear and deeply felt vision of the world, and also a remarkably skilful one. Whether he was the most significant Irish artist of his generation it is far too early to judge, but that possibility certainly exists. In any case his tragic death on the road near Clondalkin early in 1973, leaves the world of modern Irish art very much the poorer.

Two Men and a Roy Lichtenstein, *1972, by* Robert Ballagh. *(P. J. Carroll and Company, Dundalk)*

Wade was fascinated by the city, but his fascination was more than tinged with apprehension. The large 'Urban Landscape', one of a series painted shortly before his death, demonstrates this perfectly. Beneath a cold, iron gray sky a grotesque and alien life-form seems to have overrun the surface of the earth. Huge metallic maggots writhe and twist together convulsively below what may be the awning of a mass-concrete flyover. Like most of Wade's cities, this is not an environment where human beings could feel welcome. Yet it is an environment which human beings have created: the endless heap of metal pipes, the featureless roadway, the leaden sky, each are a product of modern industrialisation. The painting, for all the chill which it engenders, is still capable of eliciting a pleasurable response, for we cannot but admire the very real skill with which the artist has manipulated colours, textures, forms and space so that they add up so clearly to a single powerful statement.

In many of his earlier works Wade explored a similar theme, but in a variety of styles quite different from his last. The urban landscape was also the basic theme of his large constructions made of sawn hardboard, where rows of nail heads seemed to suggest the criss-crossing of railway tracks seen from the air.

The paintings from another series, made during the late sixties, were often truly nightmarish and apparently composed of endless heaps of rusting metal piled into crazy towers. The feeling of nightmare was often augmented in these pictures by a wilful disregard for the force of gravity, and 'stalactites' of shattered and decaying metal fragments hang disconcertingly from the sky or protrude into the picture space from the sides.

Wade was once again commenting in a direct and mordant fashion upon the insanity of a society which seems intent upon creating the most uncongenial environment possible for itself.

To a friend, Lee Gallaher, he once remarked, 'there is a jungle in everybody . . . it is the job of the artist to burn a map of it in the front of his brain.'

Robert Ballagh (1943–   )

When the American Pop artist Roy Lichtenstein made his series of 'brush-stroke' paintings during the mid sixties he was wittily commenting on art itself. These paintings, made in Lichtenstein's simple and deliberate 'comic-book' style, had as their subject matter small sections of brush work from a possible Abstract Expressionist (q.v.) painting. The 'joke' involved the very obvious dichotomy of styles between that chosen by Lichtenstein and that which he was representing. And one was also prompted to ask whether these were 'abstract' paintings or 'realistic' paintings of abstract paintings. All very confusing, and all very rarefied.

In Robert Ballagh's painting we see two men looking at one of these paintings by Lichtenstein. They are painted in a photographically realistic manner, as is the rubber plant also in the painting, and the section of Lichtenstein's picture visible is as close to the real thing as makes no difference. So here is a case of art commenting on art commenting on art. More rarefied (and more confusing?) still! And the fact that Ballagh has made his painting on a number of small canvases so that the edges of each are clearly visible further reminds us that we are looking at something artificial, and not a 'slice of life'.

Ballagh has been experimenting for some years with imagery which might generally be termed 'Pop'. He has made numerous paintings of people looking at a variety of pictures, rather similar to the one we have discussed. He has also made his own versions of the works of various earlier masters like Ingres, Goya and David, copying their compositions exactly but employing a disconcerting simplified 'comic-book' style. Art commenting upon art once more. There have also been paintings of banal, mass-produced objects like sweets—liquorice allsorts and iced caramels!

Ballagh's work is highly competent within the rather narrow field of exploration where he has chosen to work. His craftsmanship too is usually immaculate. All of which is indicative of the state of much recent Irish painting and sculpture: all traces of nationality have been carefully ironed out and the chosen means of expression is borrowed from one of the prevalent international styles.

For further reading

Bruce Arnold, *A Concise History of Irish Art* (Thames and Hudson)

Françoise Henry, *Irish Art in the Early Christian Period to A.D. 800*

Françoise Henry, *Irish Art during the Viking Invasions, 800–1020 A.D.*

Françoise Henry, *Irish Art in the Romanesque Period 1020–1170 A.D.* (Methuen and Co.)

Peter Harbison, *Guide to the National Monuments of Ireland* (Gill and Macmillan)

Professor Matthew McDermott, *Ireland's Architectural Heritage* (Folens and Co.)

G. O. Simms, *The Book of Kells* (Dolmen Press)

James White and Michael Wynne, *Irish Stained Glass* (Gill and Son)

Mainie Jellett, *The Artist's Vision* (Dundalgan Press)

Jack B. Yeats Centenary Catalogue (Secker and Warburg)

Bank of Ireland Catalogue of Works of Art (100 reproductions of modern Irish painting and sculpture, some in colour)

John Hewitt, *Colin Middleton* (Arts Council of Northern Ireland)

Introspect, ed. Patrick Pye: Magazine of the arts in Ireland, published annually

Practical Exercises

The study of Irish art suggests a number of ideas which may be of use in the practical art class. Here are just a few:

1 Class research project: investigation of buildings and other items of local interest

Every area in the country (i.e. within a radius of 30 kilometres or so from where you live) is certain to contain some items of interest—buildings, high crosses, slabs, megalithic remains etc. The most accessible and/or interesting of these should be investigated by the art class or individual (see map p.162).

Buildings: make sketches of exterior and interior views. Sketch the plan and, if possible, make a rough assessment of the main dimensions. Note any details of interest both verbally and graphically, i.e. details of decoration, use of materials, site chosen, etc. Find out as many relevant details as possible regarding the buildings' history; local libraries may be of assistance here. Other items: high crosses, slabs etc. should also be sketched from several angles. Again a descriptive account should be built up here in words and draw-

ings. Where high crosses are concerned make drawings of several of the panels and try to work out the sequence of subjects, if any.

A project like this may also prove invaluable where the answering of questions in section three of the Leaving Certificate History and Appreciation Paper is concerned.

2 Paintings: project related to investigations described above

Studies of local ruins, from megalithic passage graves to medieval castles, may suggest ideas for imaginative reconstructions in pictorial form. Some suggested titles for pictures: a monastic sculpture workshop; high crosses being carved; Normans building a castle.

The abstract and surreal concepts found in many of the illuminated manuscripts, like the books of Durrow and Kells, may suggest ideas for imaginative paintings: abstracts based on strapwork, fantastic figures or animals etc.

3 Carvings

Kitchen soap and plaster of paris are easily obtainable and simple to carve. Figures carved in soap or blocks of plaster may be based on early Celtic figures. Relief carvings made in plaster may be based on concepts from the high crosses. A class project could consist of assembling a series of such panels to form a 'high cross'; hardboard, chipboard or plywood being used as a foundation for the panels.

4 Models

Models of local and/or notable buildings and monuments like high crosses may be constructed in a number of materials: balsa wood, plywood, plaster of paris, clay etc.

Some Important Events		Building and Visual Arts	
c. 6000 B.C.	Earliest inhabitants		
c. 3000 B.C.–2000 B.C.	1. Neolithic period	c. 2500 B.C.	Newgrange Passage Grave
c. 2000 B.C.–500 B.C.	2. Bronze Age	c. 1500 B.C.	Irish metalwork exported
c. 500 B.C.–A.D. 500 c. 200 B.C.	3. Iron Age Arrival of first Celts in Ireland	c. 150 B.C.	La Tène culture brought to Ireland
A.D. 500–600 432 (462)? 563	4. Early Christian period Arrival of St Patrick Iona monastery founded by St Columba	c. 560	Monastic settlements Gallerus Oratory Stone slabs Cathach
600–800	5. High period of Irish Christian civilisation	c. 600 c. 650 c. 700 c. 790	Carndonagh Cross Book of Durrow Tara brooch and Ardagh chalice Cross of Moone
800–1000 c. 841 875–915 1002 1014	6. Period of Viking invasions Foundation of Dublin by Vikings Forty Years Recess Brian Boru Ard Ri Battle of Clontarf	c. 800 c. 923	Book of Kells First round towers Cross of Muiredach
1000–1200 1169/70 1171	7. Romanesque period Anglo-Norman invasions Visit of Henry II to Ireland	c. 1100 c. 1123 1127/34 c. 1150 1157	St Patrick's Bell Shrine Cross of Cong Cormac's Chapel Cross of Dysert O'Dea Consecration of Mellifont Abbey

1200–1700	8. Anglo–Norman period (and after)	c. 1200
		
		1212
			Building of first stone castles:
			    Trim, Carrickfergus
			Construction begun on nave of
			    Christ Church Cathedral

1315/18	Bruce Invasion		Burning of St Patrick's Cathedral
1348	Black Death in Ireland		
1477	Rule of Garret More, Earl of Kildare	c. 1470	Ballylongford Cross Carved figures from Fethard
1534	Revolt of Silken Thomas		
1541	Henry VIII declared King of Ireland		
1588	Spanish Armada wrecked off Ireland		
		c. 1600	Crosses of Jennett Dowdall
1607	Flight of the Earls		
1649/50	Cromwell's campaigns		
1690	Battle of the Boyne		
1695	Beginning of Penal Laws		
1742	9. The 18th century Swift's Drapier letters		
1742	First performance of Handel's Messiah		

Some Important Events		Building and Visual Arts	
		1771	Chambers's Casino
		1773	Ivory wins Blue Coat competition
1782	Parliamentary independence	1781	Gandon invited to design new Custom House
1798	Death of Lord Edward. United Irish rising. Death of Tone		
1801	10. Modern period: 19th and 20th centuries Act of Union		
1803	Death of Robert Emmet		
1808	Beginning of O'Connell's rise.		
		1823	Royal Hibernian Academy founded
1829	Catholic Emancipation Act		
1837	Queen Victoria's reign begins		
1840s	Failure of potato crop		
1858	Fenian movement founded	1850s	Hone in Paris
		1860s	Maclise-Murals in House of Parliament
1870	Home Rule movement	1871	Birth of Jack B. Yeats
1875	Parnell returned to parliament	1875	Hone returns from France
		1882	O'Connell Monument—Foley
		1900	J. Yeats settles in Ireland
1904	Abbey Theatre founded	1903	An Túr Gloine founded
1916	Easter Rising		
		1920	E. Hone and M. Jellett to Paris
1922	Civil War		
		1943	Irish Exhibition of Living Art founded
1949	Republic of Ireland declared		
		late fifties	L. le Brocquy's white period
1961	TV Service established		
		early seventies	Wade's urban landscapes
1972	Ireland joins EEC		Ballagh's figures looking at paintings
		1973	Death of J. Wade in motoring accident

Index